Worship as a Revelation

Worship as a Revelation

The Past, Present and Future of Catholic Liturgy

Laurence Paul Hemming

burns & oates

Published by Burns & Oates, a Continuum imprint
The Tower Building, 11 York Road, London SE1 7NX
80 Maiden Lane, Suite 704, New York NY 10038

www.continuumbooks.com

First published 2008

British Library Cataloguing-in-Publication Data
A catalogue record for this book is available from the British Library.

ISBN: 9-780-8601-2460-3

Sogar der Gottesdienst im Dom am Palmsonntag, wo noch am ehesten eine lebendige Überlieferung erwartet werden konnte, wirkte in seiner nachlässigen Liturgie wie eine Schaustellung. Veraltet alles, jedoch nicht alt; Vergangenes, aber kein Gewesenes, das sich in ein Bleibendes versammelt, um sich den Wartenden neu zu schenken.

No less the service in the cathedral on Palm Sunday, where one might most have expected to find a living tradition, seemed in the laziness of the Liturgy a mere spectacle. All was antiquated, even if not properly ancient; bygone, but not something that has been and yet is and will be yet, nothing which recollects itself as something persisting, that it might hand itself over anew to those yet waiting.

Martin Heidegger
Observation made in a notebook for Palm Sunday
16 April 1962[1]

---

1 Heidegger, M., *Aufenthalte*, in *Zu Hölderlin – Griechenlandreisen*, in *Gesamtausgabe*, vol. 75, Frankfurt, Klostermann, 2000, p. 217.

For Mark and Susan

Contents

Preface

This book began life in the Octave of Pentecost, 2007, when I was invited to give the annual Pentecost lectures to the Benedictine community at Pluscarden Abbey in the Highlands of Scotland. Pluscarden enjoys wide renown, and rightly, as a place where the love of God in the sacred liturgy of the Catholic Church is solemnly and beautifully practised. For a theologian to come to a Benedictine monastic house and lecture on the sacred liturgy is an astonishing presumption. I remain indebted to the Abbot and community for that invitation, and for the generosity and kindness with which I was met during my stay of nearly a week. The understanding of the liturgy that I unfolded then, and in what follows here, differs in important ways to that community's own, so I was all the more impressed that they were so willing to invite me to open with them the dialogue of which this book is the fruit. I was all too aware of the line of previous Pentecost lecturers, and my diminutive place in that distinguished list. I began then by begging the monks' indulgence, as I do again from my readers now – beginning, as all exposition must begin, with a request for forgiveness for all mistakes and errors here within, and for a blessing, that what is good here will bear its proper fruit.

I will repeat here a point I made then: the pope and the bishops, as the pastors of the Church, are those alone who have authority for spiritual, juridical, and disciplinary decisions about the Church's liturgical practice. They are, as this book seeks to explain, guardians of the liturgy, rather than arbiters. I write merely as a theologian – offering, I hope, prayerful and gentle provocation for the sake of deepening the love and understanding of the means of our salvation: our public worship, instituted by Christ the Lord Himself. Nothing I say has, or seeks to have, any formal status and should not be read as such; nor have I any programme for reform or 'reform of the reform', or anything of its kind. The publication of Pope Benedict's motu proprio, *Summorum Pontificum*, in July 2007, together with his own public but gentle recovery of many traditional elements in the current papal liturgy, has ushered in a new stage of the debate concerning the character and practice of our sacred worship. This book is intended to be a small contribution to that debate, and I look forward to a fulfilment of what has been hoped for by many over the last century or so: embodied once in the Liturgical Movement that characterized the earlier part of the twentieth century; renewed in the actual decisions of the Second Vatican Council, and stated in the Dogmatic Constitution *Sacrosanctum Concilium*. I hope for the placing of the sacred liturgy of the Church at the very centre of our daily life, as its *culmen et fons* – summit and source.

This book occupies a province of thought that others have also explored. Fr Aidan Nichols OP has shown the way in which the impulses for liturgical reform have their origins in a commitment to rationalism that stems, certainly from the seventeenth and eighteenth centuries, and even before.[1] The Oratorian Fr Jonathan Robinson's important work has indicated with dexterity and insight the relation that others have also tried to trace, perhaps a little clumsily at times, of the connection between the Catholic Church's sacred liturgy and historical (and contemporary) developments reflected in philosophical thought.[2] Although his method and conclusions differ in important ways from mine, there are more important similarities to be found between us, if sometimes to be read between the lines. Too many commentators (of whom Fr Robinson is not one) analyse these connections in terms of what, let us say, Nietzsche 'did', or what

---

1 Nichols OP, A., *Looking at the Liturgy: A Critical View of its Contemporary Form*, San Francisco, Ignatius, 1996. See esp. pp. 11–48.
2 Robinson *cong. orat.*, J., *The Mass and Modernity: Walking to Heaven Backward*, San Francisco, Ignatius, 2005.

Descartes 'caused' (depending on who their bogeymen are), failing to realize that philosophy as the most useless discipline 'does' nothing at all in what it effects. The work of truly great philosophical thinkers (of whom Descartes and Nietzsche are but two) is to bring to adequate description the deepest impulses and thoughts of their moment and age – in this, the work of philosophy is truly a phenomenology: it lets something be seen as it *is*, in its truth, and for *whom*, however stark and hard that truth is to bear. To lay blame at thinkers and make accusation against those who undertake this task for us is to trivialize their courage and dishonours their spiritual struggle, and the price they have to pay, in bringing to words what they themselves have had to undergo.

This is not a systematic work, and should not be read as such. It is preparatory to other writing, perhaps my own, perhaps of others, if they should join me in thinking that what it is this book attempts to speak of is important. This book (as were the lectures from which it sprang) is an attempt to show how liturgical study should form the basis, and be the ground, from out of which the science of theology is done. This is only to try to undertake what *Sacrosanctum Concilium* called for. The sacred liturgy is undergirded by nothing other than God's own historical self-disclosure: and this means in the history of Israel, and of the Church. Liturgical texts are inherently intended to be intelligible (even if that requires grace, and work; above all, work of a mental and spiritual kind), and they open the understanding – they are only 'rational' in this sense (although this is not the word I would most quickly choose). The divine (Trinitarian) self-disclosure is not to be justified or proved rationally, nor can it be corroborated or authenticated by the work of reason – rather is anything reasonable made possible by the gracious and merciful self-revealing creativity of God. To fail to understand the binding character of the order of what is prior and what comes after, especially in the order of what is revealed in faith (as even more iron in its imperative than what is given to be thought), is to fail to understand the most primary impulse of this book.

The question of which liturgical texts to quote is now a difficult one, there having been so many changes to the 'typical' forms of the

Roman rite since it took a more canonical shape after the Council of Trent (and, indeed, after Vatican II). For reasons that will become clear only in the course of the text, I have ordinarily appealed to the texts of the 1884 *Missale Romanum* and the 1623 *Breviarium Romanum*. There is no doctrinaire reason for choosing these particular editions; rather, more often than not the texts quoted from these editions are the invariable, or almost invariable, forms and compositions from the earliest written records in which we received them (sometimes they can be traced as far back as the fourth and fifth centuries). From 1911 onwards, things are not always so clear. When I have deviated from these two editions, I have tried to indicate why.

I must record some words of thanks. First, to the Latin Mass Society of England and Wales, which has in the four past decades unflinchingly witnessed to the more ancient uses of the Church, and for the friendship of some of its members both personally and for my work. Especially to the scripture scholar and exegete Margaret Barker for her kindness and enthusiasm in being willing to discuss aspects of the book with me and to open my eyes to the connections between scripture and liturgical texts; and equally to Alcuin Reid for providing many detailed suggestions and corrections. To Fr Andrew Wadsworth for his careful comments, corrections, and help with the Italian. The book is much improved for the efforts of these three, but all remaining mistakes are entirely my own. Thanks are due to Mary-Ann Crumplin who prepared the appendix of notes on many of the figures mentioned in the book. Thanks are also due to Robin Baird-Smith who as publisher of this work and as a friend provided such encouragement for it, and to Revd Nick Fawcett and Neil Higgins for their advice and care in editing the book for publication; to Ben Whitworth for reading an earlier draft and for his invaluable comments; to Ferdinand Knapp, Susan Parsons, Fr Andrew Wadsworth, Mops Millard Barnes and all connected with the Society of St Catherine of Siena, for giving in different ways unfailing love and support over the years during which what is laid out here has come to fruition, and for their contributions to the ideas developed here; to Henri de Villiers of the Parisian Schola Sainte Cecile for permission to reproduce for the cover the photograph of a Solemn Mass in

Merton College Oxford, 2007; to Bradford Houston, devout inheritor of another venerable Christian temple tradition, for his generous hospitality while I wrote this book during time in Salt Lake City; and to all those kind enough to have prayed for me from time to time while I have worked on this matter.

Biblical references in this book are mainly taken from the Douai-Rheims translation of the Bible (with Challoner Revisions, Baltimore, John Murphy, 1899 [1582, 1751]), which is based on the Septuagint and closest to St Jerome's Vulgate. The numbering of the Psalms is the Septuagint numbering, which in many cases is one number less than the corresponding number in the current Hebrew scriptures.

The text throughout this book is intended to be taken inclusively, although I have eschewed the normal paraphernalia of inclusive language. I apologize to readers for whom this is a difficulty, and there is no intended diminution of women or men in my use.

Laurence Paul Hemming
Feast of the Purification of the Blessed Virgin Mary, 2008

Chapter 1

I Saw the New Jerusalem

To pray is to ask to be made ready to hear. This book springs from the understanding that praying is a kind of hearing – not a mere opening of the ears, but a trained attentiveness in a habit acquired over years, even decades; a directedness *towards* in a particular manner. 'I pray you . . .' is a construction now rarely heard in contemporary speech, but once it meant a gracious form of address, attempting to draw towards one the attention of one greater than oneself, and an openness for them to speak, to act, to direct their attention toward the one uttering the request.

Theology – contrary to common definitions – is not speech about God. It is reflective deliberation on the work of faith. The work of faith, the *opus Dei*, as St Benedict calls it in his *Rule*, is the practice of worship, the sacred liturgy itself, and nothing less. It is through the sacred liturgy that the joining of heaven to earth comes to be understood, and culminates in making present who the Christ is by giving us understanding and experience of him. We do not pray in order to speak to God, but so that God can address us. In worship we return to God the love once offered to us and on our behalf through the sacrifice of his beloved Son. Worship, grounded in atonement, is therefore primarily toward God and only secondarily for us. The worship of the Church is divinely instituted: in Old Testament and New, God establishes not only that we should worship, but how. God establishes the Church and the hierarchy of the Church for the sake of making manifest who for us God is: 'it is to the holiness of the faithful that the hierarchical structure of the

1

Church is totally ordered'.[1] This manifestation takes place through
the cycle of the sacred liturgy: its work is to make us fit for heaven,
to enable God to make saints of us, adopted, divinized, sons and
daughters: brothers and sisters to the only-begotten who is not
adopted but is Son by right. Prayer is first and foremost the prayer
of the Church, and it is offered in her sacred precincts. Central to
every prayer and every text employed in the sacred liturgy of the
Church is its soteriological meaning – its capacity to save us – and
its anagogical meaning. 'Anagogical' means 'capacity to lift up', literally, in this case, to raise us to the heavens, to the dwelling place of
the saints on high and to the God who stretches out his hand to rule
from his cherubim throne.

The Mass of the Dedication or consecration of a church reminds
us at the point of Communion that 'my house will be called a house
of prayer, says the Lord',[2] in a direct reference to Jesus' words about
the true character of the Temple in Jerusalem. The Church makes
manifest and completes for the whole earth the meaning once
indicated by the Temple in Jerusalem, and the liturgy makes constant
reference in its annual round to this Jerusalem, the holy and perfect
city wherein the Temple is to be found: in penitential seasons the
liturgy speaks of the desolation of Jerusalem,[3] and in joyful ones, her
exultation. The Christian is, through the work of the sacred liturgy,
inscribed into the heavenly Jerusalem and is made one of her citizens.
The true Jerusalem is the pole of the earth, its true centre, and where
the meaning of the whole cosmos becomes manifest through God's
presence in the sanctuary, which is the temple and the church.
Anciently the Temple in Jerusalem is the symbolic manifestation of

---

1 John Paul II, Apostolic Letter *Ordinatio Sacerdotalis*, Vatican, Libreria Editrice Vaticana,
   1994, §3. 'Ceterum ad fidelium sanctitatem funditus ordinatur hierarchica Ecclesiæ
   constitutio.'
2 *Missale Romanum* (1884), Mass of the Dedication of a Church, Communion Antiphon
   (cf. Matthew 21.13). 'Domus mea, domus orationis vocabitur, dicit Dominus.' The
   chant adds, 'within it everything that is asked is accepted, and whoever goes in seeking
   will discover, and to him who knocks, it shall be opened'.
3 *Breviarium Romanum* (1623), note especially the responses at Tenebræ of the sacred
   triduum, and the prophecies from Ezekiel about the desolation of Jerusalem and her
   restoration during Advent.

the Garden of Eden: worship has (or should have) the effect of returning us to the paradise of Eden.

The liturgy which celebrates the anniversary of the dedication of a church makes clear the connection between our places of worship and the cosmic order itself: 'I saw the holy city, the new Jerusalem, coming down out of heaven from God, prepared as a bride adorned for her husband'.[4] The central words are: 'I saw'. By means of the presence of the physical and sacred place of a church we are to be made able to see. What we are to see, however, is not the Bridegroom himself – something else makes this visible to us (the liturgical actions that take place within the church). Rather, the physical church makes present the place wherein the Bridegroom is to arrive. The church is indicated as a place 'having been prepared' *(paratam)*. To have been prepared means to have been established by divine ordinances as fit, according to what God has apportioned for it. The ordinances of the New Jerusalem correspond to the ordinances for the establishment of the 'holy city', built on a mountain, which is the site for the temple of the Lord, the place of encounter and reconciliation between God and men. What is the essence of the prayer in the place made holy to the Lord? The liturgy tells us 'this place in which the priest prays is holy. [He prays] for the faults and sins of the people.'[5] The priest in question is Christ, the Bridegroom, who is also the high priest. The temple is the place where atonement takes place; it is the place not only where the Bridegroom appears, but where heaven and earth are reconciled.

For Catholics the ritual of atonement is signified by the offering of the Mass, where Christ is at one and the same time priest and victim. The prayer in question is the sacrificial offering of Christ himself in the *singular* sacrifice of the endlessly repeated Mass, and the responsory which indicates this is sung in the offices that precede and follow

---

4 The Apocalypse of John, 21.2. *Breviarium Romanum* (1623), Office of the Dedication of a Church, chapter at Vespers and Lauds. 'Vidi civitatem sanctam Jerusalem novam descendentem de cœlo a Deo, paratam sicut sponsam ornatam viro suo.'

5 *Breviarium Romanum* (1623), Office of the Dedication of a Church, responsories at Terce and Sext (the offices to be said or sung before and after the conventual, or principal, Mass).

the presupposed time of the solemn offering of the actual Mass for a newly dedicated church (and in the Mass on each year in which the anniversary of the dedication is kept). The responsories frame and indicate the meaning to be conveyed.

The feast of the Dedication of a Church is to be kept annually, especially in the cathedral as the seat of the bishop, or in the monastery, and it was until very recently kept for an 'octave' of eight consecutive days. Keeping a feast of dedication for eight days originates with Solomon's dedication, renewed at the rededication of the Temple in Jerusalem after it had been desecrated by the Roman vassal king Antiochus Epiphanes,[6] and the restoration in the Temple of the altar of sacrifice – and so we can see here the relation between the Christian keeping of octaves and its origination in the Temple in Jerusalem. In the keeping of the octave of the feast of dedication, the church as that place prepared according to divine ordinances for the presence of the Bridegroom and where the offering of the high priest is made, is indicated as the sign of the *true* rededication of the Temple. The church is not the heavenly Jerusalem: it is its sign, a sacramental means by which each of us can say 'I saw' the new Jerusalem descending from heaven to earth. The church as sanctified place makes possible this descending, and as such it makes possible – for those made fit to do so – an encounter with the Bridegroom who at the same time as High Priest reconciles them to God and atones for their sins.

The first Christian feast of dedication is the historical octave of Easter, the eight days between the resurrection and Christ's second appearance to his disciples, and so the octave of the dedication of a church parallels and is directly related in meaning to the annual liturgical keeping of the octave of Easter. We understand Jesus' own connection with the feast of Dedication of the Jerusalem Temple from a passage early on in St John's Gospel: challenged as to whether he is the Christ, Jesus declares that he is the one who enters in through the door in order to be shepherd of the sheepfold: at the same time, he predicts his death as one who lays down his life for the sheep.[7] After

---

6 The biblical record of this is contained in the books of the Maccabees. Cf. also 1 Kings 8.65–66.

7 John 10.7, 18.

this encounter, St John tells us that Jesus leaves his questioners and goes into the Temple by Solomon's porch. The question of Jesus' identity – who he believes himself to be – is to be resolved through his identification of himself with the Temple in Jerusalem.

In St John's Gospel the account of Jesus' resurrection appearances begin with the Lord appearing to Mary Magdalene, telling her not to touch him because 'I have not yet ascended to my Father', with the suggestion, therefore, that it *will* be possible to touch the Lord once he has ascended.[8] Touch here means 'understand through tangible signs', as we shall later see. Mary reports to the disciples, 'I have seen the Lord'.[9] The risen Christ then appears to those who were in a place where the doors were shut. To any Christian hearing this Gospel in the early Church two things would have been obvious – one, that this appearance is fundamentally Eucharistic, for the liturgy of the Eucharist is that liturgy which takes place in secret, behind closed doors, in a place reserved to be witnessed by the baptized alone and undertaken in the sanctuary, the most sacred place in the temple, the holy of holies, the place of the divine presence, where only the high priest may enter. Secondly, that the *place* is indicated as the place of the encounter with the Bridegroom, the Temple in Jerusalem. Christ is himself and has in his own person become the Temple; that one who, the physical Temple having been destroyed, he claims will be built up again in three days. St John is the evangelist who identifies the body of Jesus with the temple,[10] and who tells us that this is to be remembered and understood only when Jesus rises from the dead: 'When therefore he was risen again from the dead, his disciples remembered that he had said this: and they believed the scripture and the word that Jesus had said.'[11] Jesus indicates his identity with Jerusalem in the words he says at this point: 'peace be with you',[12]

---

8 John 20.17.

9 John 20.18.

10 Cf. John 2.19–21: 'Jesus answered and said to them: destroy this temple; and in three days I will raise it up. The Jews then said: six and forty years was this temple in building; and wilt thou raise it up in three days? But he spoke of the temple of his body.'

11 John 2.22.

12 John 20.19.

indicating that he is the one who speaks the peace indicated by the name of the city of Jerusalem.[13]

The account in St John's Gospel of the return of Jesus to the disciples on the eighth day is itself a Eucharistic reference – the eighth day is also the day of the resurrection (the day on which the Eucharist is always to be celebrated), but it indicates as well the Jewish keeping of the octave day of the rededication of the Temple, which is here to be understood as Jesus' body, restored after its defilement and desecration in its scourging and crucifixion, and indeed in its having been killed (thereby ending the Jewish prohibitions concerning contact with the dead). Thomas the Apostle's abandonment of his disbelief through intersecting his own body with that of Jesus (placing his finger into the wounds and his hand into the side of Jesus) is the fulfilment of Jesus' own prediction of what his disciples will remember *and will believe*. The Temple, like the place where Jesus appears to his disciples, is also a place whose doors are closed to those not part of the covenant restored in the person of the Christ. What is given in the *place* behind closed doors which allows the heavenly Jerusalem to be seen – the church as the analogue of the Temple – is the coming of the Bridegroom to all future believers. The antiphon for the Invitatory psalm at Matins of the feast of Dedication of a Church makes this connection explicit: 'holiness becomes the house of God: that we may adore from within her Christ her spouse'.[14] The collects and other prayers during the octave of the feast of dedication all refer to the church whose dedication is to be celebrated as 'this temple'.[15] The

---

13 Various etymologies have over the centuries been suggested for the name of the perfect city. The Christian liturgical texts indicate, however, a strong preference for the name having a connection with peace, suggesting that this is a long-held tradition within the church.

14 *Breviarium Romanum* (1623), Office of the Dedication of a Church, invitatory antiphon at Matins: cf. Psalm 92.5.

15 In the revised office of the 1970 Missal and Breviary the references to the temple are much more muted. There is a shift from the eschatological dread character of the meaning of the temple, so that whereas the introit originally said 'terrible is this place: it is the house of God and the gate of heaven' (*Missale Romanum* [1884] Mass of the Dedication of a Church. 'Terribilis est locus iste: hic domus Dei est, et porta cœli.') in the revised rite it reads 'wonderful is God in his sanctuary' (*Missale Romanum* [2002], Common of the Dedication of a Church, Anniversary Mass. 'Mirabilis, Deus, de sanc-

very designator 'this' (*hoc*) indicates the fundamental connection between the Temple established by Solomon, the temple of Christ's body and the Temple made manifest in the coming to earth from heaven of the new Jerusalem.

Liturgically, the octave of Easter is at one and the same time the *real* octave of the rededication of the Temple, which expresses the original connection between the foundation of the first Temple and its re-establishment in the body of the Lord. The ancient liturgical texts of the feast of Dedication of a Church reflect this unity. The readings at Matins on the first day of the octave from 2 Chronicles give an account of Solomon's establishment and dedication of the Temple. They begin by telling us 'when Solomon had completed the founding prayers, a fire descended from heaven and devoured the holocaust and the animal sacrifices, and the majesty of the Lord filled the house'.[16] The house is the Temple. Octaves, or periods of eight days of celebration, which until recently were a widespread feature of the Catholic calendar (and which we will consider in more detail later) therefore all refer both to the way in which in the resurrection the real meaning of Christ's physical body is made manifest as a continuity with the temple worship of Israel, and the ways in which (and this means the persons and places through whom) all this is to be seen: *I saw* the new Jerusalem descending from the heavens.

The Temple in Jerusalem was the place where the eternal covenant between God and man is kept and made liturgically present. The Temple was the place where the meaning of the whole cosmos was both revealed and explained, and where the reconciliation of the unseen God and man (who lives in the realm of the visible) is undertaken. The collect for the dedication of a church makes this explicit: 'O God who invisibly holds together all things, and yet for the

---

tuario tuo'). The revised collect is significantly shortened, and the less eschatological emphasis of the whole revision is encapsulated in the brief reading at Sext: 'you are the temple of the living God' (*Liturgia Horarum*, 1970, Common of the Dedication of a Church, lectio brevis at Sext. 'Vos estis templum Dei vivi.')

16 *Breviarium Romanum* (1623), Office of the Dedication of a Church, reading from the first nocturn of Matins. 'Cum complesset Salomon fundens preces, ignis descendit de cœlo, et devoravit holocausta et victimas: et maiestas Domini implevit domum.'

salvation of the human race show the signs of your power, by your inhabitation of this temple make visible your power.'[17] The invisible God, and the hidden meaning of the cosmos, is disclosed by the visible sign of the church and the visibility of the worship that takes place within it. The church is to be understood as a sign, a formal indication, something like a sacrament, of the heavenly Temple. Traditionally, certainly up to the baroque period, the construction of churches, especially principal churches, was crowded with symbolism and coded meaning. Nevertheless, the liturgy reflects and amplifies the understanding that the church is an analogue of the Temple; a place of prayer, where the prayer in question that is made by the priest (and therefore Christ the High Priest) in atonement for the sins of the people is heeded; a sanctuary of holiness and set aside for the Lord; built upon a firm rock; a place made of precious stones and adorned with gems, made fit to receive the Bridegroom who is Christ; the gate of heaven; a place where the holy name of God will be invoked.

The liturgy indicates in full the connection between the Temple in Jerusalem and the sacred place of a particular church. The collect for Mass of the dedication of a church indicates that this Mass is to be kept 'year on year': we have seen how the first feast of dedication coincides with the meaning of the Lord's own resurrected body and is inscribed in it. All the liturgical prayer that is made in the church is rooted in the description of prayer as pleading of atonement by the Lord. The annual character of the feast of dedication is not simply an analogue of the annual feast of Dedication of the Temple in Jerusalem, in the same way as the octave of the feast of dedication is coincident in its origin with the octave of Easter, rather, *as* an annual event it is *coincident* with the very meaning of the Day of Atonement itself. The feast of dedication recalls that the eternal covenant of the atonement must be honoured and renewed. The collect for the

---

17 *Missale Romanum* (1884), collect on the day of the dedication of a church. 'Deus qui invisibiliter omnia contines, et tamen puo salute generis humani signa tuae potentiae visibiliter ostendis: templum hoc potentia tuae inhabitationis illustra, er concede; ut omnes, qui hunc deprecaturi conveniunt, ex quacumque tribularione ad te clamaverint, consolationis tuae beneficia consequantur.'

annual feast itself reminds us that the 'year by year' renewal of the day of consecration at the same time 're-presents us unimpaired to your sacred mysteries', which means that in virtue of the prayer offered by the Bridegroom and High Priest (who represents and makes on their behalf the prayer of the people), we ourselves can become ones who 'enter into this temple with beneficent petitions' so that we 'obtain them in joy'.[18]

18 *Missale Romanum* (1884), collect of the Common of the Dedication of a Church. 'Deus qui nobis per singulos annos huius sancti templi tui consecrationis reparas diem, et sacris semper mysteriis repræsentas incolumes: exaudi preces populi tui, et præsta; ut quisquis hoc templum beneficia petiturus ingreditur, cuncta se impetrasse lætetur.'

Chapter 2

Briefly, the Roman Rite

For Catholics the period after the Second Vatican Council has seen some of the greatest liturgical change. A question implicit in the current situation of our liturgy is: surely the development of the Roman rite, as of any other *historical* phenomenon, is a *human* development, and therefore subject to human decision and constraint? Martin Mosebach points out that the Mass has had substantially the same form for a very long time. He adds, 'we are as historical beings, subject to the age in which we find ourselves, to which we belong, we have to see with its eyes, hear with its ears, and think under the law of its mentality'.[1] Our current age sees everything as an object of manufacture, as something which can be got hold of and improved, or altered, to produce *better* or *more effective* outcomes. This is our present fate, especially in the West, to understand all things in this way – and it is inevitable that we should transfer even to our sacred worship the same outlook. To learn to be entrained to something that precedes and outlasts us, and that, rather than being shaped by us is what most shapes us in God, is a task. I do not propose to examine in detail the course of the liturgical reform, or its motors – others have done that, some with considerable insight and flair.[2] Mosebach

---

1 Mosebach, M, *Häresie der Formlosigkeit: Die Römische Liturgie und ihr Feind*, Munich, Hanser, 2007 (2002). 'Wir sind als geschichtliche Wesen alle dem Geist der Epoche unterworfen, der wir angehören, wir müssen mit ihren Augen sehen, mit ihren Ohren hören und nach dem Gesetz ihrer Mentalität denken.'

2 See especially Gamber, K., *The Reform of the Roman Liturgy: Its Problems and Background*, San Juan Capestrano, Una Voce, 2003.

explains the answer to this preliminary question when he concludes 'alterations to an ancient action, that occur through the shaping hand of history, have no author', or, we might say, no *human* author. The Spiritual hand that shaped the Roman liturgy over centuries did so in conformity with divine ordinances: it was itself a revelation.

During the period of reform the interiors of many of our churches have been radically altered – altars have been moved so that the priest stands behind them in the celebration of the Mass (rather than face East, usually the same direction as the people),[3] and new churches have been built according to experimental and non-classical plans. Mass is to be heard in the vernacular languages rather than Latin. If there is music at all, the congregation is asked to join in the singing of modern hymns. These are only the most obvious changes: the real changes to the liturgy are to be found in the texts. By texts I do not simply mean the words of the prayers, the collects, antiphons, and other parts of the liturgy. Part of the textual character of the liturgy is also the rubrics – the words in red in the liturgical books (hence the name rubric, from Latin *ruber*, describing when something is red). Often the rubrics in the older liturgical books are simple *aides mémoire*, which indicate not so much what is not be done as the occasions when something is to be done differently. The performative aspect of the liturgy is integral to its meaning, and yet often why something is to be done (or omitted) is not immediately obvious, or widely understood. Nevertheless what is to be done, and how, and when, is part of the whole textual character of the rites.

A further part of this textual character of the liturgy as a whole is the vestments, the furnishing and ordering of the church interior, the shape and character of the sacred vessels, the materials from which all is made, its exact placing and so forth. Everything in a church intends a meaning, so that the whole of the liturgy, its chant, what is performed, by whom, and how, where, and when, form a whole textual complex with intricate significance. The meanings intended have been built up over centuries, but much of it was taken over from the understanding

---

3 For a full discussion of this see Lang, U. M., *Turning Towards the Lord*, San Francisco, Ignatius, 2004.

and connections the early Church had of, and with, the religion and history of Israel. It is often presumed that the model of worship developed by the early Christians was based on the Jewish synagogue (and many theologians and commentators can be found who assert this to be the case, or who simply presume it), but increasingly, the real roots of Christian worship can be shown to be the Temple in Jerusalem.[4] The Temple was destroyed in AD 70 by the Romans, and the (Rabbinical) Judaism that succeeded its destruction represents the inheritance of only part of a more differentiated religion. The early Christians considered themselves to be the true successors not so much of the worship of the synagogue, but the Temple. In this they believed themselves to be reflecting a tradition they had received directly from Jesus and what he communicated, often in secret, to the Apostles. Historically the liturgy of the Western Church (as indeed in the East) abounds with references to, and indications of, this belief.

The common conception of the early Church as in many ways adhoc, as groups of Christian men and women coming together informally to sing hymns, pray, break bread and bless wine, is quite false. Persecution, and the precious and sacred character of what took place behind the 'closed doors' of the Christian assembly, meant that until the period of persecution passed (with the conversion of Constantine), and even then only very gradually, much that constituted the Christian practice of worship was not committed to writing. It was not only for fear of persecution that the nature and details of worship were kept secret: what was so sacred was not to be publicly spoken of or openly discussed. Consequently, much of the historical record is allusive, only elliptically explained, if it is explicated at all. This continued a tradition originating with Israel herself: some of the scriptures were forbidden to be publicly known, written, or commentated upon. In addition the liturgy itself developed only slowly

---

4 See especially the work of Barker, M.: *Temple Themes in Christian Worship*, London, T&T Clark (Continuum), 2007; *The Great High Priest: The Temple Roots of Christian Liturgy*, London, T&T Clark (Continuum), 2003. In this the worship of the Church has a parallel with the synagogue, for as the worship of the synagogue is rooted in the Temple, so too is that in the churches.

over time, fulfilling, amplifying, even forgetting, the traditions established in the emerging Christian Churches.

This book is concerned with the Roman rite, the rite that emerged from the Church and diocese of Rome.[5] There are many other rites which are not Roman in origin – in the East the Liturgy of St John Chrysostom or Liturgy of St Basil the Great, or the Liturgies of the Armenian and the Ethiopian Churches.[6] In the Catholic Church, however, there are a large number of rites quite distinct from the Roman rite: the rite of the diocese of Milan or Ambrosian rite; or the Mozarabic rite, widespread across the whole of the Iberian peninsula up until the twelfth century, when it was reduced to a chapel in the cathedral in Toledo and six other parishes in that diocese. Both of these rites survive in a modified form to the present day. In the East, the Eastern-rite Catholics in the Ukraine use forms of the liturgical books also in use in the Russian Orthodox Church, or the Chaldean rite in Iraq, the Melkite and Maronite rites in Lebanon and the Syro-Malabar rite in Southern India.

The Roman rite is the name, not for a single, homogeneous, rite, but for the historical family of rites that all developed from and owe their origin to the rite of the Church and diocese of Rome. The Roman rite encompasses not only what has often been called the Tridentine rite that emerged from the Council of Trent with the Missal of St Pius V of 1570, but also the various diocesan rites, the rites specific to monastic orders and houses and other religious orders. Thus the Dominican rite is a variant of the Roman rite, as is the monastic rite of the Benedictine Order. Others are the Carthusian, Cistercian and Carmelite rites, each with its own distinctive features and disparities.[7]

Many dioceses had distinctive rites. Best known in Britain was the Sarum Use (or rite) in the diocese of Salisbury, but in fact a

---

5 For a truly comprehensive account see Righetti, M., *Storia Liturgica* (vols 1–4), Rome, Ancora, 1998 (1964). The most comprehensive historical discussion of the texts of the Roman Missal is by Jungmann SJ, J. A., *The Mass of the Roman Rite: Its Origins and Development*, trans. Brunner CSSR, F. A., Blackrock, Four Courts Press, 1986 (1950).

6 Cf. King, A. A., *The Rites of Eastern Christendom*, Rome, Catholic Book Agency, 1947.

7 Cf. King, A. A., *Liturgies of the Religious Orders*, London, Longmans, Green & Co., 1955.

number of medieval dioceses in Britain had their own rites or 'uses' – all variants of the Roman rite – up until the Reformation of Henry VIII.[8] The better known are those of Hereford and York, and the monastic Custom of Westminster. A good deal of Anglican scholarship of the nineteenth and early twentieth century produced fine scholarly editions of these rites and uses, many of which were published by the Henry Bradshaw Society. The same was also true of mainland European dioceses, many of which remained in use after the Council of Trent which, although it resulted in a definitive set of the liturgical books, granted that any rite or use that had been in existence for at least two hundred years could remain in use.[9] Many did remain in use. These rites, often very close to the Roman rite in much of their content, nevertheless had quite distinctive ritual aspects or chant specific to themselves. Thus the rites of Trier and Braga, or the Strigonian rite of Estergom (Budapest), to name only three. The Use of Braga was only restored, after much careful scholarship, in 1919 and 1924, to be abandoned in 1971.

Nevertheless the basic structure of the recitation of the psalter at the various hours of the Church, the lectionary of readings throughout the year at Mass, and the collects and other prayers, show a high degree of congruence. All the forms of the Roman rite used the Roman Canon or prayer of consecration in the Mass until the introduction of additional Eucharistic prayers or 'anaphoras' prepared for liturgical use in 1968 and added to the Roman Missal of Paul VI in 1970.

---

8 I have used the term 'rite' almost interchangeably with the term 'use' throughout. Really a 'use' is a variant of a 'rite', whereas a rite as such is a distinct form of liturgical and historical practice. Whereas we speak of the Ambrosian rite, we should really speak of the York or Carthusian *use* of the Roman *rite*. What is confusing is that there really is no such thing that we can point to as the Roman rite *per se*, except insofar as we could point to the liturgical books of the Tridentine and postconciliar reforms (themselves very much a 'subset' of all that goes under the name of the Roman rite). Still more confusingly, for many liturgists a 'rite' can be as simple as a formulary, or an action (thus the words *Ite, missa est: Deo gratias* can constitute the 'rite of dismissal').

9 Cf. King, A. A., *Liturgies of the Past (Rite of Aquileia, Rite of Benevento, Gallican Rite, Celtic Rite, Rites of Mediaeval England, Rite of Nidaros – Trondheim)*, London, Longmans, Green & Co., 1959; *Liturgies of the Primatial Sees (The Rites of Lyons, Braga, Milan and Toledo)*, London, Longmans, Green & Co., 1957.

There was even wider variation in the chant. The Roman chant books are the *Gradual*, giving the chants for use in the Mass, and the *Antiphonary* for the offices (combined in the Solesmes reform of the late nineteenth and early twentieth centuries into the *Liber Usualis* or 'book of Use' so dear to many parish musicians and liturgists). Although many parts of the chant – especially for the more solemn parts of the calendar or liturgical year – are identical or close to identical across all the forms of the Roman rite, there were additional aspects unique to places. For instance the Sarum rite (and some other English diocesan rites) included 'Tropers' or books of additional chants comprised of commentary, which interspersed or 'troped' glosses sung in between sections or verses of the Gospel at solemn forms of the Mass.[10]

The liturgical books that followed on from the Council of Trent became normative across the Catholic Church in the West, and were taken to every land that did not have an older rite of its own – Africa (in places where no ancient rite existed already), Asia, Latin and North America, and the Antipodes. In fact the 'Tridentine' rite is in many ways a truncation of other forms of the Roman rite, and, as László Dobszay has pointed out, 'the "Tridentine" liturgy was the rite of the Roman Curia', evolving from forms in the eleventh and twelfth centuries 'on the basis of old Italian and Roman traditions.'[11] It is shorter than other forms, and its ritual at Mass and the offices is often simpler. Dobszay adds that 'many rich elements of the Holy Week liturgy, for example, fell victim to the Curial reform' of this version of the Roman rite.[12]

The most important texts of the Roman rite date back, almost unchanged, to the earliest extant liturgical books. Among these texts are many of the collects and other related prayers, like the postcommunion prayers and 'secrets' (prayers said over the gifts immediately prior to the consecration); many of the arrangements of the texts of

10 See for a discussion that focuses on musical questions Harper, J., *The Forms and Orders of Western Liturgy from the Tenth to the Eighteenth Century: A Historical Introduction and Guide for Students and Musicians*, Oxford, Clarendon Press, 1991.
11 Cf. Dobszay, L., 'The Bugnini-Liturgy and the Reform of the Reform', in *Musicæ Sacræ Meletemata*, vol. 5, Front Royal, 2003, p. 152.
12 Dobszay, L., 'The Bugnini-Liturgy and the Reform of the Reform', p. 153.

the chants, associating particular psalms or texts taken from psalms, or from sacred scripture with particular parts of the Christian year; or again the antiphons associated with particular psalms and above all the actual arrangement of the way the psalms are to be said in the hours of the Church. The liturgical books containing these texts stem from the seventh and eighth centuries, but often can be corroborated to texts as early as the third, fourth, and fifth centuries. If we have evidence for different arrangements of the material – the psalmody, antiphons, and the collects – that predates the extant books we now have, this evidence can be shadowy and inconclusive. Of course as new feasts and celebrations were added over the centuries new compositions appeared, but these invariably were composed to reflect the genius and form of the texts to which they were added – a superlative case of which is the Office and Mass of Corpus Christi, parts of which survived the 1970 reform (and which succeeded an earlier medieval version), almost certainly composed by St Thomas Aquinas.[13]

There are several liturgical books of the Roman rite. The Missal is one with which most readers of this book will be familiar, perhaps in the forms it has taken from the twentieth century onwards of 'people's missals'; books which, when the Mass was still universally in Latin, were often bilingual and contained much additional, explanatory and catechetical, material. There are currently two forms of the Roman Missal authorized for use in the Catholic Church: the version of 1962, which is used in accordance with Benedict XVI's motu proprio *Summorum Pontificum*, and the (2002) third typical edition of the Roman Missal first introduced by Paul VI in 1970. The 1962 version of the Missal is sometimes known as the 'Tridentine Rite' or the *usus antiquior* ('more ancient use') of the Roman books. It is the last in a series of revisions to the Missal issued after the Council of Trent by St Pius V in 1570, under the bull *Quo Primum*. This Missal was variously revised in 1604 by Clement VIII, 1634 by Urban VIII, 1884 by Leo XIII and St Pius X (though not issued until under his successor Benedict XV in 1920). The texts of the 1920 Missal did not differ markedly from that of 1884, but

---

13 Cf. Rubin, M., *Corpus Christi: The Eucharist in Late Medieval Culture*, Cambridge, Cambridge University Press, 1991, pp. 185–98.

there were changes to the rubrics and the calendar, which we will discuss. Further revisions were made in 1955, and then Blessed John XXIII issued a revised Missal in 1962. There are some significant differences between the Missal of 1570 and that of 1604 and 1623 (especially in the calendar), but there were no significant ritual or textual alterations (although there were additions) until after the Missal of 1884 (in fact from 1920 onwards). The Missal of 1570 was the first Missal formally issued by Rome as a 'typical rite' for use across the Latin Church, although rites that had been in continuous use for two centuries or more were permitted to coexist alongside it (and did). This Missal is very similar to an earlier Roman Missal of 1474, and is recognizably the inheritor of the earliest extant forms of the texts of the Roman rite.

In 1951 and 1955 there were alterations, mainly to the Holy Week rites and the Vigil Mass of Pentecost, and these were consolidated, together with other changes, into Blessed John XXIII's Missal of 1962. The further revisions to the order of Mass in 1965 and 1967 really represent the first postconciliar reforms. In 1969 Paul VI issued a new Order of Mass, and in 1970 an entirely new Missal, which had been radically altered, both in its texts and in its ritual. Again there have been minor textual revisions, so that the current version of this Missal is the 2002 edition.

In addition to the Missal and of almost equal importance for daily use is the Breviary, or texts for use in the offices. St Pius V issued the version of the Breviary that corresponded to the 'Tridentine' Missal in 1568 – again important revisions were made by the two popes who initially revised the 1570 Missal, Clement VIII and Urban VIII. After 1623, and like the Missal, the text continued largely unaltered except for minor additions until the reform of 1911 when (unlike the 1920 Missal) there were really very important textual changes and it ceased to be recognizably the same book. There were major changes to the 1911 book in 1955 (although in such a way that the pre-1955 book could be adapted to reflect them), and all these were consolidated into an essentially new breviary under Blessed John XXIII in 1961. Paul VI issued an entirely revised and transformed breviary, now called the *Liturgy of the Hours* (*Liturgia Horarum*) in 1970, which has only had very minor subsequent alterations.

The offices of the Breviary are organized around the recitation of the psalms, anciently based on the idea that the 150 psalms in the ferial office are distributed across a single week. Until 1911 the weekly cycle of psalms was mainly distributed between the two offices of Matins and Vespers, with Psalms 1–108 belonging to Matins (omitting the psalms used at the other offices) and said in succession between Sunday and the following Saturday, and in a similar pattern Psalms 109–147 at Vespers. Lauds began with Psalms 92 and 99 on Sundays and feasts, and Psalm 50 on other days, followed on every day with Psalms 62 and 66 (said together without a break), a variable psalm and Old Testament canticle on each day, and then ending with the series 148–150, the 'Lauds' psalms which repeatedly use the word *laudate*, O praise! The little hours are all based around Psalm 118, said in full each day, with some additional psalmody at Prime. Compline has four psalms. This structure was significantly modified in 1911 (although the distribution of the psalms was less disturbed for feasts). In the1970 breviary the psalms were distributed across four weeks, not one, and the ancient ordering is gone.

The office of each day begins with Matins, known in Monastic Use as Vigils or the night office, and in the postconciliar liturgical books as the 'Office of Readings' (no longer required to be said during or near the night): each day this is proceeded by a single psalm (the 'invitatory' psalm – so called because it is the invitation to the office of the day: in the 1970 Liturgy of the Hours this could also be moved to be said before Lauds). Each psalm or group of psalms has an accompanying refrain, or antiphon, which is said before and after the psalm. The antiphons are sometimes 'common', that is they do not vary, or 'proper', that is they relate to a season, feast, or office for a specific kind of celebration or commemoration. Matins is a lengthy office consisting of 'nocturns' of many psalms (twelve, six, or three) and then, in each nocturn, three readings. After each reading there is a responsory, or series of verses that are sung to a rich chant, or that can be said. The 'ferial' or ordinary office on weekdays has only one nocturn; the festal, common, and Sunday offices almost always have three. In the first nocturn the readings are from scripture, but if there is more than one nocturn the readings are also taken from the

Fathers – in the second nocturn explaining the character of the feast, and in the third from homilies and texts commenting on the Gospel reading from the Mass.

Next after Matins is Lauds, the office that is parallel in structure and shape to Vespers, by long tradition sung at sunset (although in use it drifted at times even into the morning). The name Lauds refers to the three 'laudatory' psalms that until 1911 ended every celebration of this office, Psalms 148–150. Vespers takes its name from the Latin word for evening. Lauds, essentially a continuation of the night or vigil office, celebrates and praises the rising of the sun as an analogue of the resurrection: Vespers gives thanks for the ending of the day and in the dying of the light keeps faith that the light will rise again by morning. Vespers and Lauds have almost identical structures: five psalms or groups of psalms with five antiphons (on feasts almost invariably the same antiphons are used at Lauds and Vespers with the psalms), a brief scripture reading, or 'chapter', a hymn, responsory and then a canticle from St Luke's Gospel. At Lauds this is the 'song of Zacharias' or Benedictus (so named after the first word in Latin in the canticle) and at Vespers the 'song of Mary' or Magnificat.[14] On ferial and penitential days the offices end with a series of responses (*preces*), and then with a series of commemorations. This structure was much simplified after 1970, with the hymn being moved to the beginning and the number of psalms being reduced to three, or three parts of psalms.

After Lauds comes the first of the 'little hours', Prime, in many ways parallel in structure and shape to Compline, the hour that ends the liturgical day. The office of Prime was 'to be suppressed' in the liturgical books of the Roman rite by order of the Second Vatican Council, despite its great antiquity (originating in the fourth century).[15] In both the offices of Prime and Compline, the prayers

14 Luke 1.68–79; Luke 1.46–55.
15 *Sacrosanctum Concilium*, §89, d. 'Hora prima supprimatur'. This word does not mean 'abolished' in the strong sense, but simply 'reduced' or held back in significance. Many argued (like the Martimort and the Jesuit Robert Taft) that Prime was a duplication of Lauds, which entirely falsifies its history and use. In 1955 (along with many other

and psalms are less variable (at Compline the psalms did not vary at all until the reform of 1911, when they were also reduced in number from four to three). Finally there are the three 'little' hours, identical in structure: Terce, Sext and None. In monastic houses, cathedrals and conventual churches, Terce preceded the principal sung or solemn Mass of the day except on specific occasions where the rubrics indicated otherwise. Sext concluded the morning's work, and None was said at some point after lunch.

The texts of the Missal and the Breviary are closely interlocked, and comment on each other with an at times intense closeness: on all days that have a Gospel text proper to them (feasts, commons, Sundays, the days of Lent), the readings of the last nocturn of Matins are taken from homilies on the Gospel passage. Before the advent of printing, when the liturgical books were large manuscripts for communal use in the choir-space of churches, the texts for the singing of the offices and Mass would have come from the same books and would not have been distinguished or distributed in the way they now are. In fact the cycle of the liturgy – the Mass and the hours or offices – is a *single* cycle and is the whole of the choir liturgy for each day (with in many places an additional obligation to recite the parallel cycle of the Little Office of the Blessed Virgin Mary, notably among the Carthusians, and on particular occasions the Office for the Dead).

This indicates a further, important, fact: the ordinary and proper forms of the Mass and of all the offices (with the possible exception of Terce, Sext and None) is the sung form. The sung form includes the ritual for use in Choir at Mass and at each office. We will consider the philosophical and theological meaning of singing later, but the sung form of the offices in particular ritually represents the adoration of the angels before the cherubim throne. The psalms frequently

---

revisions) the recitation of the Athanasian Creed (almost certainly not composed by St Athanasius but more likely dating from fifth- or sixth-century Gaul), said on Sundays after the psalms, was abandoned at Prime. One of the clearest Western statements of the doctrine of the Divine Trinity, the loss of this creed to liturgical use has had a profoundly detrimental effect on the capacity of the parochial clergy to preach the most central doctrine of the Christian understanding of God.

employ a Hebrew word meaning, properly, temple-singing, indicating that the psalms were intrinsically ordered to liturgical use from the beginning. Historically, the normative form of the liturgy is therefore that of the principal houses of a diocese, monastery or religious order, in cathedrals with the bishop or canons presiding, or in monasteries and convents presided over by the abbot or prior, and so making the Temple of God visible in that place (and sanctifying it). The said forms of the liturgy – low Mass or recitation of the office 'privately' – are entirely derived from, and should always be oriented toward, and take their full meaning from, the sung and solemn forms.

Until the reform of the Missal and Breviary after the Second Vatican Council, very often the first pages one would have encountered on opening the books would not have been the rubrics, or an exposition of their use or theological meaning (the 'General Instructions' that now begin the official versions of these books) but a series of tables and charts to indicate how to relate the contents of the book to the passage of time. In other words, the most important aspect of the liturgical books is their relation to time, and to the sanctification of the passage of time in relation to the place in which the recitation is made.

We will not be considering in any depth the other liturgical books, but it is worth providing a brief description of them. The Processional provides the texts and manner of processions, and in some variants of the Roman rite includes variations and additional chants for use at Mass, for specific actions during the year, and in the offices. The processions usually take place after Terce, or after Mass on Sundays and major feasts. The Pontifical and Pontifical Missal provide the additional forms and texts used by the bishop at Mass, and for the sacraments and sacramentals reserved to the bishop – anciently Confirmation (which formerly could be administered by priests if there were danger of death, and now can be administered by them on other extraordinary occasions), ordinations, the putting into vows of members of religious orders, and certain kinds of blessing. The Ritual provides the forms of the sacraments of Baptism, marriage, unction or anointing of the sick, the funeral rite, a vast array of blessings, some exorcisms, and particular ceremonies for which few now have any use, like the lifting of interdicts on geographical regions. The Martyrology, divided by the days of the year and in the older liturgical use read each day (for the day following) at the end of Prime, provides a list of the saints and in many cases the legends or hagiography associated with them. The Martyrology was the last of the liturgical books to be reformed after the Second Vatican Council, being published in Latin only in 2002.

I do not propose to trace, or even account for, the history of liturgical change between 1911 and 2002. Alcuin Reid's masterly work *The Organic Development of the Liturgy* has done a very fine job in explaining what took place and how up until the beginning of the Second Vatican Council.[16] Full, systematic evaluations of the postconciliar reform have yet to appear, but the work of Lauren Pristas has shown at least some of the theological effects.[17] Significant commentaries have been written on the reformed texts.[18]

It is arguable that the most important alterations to the liturgy were not the ones that began in 1964, in the wake of the Second Vatican Council, but much earlier, in fact beginning during the pontificate of St Pius X. Many of these changes were developments in the wake of the Liturgical Movement, which had its roots in the zeal of Dom Prosper Guéranger, who in 1841 had begun a huge 15-volume commentary on the Liturgy, *The Liturgical Year*.[19] For many, the Liturgical Movement began formally in 1909 with Cardinal Mercier's 'National Congress of Catholic Works' with its call for the text of the Mass and of Sunday Vespers to be available to all the faithful in the vernacular. Other prominent figures in the Liturgical

---

16 Reid, A., *The Organic Development of the Liturgy*, San Francisco, Ignatius, 2005 (2004).
17 Pristas, L.: 'The Pre- and Post-Vatican II Collects of the Dominican Doctors of the Church', in *New Blackfriars*, November 2005, pp. 604–21; 'The Orations of the Vatican II Missal: Policies for Revision', in *Communio*, vol. 30 (Winter, 2003), pp. 621–53; 'The Collects at Sunday Mass: An Examination of the Revisions of Vatican II', in *Nova et Vetera*, vol. 3 (Winter, 2005), pp. 5–38; 'Theological Principles that Guided the Redaction of the Roman Missal (1970)', in *The Thomist*, vol. 67 (April, 2003), pp. 157–95.
18 Perhaps the most comprehensive is by Martimort, A. G. with others, *The Church at Prayer* (4 vols), London, Geoffrey Chapman, 1988.
19 Guéranger OSB, P., *L'année liturgique* (15 vols), Paris, Oudin, 1875 (1844–8).

Movement included Abbot Ildefons Herewegen of the Abbey of Maria Laach (who in 1918 began what was to become the 'dialogue Mass' or Mass where the whole community made the responses to the priest), Romano Guardini and Dom Odo Casel (also a monk of Maria Laach), Dom Lambert Beauduin and the historian Joseph Jungmann.[20] Without doubt the Liturgical Movement generated huge benefits for the lay faithful, especially in the quality of the missals and catechetical material that appeared in its wake. A major premise of many of those connected with the Liturgical Movement was, however, that the faithful, and many of the clergy, did not fully or adequately understand the liturgical actions in which they were participating. To say the very least, where this view was prevalent it was itself a misunderstanding: historians like Sheridan Gilley have demonstrated that, for instance, in Ireland there was a wealth of activity – guilds, societies, and other religious organizations – dedicated to assisting the faithful in understanding and participating in the sacred liturgy.[21] Ireland was anything but unique, and this instinct that drove the Liturgical Movement should better be traced to theological anxieties among the theologians themselves about what the liturgy is and how it is to be understood.

---

20 For a preconciliar history of the Liturgical Movement which exhibits the bias that came to predominate (of the liturgy as something needing to be adapted, especially in the light of a reformed understanding of scripture, if it were ever effectively to be brought to the masses) see the work of the American Lutheran Koenker, E. B., *The Liturgical Renaissance in the Roman Catholic Church*, Chicago, Chicago University Press, 1954. For an assessment of Koenker see Reid, A., *The Organic Development of the Liturgy*, pp. 192–4.

21 In a paper given to the CIEL UK conference at Marsh College, Oxford in 2006, not yet in print.

Chapter 3

Reasonable Worship

This book argues that the call for liturgical reform, especially in the form that it began to take after 1903, and with full force in the period 1965–70, was driven by an underlying rationalism. Rationalism is the understanding that everything, all truth, arises on the basis of what can be foreseen by man, what is calculable and predictable for him in advance of its occurring. To reason means 'to think', but in a particular way: to think 'constructively', from one premise to the next. The rational is the essentially calculable (indeed the verb *ratio* in Latin can mean either to think or to count, in the same way as 'to reckon' in English can mean 'to think' or 'to count up' – accountants 'reckon'). The rational always moves from the past to the future: it builds future knowledge on the basis of what we already know, and have already secured to be true. This is why the scientific method is a rational method. Descartes' understanding of God was – although derived using seemingly impeccably Christian credentials – an essentially rational conception of God. The God that 'causes' the human self (the one who can say *I think, therefore I am*) is the 'only' kind of God that could have given rise to such a being. In this, Descartes said very little about the nature of God: he made a particular argument from the infinity of God compared to the finitude of man, an argument derived from the claim that God is infinite to be found in many earlier authors (especially St Thomas Aquinas and Suàrez) but profoundly different in its effects.

If the meaning of what it is to be human, and indeed the meaning of what it is to be divine, has already been secured in (philosophical) thought, then, strictly speaking, any other source of understanding of humanity or God (or creation and the world) will have little or nothing to say to you – indeed, quite the reverse, you will measure *every* other kind of discourse about God, humanity, and the world against what you already know. The liturgy is, however, another source of understanding of God, man, and the world. As a source of understanding it is inherently structured towards the intellect of man. It is not, however 'rational' in the sense that what it says is a means of calculation and prediction for man. Quite the reverse, the liturgy constantly changes and surprises us; it disturbs the rational, predictable, order of things in order to open the understanding still more widely to the things of God. What God has to say in his address to a man is always surprising, never exactly what he would have expected or could have thought to hear. The liturgy comes from the future, in fact from the end of time. It draws those whom it addresses toward God, who calls mankind into a life that is not based on man's past, and previous experience, but on man's destiny, and it speaks *from out* of where man is called to go. It speaks from ahead of, and beyond, man, both individually and as a whole.

The rational is what can always be grasped merely by the means of the mind: the truth that it knows is preoccupied with the past, and with what is *already* known. Liturgy takes over and completes a structure of truth that was originally embodied in myth. For the pagan Greeks, every myth appeared in multiple forms, and was said in multiple ways. In this it spoke of the truth that the gods knew, which took different forms on the face of the earth. Myth, unlike reason, was also preoccupied with the future, because, the Greeks held, the gods could see what men could not. The name given to Zeus by Homer and the poets is 'wide-seeing' or 'far-seeing'. The gods let man into his future.

Many of the myths, of the gods especially, have many endings and can be told in multitude ways. In the same myth even the names of the characters can change. In different versions of his birth, Dionysus is the son of either Semele or Persephone – so much so that Dionysus is himself known as *Dimetor*, 'twice-mothered'. Doubling clings to Dionysus: he is plucked from his mother's womb as she is destroyed (by demanding to see Zeus in his full glory) before he has come fully to term, and saved for birth a second time by Zeus (his father) sewing him into Zeus' thigh (a mythic coyness); he is also known as 'twice-born'. The poetic verse-form which is his own is the dithyramb, the 'double-door'. His deaths are multiple, as is his rebirth.

Myth reveals what it is to disclose and so speak of as the true, not as the rational statement does, through a *single* 'truth' to be appropriated, but through doubles and multiples of means. These yield that the true manifests itself in different ways according to actual places, and persons, and times. Truth given in this way by myth is not 'free' or relative, or empty, or plastic in form; rather, myth always presupposes that it appears in world, that world gives myth to be in many ways. The multiformity of myth allows world to be seen as the 'wherein' myths unfold. That the myth is told *here* in one way and now *here* in another indicates in a most formal way the canopy of world in its breadth, and as letting the variety of meanings of a truth come to be.

What is essential in every mythic saying is some truth that can be got through to, and reached, only with difficulty, only by seeing it from many sides and in many places. What myth discloses takes much time, and a familiarity with many places, to know. To seize what is essential in myth is not momentary (as rational knowledge is) but can only be long drawn out and has, not a moment, but *place* and *while*. Myth, in its speaking, always presupposes the existence of the world and its various places in which the myth is to be told.

If myth is no longer binding for man because the pagan world has been eclipsed, and myth no longer indicates who the gods are as ones who foresee the future and the unknown for man, or who man himself is, and how it is with his world, then surely is not the mathematical character of reason much more binding? Does not logic count for something, and compel us in some way? Martin Heidegger comments that 'mathematical knowledge is in itself, in its content . . . the emptiest knowledge in what it lets itself think, and as this is at the same time the least binding for man'.[1] In fact Christian liturgy occupied and perfected the understanding of truth that is given in a more limited way in myth.[2] The pagan mythology gave way to what is revealed by God in Christ. In no sense did Christianity take over the content of the pagan myths, but because the understanding of truth (as oriented toward the future) given in myth had been disclosed, the perfect revelation in Jesus Christ was able to show the origin and unity of what myth dimly gestured towards in the eternal covenant with the Father: a *future* hope, one that is disclosed *from the future*, from ahead and beyond. The revelation in Jesus Christ revealed man's destiny, and the destiny of the whole cosmos, as the perfection of all things at the end of time.

My concern is not so much with the history or even the motives of the period of reform from 1903 to 2002, as with its effects on the liturgy itself and its capacity to undertake its sacred work of revealing the person of the Father through the person of the Son, and the meaning and destiny of man and the cosmos in which he dwells. Underlying this is a view that the reforms were often carried out with the best of intentions, but with surprising and often unintended consequences. Several commentators have noted that the period of liturgical reform coincides with the exercise of greater papal authority over the liturgy. Alcuin Reid draws attention to the significance of the reforms of St Pius X (which we will examine in greater detail as we proceed) when he says: 'that a pope could discard ancient liturgical Tradition by sole virtue of his own authority is found nowhere in liturgical history before',[3] a point explored with devastating breadth by Geoffrey Hull in his astonishing book *The Banished*

---

1 Heidegger, M., *Die Grundbegriffe der Metaphysik: Welt – Endlichkeit – Einsamkeit*, in *Gesamtausgabe*, vol. 29/30, Frankfurt, Klostermann, 1992 (1983), p. 25. 'Die Mathematische Erkenntnis ist in sich ihrem Gehalte nach . . . die leerste Erkenntnis, die sich denken läßt, und als diese zugleich für den Menschen die unverbindlichste.' Heidegger adds that this is why mere 17-year-old mathematicians can make great discoveries.

2 It was an instinctive understanding of this that motivated so much of the research of Dom Odo Casel, although he did not explicitly thematize the question of truth in the relation of myth and reason to the future and the past in this way.

3 Reid, A., *The Organic Development of the Liturgy*, pp. 77–8.

Heart.[4] Nowadays the most ardent proponents of liturgical modernization are almost invariably those who most dislike the exercise of papal authority, entirely lacking the historical sense to realize that what they most desire only became possible through the exercise of what they most disdain. Where real care must be exercised, however, is in understanding what gave rise to that possibility: the papacy did not usurp a power previously unknown to it, rather has the papacy been driven by historical circumstances – the Reformation, revolution, the Napoleonization of Europe, to name but a few. Above all, and despite its resistance, the papacy has also been shaped by the metaphysical outlook that drives modern man to seek domination over all things, the triumph of power itself. In fact, understood like this, the papacy remains a place of resistance and refusal of the planetary drive to instrumentalize all things to the will of man, but is still caught up in it, no less than are the rest of us.

We will consider St Pius X's reforms again, but the first document he published on these matters, calling for the restoration of the Church's music, was in 1903, with the motu proprio, *Tra le sollecitudini.*[5] This document initiated the use of the words *partecipazione attiva*, the 'active participation' that has been taken up again and again as a slogan in the course of liturgical reform, and especially by the Liturgical Movement, which we will discuss from time to time. *Tra le sollecitudini* is rare, even now, among Vatican documents in having been published first in Italian, only appearing in an official Latin version later. The Latin form of the document altered the Italian phrase 'active participation' by speaking merely of *participatio* – 'participation', dropping the notion of 'active' agency that has, nevertheless, ever since attended the idea. To join in you have to *do* something. We must not blame St Pius X himself – the phrase caught a mood that

---

4 Hull, G. S., *The Banished Heart: Origins of Heteropraxis in the Catholic Church*, Sydney, Spes Nova League, 1995.

5 Pius X, motu proprio of November 22nd, 1903, *Tra le Sollecitudini*, in *Acta Sanctæ Sedis*, vol. 36, Vatican, 1904. The Italian text is at pp. 329–39 (see p. 331); the Latin at pp. 387–95 (cf. p. 388). The reason the text is in both languages is almost certainly that the text was originally prepared as an instruction to the clergy of the patriarchate of Venice, from which place he came to be pope.

was already abroad. You can't be present to something unless you are doing something to indicate your presence. Nietzsche would have applauded (there is no doer prior to the deed). Later in the period of reform the documents speak constantly of *actuosa participatio* – active participation – most notably Pius XII's 1947 encyclical letter *Mediator Dei*, itself a milestone in this process.[6] The Dogmatic Constitution on the Sacred Liturgy of the Second Vatican Council, *Sacrosanctum Concilium*, certainly emphasized 'full, conscious, and active participation in liturgical celebrations which is demanded by the very nature of the liturgy, and to which the Christian people, "a chosen race, a royal priesthood, a holy nation, a redeemed people" (1 Pet. 2.9, 4–5) have a right and obligation by reason of their baptism'.[7]

The development of liturgical reform from 1903 onwards, and the phase of the Liturgical Movement which began about the same time, both began by being oriented toward involving the faithful more deeply in the liturgical life of the Church. There was a genuine desire to make the liturgy in its full history and complexity more accessible and more available to the faithful. With this desire came the need to relate the explanation of the liturgy to 'modern man' – the 'man of his times' that turns up as the subject of Romano Guardini's hugely influential little books *Vom Geist der Liturgie*, whose title is usually translated as 'The Spirit of the Liturgy'. Guardini was a founder figure and leader of the Liturgical Movement. Translated like this, the title suggests that the book discusses something that is a feature or characteristic of the liturgy itself, but even a cursory reading of the book reveals that the title actually indicates the book's preoccupation is not so much with the liturgy as such, as with the way that it is received, and so understood, by 'modern man'. This concern became a central focus of many of the leading figures of the Liturgical Movement. The word

---

6 Pius XII, Encyclical Letter *Mediator Dei*, November 1947, in *Acta Apostolicæ Sedis*, vol. 14, pp. 521–95, p. 551 *et passim*.

7 Vatican Council II, Dogmatic Constitution on the Sacred Liturgy *Sacrosanctum Concilium*, 1963, §14. 'Valde cupit Mater Ecclesia ut fideles universi ad plenam illam, consciam atque actuosam liturgicarum celebrationum participationem ducantur, quae ab ipsius Liturgiae natura postulatur et ad quam populus christianus, "genus electum, regale sacerdotium, gens sancta, populus adquisitionis" (1 Pet. 2.9, 4–5), vi Baptismatis ius habet et officium.'

Geist in German has a huge range of meanings – it can mean spirit, but also mind, intellect, understanding, to name but a few of the possibilities. Guardini's use of *Geist* suggests something more like 'the means of understanding' of the liturgy. In the book, he discusses the actual texts and material of the liturgy almost not at all. While he recalls that the liturgy 'has no purpose because it is indeed not there for the sake of men, but of God',[8] in fact he is totally occupied with the idea that 'before all else the whole assembly must take an active part . . . all those present must take part'.[9] Guardini betrays the underlying rationalism of this view in his description of the self-understanding of the 'modern people' he so often refers to. On the one hand, he emphasizes that the liturgy is not celebrated by any individual, 'but by the whole company of the faithful'.[10] On the other hand (in a way that exactly parallels the Cartesian understanding of the rational self or 'subject' that we will examine shortly), he argues that 'the individual is truly a member of the whole, but not merely a member, he is not dissolved in the whole. He is joined to it, but in such a way that he remains throughout what he is, self-standing, remaining his own person.'[11]

This is the thoroughly modern, subjective, understanding of the human being – that one who, independent and self-established, *then* enters into social (here conceived as liturgical) relations. This same individual, whom Guardini had identified as the basis for the Liturgical Movement, made his appearance as one of the driving reasons for liturgical reform in *Sacrosanctum Concilium*, speaking in its very opening paragraph of the need to reform the liturgy to accommodate it to contemporary humanity and the 'requirements of the age'.[12]

---

8 Guardini, R., *Vom Geist der Liturgie*, Freiburg, Herder-Bücherei, 1959 (1917), pp. 96f. 'Die liturgie [kann]. . . keinen 'Zweck' haben, weil si ja eigentlich gar nicht um des Menschen, sondern um Gottes willen da ist.'

9 Guardini, R., *Vom Geist der Liturgie*, p. 34. 'Vor allem muß die ganze Versammlung lebendigen Anteil nehmen. [. . .] Alle Anwesenden müssen beteiligt sein.'

10 Guardini, R., *Vom Geist der Liturgie*, p. 45. 'Sondern von der Gesamtheit der Gläubigen.'

11 Guardini, R., *Vom Geist der Liturgie*, p. 45. 'Der Einzelne ist wohl Glied des Ganzen, aber nicht nur Glied; er geht im Ganzen nicht auf. Er ist ihm eingefügt, aber so, daß er durchaus bleibt, was er ist, eigenständige, in sich ruhende Persönlichkeit.'

12 Vatican Council II, Dogmatic Constitution on the Sacred Liturgy *Sacrosanctum Concilium*, 1963, §1. 'Ad nostræ ætatis necessitates.'

Guardini speaks of the problem of the particularity of the liturgy in its address to every individual, but in such a way that suggested to later liturgical thinkers not that the individual should adapt himself to the liturgy, but that the liturgy may need to be adapted to modern man. Active participation became a goal towards which the liturgy needed to be driven, and adapted wherever it could be identified that it fell short of that goal.

Fr Aidan Nichols, in an attempt to mitigate this interpretation, has suggested that *actuosa participatio* did not so much mean *active* as *actual* participation,[13] but even here, one must ask (and theologically), actual participation in what? Valiant attempts to interpret *actuosa* as *actual* as a way of resisting the underlying imperative to be 'active' and 'doing' tend to fail because if the Latin allows for this ambiguity, the original Italian is quite specific: *attiva* meant active, even if (in Latin) *actuosa* does not mean *activa*. What 'active' meant in 1903 is much closer to what 'actual' means now – in this sense Nichol's emphasis is not wrong.

We have been strongly schooled by the implementation of liturgical reform to interpret *actuosa participatio* as intense, conscious, agent, participation in the rites – the right and ability to say and perform the actions of the liturgy for ourselves. In reality this is about the one thing that *actuosa participatio* cannot mean. It means rather, fully to participate in what the rite itself participates *in* and makes us present *to*. In what we now call the Liturgy of the Word of the rite of Mass, this is the history of God's revelation of his plan of salvation for all, and the culmination of that plan in what is revealed through the life and teaching, death and resurrection of His Son. In the Liturgy of the Eucharist, our participation comes to be in the conversation that takes place between Father and Son in the sacrifice of the cross and in Christ's rising again. The 'agent' of the liturgy is not even the celebrating priest or bishop, let alone any other minister or layperson, but Christ, in relation to his Father.

---

13 Cf. Nichols OP, A., *Looking at the Liturgy: A Critical View of its Contemporary Form*, San Francisco, Ignatius, 1996, pp. 65–9; Reid, A., *The Organic Development of the Liturgy*, p. 64 *et passim*.

Actuosa participatio is not a description of what we must be *doing*, but a synonym for our life in the Spirit, the means by which we are drawn (and so 'done to'), and so we are placed *into* the life of the Divine Trinity, the life we are made present to and made able to share by the enacted work of the liturgical rites (a work of Christ's). In truth, in face of the cross, we can only be drawn into what passes between the Son and the Father insofar as we are given grace in the Spirit to pray and attend. The psalms themselves speak of what it really is to participate: 'Jerusalem is built as a city whose fellowship (*participatio*) is complete'.[14] Jerusalem, the Holy City, is the place *wherein* we can be ones participating in the marriage of the sacrificial Lamb. We must enter the new Jerusalem, enter into her Temple (liturgically speaking), to participate in her Covenant.

It is for this reason that none of the words pronounced in the rite are properly *our* own (whoever 'we' are – bishop, priest, minister, layman), they all belong to Christ either directly or dependently. Only what passes between the Father and the Son has the power to save us: there is nothing at all we can *do* for ourselves, standing at the foot of the cross. We are helpless to save ourselves. The words of the liturgy are Christ's, either because they are his own words taken from the Gospels, or because they point to him (they are words taken from scripture as it itself witnesses to the history of our salvation) or because our petitions and prayers are consonant with the entirety of the tradition. The liturgy presupposes that the prayer that takes place in church is the high-priestly prayer of Christ to the Father which is made through Christ's sacrificial self-offering of himself *to* the Father. It is this priestly prayer that makes all other prayer possible. The words uttered in prayer, and how they are disposed, are therefore of paramount importance. Especially, the priest and his assistants are not free with respect to these words: they must utter what is needful.

When Pope Paul VI spoke of the meaning of *actuosa participatio*, he described it with the words 'now all must listen and pray'[15] – this

---

14 Psalm 121.3. 'Jerusalem quae aedificatur ut civitas cuius participatio eius in idipsum.'
15 Paul VI, audience of 17 March 1965, in *Osservatore Romano*, 18 March 1965, p. 1. 'Ora no, deve ascoltare e pregare.'

applies as much to the bishop, priest and sacred ministers, as to the people. Even if we have something to do or say we first attend and listen. It is by praying the liturgy, above all the Mass, that we are made present to the sacrifice and its power to save us. Hence why so many of the prayers, especially of the Missal, traditionally have emphasized our need for help in this work of prayer and attention.

Participation understood like this is quite difficult, requiring much more than just *doing* or *saying* or *singing*. It requires 'seeing into', and even behind, what is done and said and sung, and so understanding its sacred meaning. It requires careful catechesis and much concentration. Actually it requires a great deal of silence and stillness.

How is it that active participation has come to have a meaning so very different from the one I have described? The way in which active participation has been interpreted – as our 'doing' the liturgy – betrays an underlying rationalism in understanding what the liturgy itself is to do. This rationalistic outlook says that in order to participate 'effectively' we must know in advance and already have grasped the meaning of what it is we are involved in. The liturgy is to be experienced, participated in and actualized (made real, we might say) by a self that precedes the liturgical event in question. This self is the modern self known and understood in contemporary philosophy and psychology, the 'subject'; that 'one' essentially described by the philosopher René Descartes and named by Romano Guardini as 'self-standing'. Descartes' declaration *cogito, ergo sum*, 'I think, therefore I am', is not a deduction coming at the conclusion of a syllogism, nor the consequence of a proof, but absolutely the reverse. It is, for Descartes, first in the order of things of which I can be certain. The self from thereon in is always present in advance of everything else it knows. This is in contrast to the understanding of the self that preceded Descartes, based on the ancient conception of the self, that the self is not 'there already', but is actually activated and constituted *by* what it knows.

In his *Meditations on First Philosophy*, after having established the self as first in the order of things of which I can be certain, the second indubitable thing Descartes discovers is God. This discovery of God is, however, the discovery of the idea of God, and moreover, the necessity of God and that I know God to be God has been located in the same ideal realm where I established the self as certain. There is now an 'interior' world which the psyche inhabits and truly is. Everything exterior, as Descartes reminds us several times in his *Meditations on First Philosophy*,[16] is still dubitable and capable of being known only with error. His concern to establish the indubitability of God is quite simple; God is necessary to guarantee the truth of what has now become the exterior world. If it were not for the idea of God, truth would simply assume the character of sets of non-objective psychological rules. Philosophy would thereby cease to be 'first philosophy', and would become simply 'psychology'. It is only after the establishment of the indubitability of the idea of God that I can proceed to establish knowledge about the world that is free from error.

If we are to assume that the modern conception of the person is sufficient for understanding our self-constitution in faith, we must come to terms with the fact that this conception which is epitomized and described by Descartes has radically separated the constitution of the self from God. Only *subsequent* to the *cogito*, to self-positing, is God discovered at all. For Descartes, God is only in consequence not even of who, but only of *that* I am. Despite the fact that Descartes believed that he could through the *cogito* establish God as more certain 'even than the truths of geometry', about the only person ever convinced by Descartes on this account was himself. It remained to Nietzsche to hammer out philosophy as a pure psychology, and to declare the God who Descartes had established as certain, as certain to be dead. From now on truth (for Nietzsche) is characterized in terms of power, which is the way an interior psyche exerts its force and self-enactment on an exterior world, a world which from now on is to be constructed and produced, and so is not an already-given.

Liturgical prayer works in exactly the opposite way, and the person it presumes is a new person made in Christ, in fulfilment of the relationship already begun in, and constituted by, Baptism. Constituted

---

16 Cf. Descartes, R., *Meditationes de Prima Philosophia*, in Adam, C. and Tannery P., *Œvres de Descartes*, Paris, Vrin, 1996 (1965: 1641), vol. 7.

here means 'made possible'. However, even Baptism refers to a birth from ahead and beyond us, in fact *from above*: in Baptism we are oriented toward the future, toward that place from where we receive our true identity, and so are oriented toward what we will become, not what we are now. Here, not just the priest, nor even the other ministers of the liturgy, but all who participate in liturgical prayer simultaneously are called to a participation that joins each of us to the body of Christ, and through that joining, to each other. Our work is a work of self-displacement, so that it is *Christ* who speaks in the scriptures and through the recitation of the psalms, *Christ* who dwells amongst us as Bridegroom, as high priest, and in sacrament, *Christ* whom we find in those who are also present with us in the liturgy.

To know 'about' the God disclosed through the liturgy is not the same as knowing God *in* the liturgy. In, let us say, a course of Religious Studies, it might be possible to discover that Christians think of God as Trinity whereas Jews or Muslims do not, and to explore the differences. This is to know 'about' the Trinity. To know the Trinity, to know God *as* Trinity, is to know through faith in Jesus Christ that God as Father calls me through the Spirit to be an adopted son or daughter. To know, to believe, to trust, that Jesus is the Son of God is to know that I too can be filiated to God. The experience of participating in the liturgy is the practical working out of that knowledge. It is knowledge that can only be gained by, and rejoiced in, through faith. Through faith, and by Baptism, we enter *into* the life of God by means of the liturgy. The liturgy discloses an understanding of God as he reveals himself to *be*, in Christ, in a knowledge that can only be gained through faith, not deduced or derived by reason or a rational act of self-positing (I think: I am).

What arises liturgically is a new relationship that did not exist prior to faith and Baptism. It is therefore radically different to the self's self-understanding in contemporary culture. The self is no longer, in the liturgy, self-constituted, nor can it understand itself ever as self-positing (as a Cartesian *ego*). In consequence of the redemption wrought in Christ, the self must always be understood as constituted through a pilgrimage of discovery. This discovery discloses the self's reality as properly interior to the divine life, the life of God as Trinity through what is revealed in the liturgy. It should therefore become clear what is meant by knowledge of the Trinity. This is not knowledge 'about', because my self-knowledge is part of the content of my knowledge of the Trinity, or rather, my self-knowledge is constituted through my being known and loved by God.

This understanding of the self is so radically different to what we are used to, or rather, to how we are used to thinking of ourselves, that it can seem like the stating of an ideal, rather than a real relation. In truth, however, this is the very deposition of the ideality of the self. As self-positing the self always asserts and posits itself as the sole certainty in a realm detached from the world, and indeed from God – an ideal realm. Having so posited itself as certain, it then proceeds from the certainty of ideal world to the dubitability of the real one. In contrast to this idealism, the intra-Trinitarian structure of the self can never be ideal, but must take the world as the place where the practice and experience of intra-Trinitarian life is played out. Creation here becomes, not something whose status can ever be dubious or doubted (in the way that it is central to Descartes' method of doubt), but rather, the God-given place of the encounter with God through Christ in the liturgy. Creation becomes the matter and stuff of a conversation with God wherein our intra-Trinitarian belonging is both lived and has to be fulfilled.

Nowhere is this interrelational character of life, constituted from out of the Divine Trinity, more visibly demonstrated than in the most solemn celebrations of the Church's rites, especially in the pontifical form of the Mass, and the solemn form of the Mass with deacon and subdeacon, as well as in the solemn forms of the offices on great feasts, where there are two, four, or even six assistants. The rites *require* the cooperative work of those around the altar in ensuring that the work to be carried out is *done*. Countless commentators have explained that the activity of the rites around the altar unfolds a vision of the ministrations of angels to Christ around the unbloody altar of heaven: the pleading of the lamb before the cherubim throne (the prayer of the High Priest in the New Jerusalem). This is the representation in the church of the Holy of Holies as the temple 'place of the Presence'. The type of this is the vision in the book of Revelation as the type of Christian liturgy, again whose summit is the most solemn forms of the rite of Mass.[17] Margaret Barker notes that 'In temple tradition, those born from above were the angels, the true teachers, and this is what the Christians claimed to be'.[18] To be born 'from above' is to be born not *ab initio*, from a rational Cartesian mental act of self-authentication, but eschatologically, from beyond (we might say, *ab infinito*) and so from out of the end of time (from Baptism).

The solemn rites display and make visible what the life of angels will be like. When we witness them we witness how we are to co-operate around the heavenly altar to make manifest the meaning and presence of Christ. At the same time, this is why the rites have actions and gestures that are not spontaneous but required and laid down – they are the analogue of the virtues and the grace we must acquire to *become* what we will be at the end of time, before the altar and the throne. We must put on these actions and gestures, which means we must learn them as coming from beyond and outside us, not from within. This is also why those around the altar are vested. Not that they should glory in what they wear, but because they are ones made glorious in Christ, resurrected as *glorified*. Our baptismal robe of white is further made to shimmer.[19] St Thomas Aquinas speaks of how the angels shimmer with light, not shining by emitting light, but shimmering, which means retaining to themselves the light by which they are illuminated. This description mirrors the biblical and historical accounts of appearances of angels and the resurrected (of which the type is the Transfiguration).[20]

The vestments at the altar are not mere coverings or aggrandizements. Rather – in that they are variously held, lifted, taken off and

---

17 Cf. Revelation 4.1–11.

18 Barker, M., *Temple Themes in Christian Worship*, p. 45.

19 Cf. *Rituale Romanum*, 1884 (1752), Rite of Baptism. 'Accipe vestem candidam, quam perferas immaculatam ante tribunal Domini nostri Jesu Christi, ut habeas vitam æternam'. ('Receive this white vesture, see that you carry it unstained before the judgement seat of our Lord Jesus Christ, that you may have eternal life.')

20 Cf. Matthew 17.2 (Mark 9.1). 'And [Jesus] was transfigured before them. And his face did shine as the sun: and his garments became white as snow.'

replaced, folded, unfolded, exchanged and supported by the ministers and servers of the altar, or used to veil, conceal, and unconceal what they adorn – they articulate a complex and sophisticated language of the relations between persons, and of the meaning of the sacred vessels, and so reveal the gradations of the ranks of priesthood (remembering that the diaconate refers to the Levitical priesthood) and grades of angels that were a common feature of Christian discourse until comparatively recently, falling into the background only with the end of the high middle ages. Inasmuch as this language is derived from the divine commands given to describe the nature and character of sacred vesture in the Temple, they indicate a divinely revealed origin, not just a human manufacture.[21]

If the sanctuary represents the vision of the holy of holies, it also renders it audible. The language of prayer, rendered as singing, breaks the structures of rationality and representation that constitute the human person subjectivally, so that what is produced to be heard and understood is *not* the product of the human will, but the resonance of the human voice through the sung invocation of the divine. The musicologist Marcel Pérès has examined in detail the Cistercian musical reforms of the thirteenth century, and from his researches concludes that 'the theoretical preoccupations of the Cistercians were not vain speculations; the intention of the reformers was directed at the incarnation of the Word through the agency of the most basic laws of the resonance of the human voice'.[22]

Armed, however, with an understanding of human being and its relation to God; governed, not by a modern conception of a spatio-

---

21 It is disastrous that in the reforms of the twentieth century this language of the vestments was truncated and lost, beginning with the abandonment in the 1950s of the use of folded chasubles in the liturgy of Lent and Advent, the disappearance of the humeral veil at the solemn form of the Mass in 1965, and the significant truncation of the vestments of bishops. The quality of modern vestments all too rarely makes the wearer a fit inhabitant of the heavens.

22 Pérès, M., *Chant Cistercien du XIIIe*, Paris, Fondation, 1992, p. 3. 'Les préoccupations théoriques des cisterciens n'étaient pas de vaines spéculations: les réformateurs avaient pour dessein l'incarnation du Verbe par l'intermédiaire de lois de résonance les plus fondamentales de la voix humaine.' Cf. Michel Huglo and Marcel Pérès, *Aspects de la Musique Liturgique au Moyen Age*, Paris, Éditions Créaphis, 1991.

temporal universe, but by the ancient cosmology in a musical system still owing much to Pythagoras; and certainly not owing anything at all to the way in which musical relations were mathematically harmonized in the baroque period,[23] the Cistercians constituted by the harmonious collaboration of architecture and sound an icon of the heavens which was also a figuration of the mystery of salvation.

The principles that underlay what Pérès describes were already established in Christian practice: in the first place, the singing of the chant was understood as constitutive of world as such, not *a* world, an imaginary place, but the *real* cosmos *entire*. This is not a community that a Cartesian agent subject enters into from without, from the ideal place of a mental act. Rather, through the work that it undertakes (prayer itself, as singing) the participant is disclosed to be already a member of the company of heaven, an angelic figure, which is why the choir should be vested. Singing here is analogous to the unity of the heavens even in their movement – an understanding derived directly from the Pythagorean and ancient understanding of the work of music as reflecting the movement of the heavens, a work that *lifts* the person into the heavens, and so to the outermost limit of the heavens, from ancient times considered to be the very 'seat' of the divine. This is the *performance* of the 'anagogical' as that lifting up that was described earlier.[24]

This viewpoint, derived from pre-Christian antiquity, becomes Christianized in the sense that the heavens are understood as not of themselves eternal (as, for instance, Aristotle had held) but as originating from God. The chanting of the psalms, and the participation in the sacrifice of Christ, constitutes the form the participant takes within the heavens in his or her relation to the God who alone creates *ab initio*. This form is that of Christ. In the second place, however, the Cistercian reform aimed to make much more explicit the natural harmony between the heavens and the earth that the atonement in Christ had restored. Pérès makes the point that the great Cistercian

---

23 The resolution of musical intervals and the 'Pythagorean comma' through altering the pure relations between notes by thirteenths and seventeenths in the solution of 'equal temperament'.

24 See p. 2 above.

abbeys – Fontenay, Sénanque, Le Thoronet, Fontfroide and so on – were constructed to possess particular acoustic properties that amplified the human voice in such a way as to add harmonies to it that would not otherwise be apparent to the ear. Pérès adds: 'Without recourse to the artifices of polyphony, a single voice, or the chorus in unison, are able to produce harmonies that are not the work of the human will, but the effect of the fundamental laws of the vibration of sound-bodies, physical harmony, the impulse of matter that, by means of the absolute logic of its laws, renders the perenniality and the magnificence of the thought of God to the human ear.'[25]

This form of social relation (as an audition of the society of heaven, not earth), makes present, and audible (but does not 'construct') our common being in God, initiated in Baptism, achieved through grace, through the gift of faith and the strenuous perfection of the virtues, but is never accomplished by a 'cogitative act' of reason or deduction. This divinized society, as singing-with-others, can never be either egotistical, nor interpersonal, for *my* singing is never directed towards the *thou* (towards 'you'), but is always a taking up of words that are presumed really to be a conversation between the Son and the Father, into which *we* are to be inserted. We relate to God by singing the words that are exchanged *within* the divine life, the Godhead as such: we are included in this *through* the Spirit, and so through the relations between Father, Son and Spirit. This is why *what* we sing must be capable of being read as this conversation: the type of this is the psalms, whose words form the backbone of all chant.

In the liturgy, as citizens and subjects of the new, heavenly, Jerusalem, our true birth (Baptism) is heavenly, from *above*, and *beyond*, not below, and in the past. It is for this reason that (in except three cases) the Church celebrates liturgically the day of death of the

---

25 Pérès, M., *Chant Cistercien du XIIIe*, p. 5. 'Ainsi, sans avoir recours à l'artifice de la polyphonie, voix seule ou chœur à l'unisson peuvent faire entendre des harmonies qui ne sont pas l'œuvre de la volonté humaine mais l'effet des lois fondamentales de vibration des corps sonores, harmonie physique, élan de la matière qui par l'absolue logique de ses lois rend accessible à l'entendement humain la pérennité et la magnificence de la pensée de Dieu.'

saints as the 'heavenly birthday', not the actual date of physical birth. The exceptions are: the birth of the Christ, who is descended from heaven and is of heaven by right; Mary the Mother of God who is conceived immaculate and preserved from sin throughout life, whose assumption reveals her already to belong more to heaven than to earth; and John the Baptist, who was sanctified in his leaping in the womb at Mary's salutation of his mother, Elizabeth, and who was at that moment justified and freed from original and all future sin until his martyrdom.[26]

Is not the modern conception of the human person also relationally constituted? Is not the modern preoccupation with 'the other', or the 'philosophy of intersubjectivity', the assertion of this relationality, which provides a basis for a relationship with others, and for its directedness towards the Other who is God? The answer to this question must be no.

In the first place, in the understanding I have described, God is no longer 'other' to me, even in an I–thou relationship. God's interior self-relation in the Persons of the Trinity, through the redemption wrought in Christ, now *includes* me insofar as I am called to live within it, and *know* myself to be so living. This is in consequence of the death and resurrection of Christ, within which mystery I am included through Baptism. God is not I–thou to me, but now I live through the Son in the power of the Spirit toward the Father: insofar as I receive the Spirit in Baptism and Confirmation, I live in the Christ I come to know in the liturgy, and so I am brought to meet the Father. Insofar as I am in Christ, I am caught up into the divine, Trinitarian, life. There are not four terms here always becoming three: my whole being-constituted is now in virtue of life in the Trinity. Moreover I do not encounter God *afresh* in an I–Other relationship, but my every participation in the liturgy re-enacts what was already made true in Baptism: it re-enacts, brings into existence, and enfleshes the baptismal event and makes it real, above all in the event of the Mass and my receipt of the Eucharist. I live my Baptism,

---

26 Cf. Luke 1.42–4. 'And it came to pass that when Elizabeth heard the salutation of Mary, the infant leaped in her womb. And Elizabeth was filled with the Holy Ghost.'

above all through my very embodiment (whilst gaining an understanding of what it will be to have a new body on a new earth under
a new heaven), and not in any ideal space. My Baptism is the conditioning possibility of my vocation as a Christian.

Chapter 4

A Liturgical Theology

The Dogmatic Constitution *Sacrosanctum Concilium*, the first documentary act of the Second Vatican Council, stated that:

> The study of sacred liturgy is to be ranked among the compulsory and major courses in seminaries and religious houses of studies. In theological faculties is it to rank among the principal courses. It is to be taught under its theological, historical, spiritual, pastoral, and juridical aspects. In addition, those who teach other subjects, especially dogmatic theology, sacred scripture, spiritual and pastoral theology, should – each of them submitting to the exigencies of his own discipline – expound the mystery of Christ and the history of salvation in a manner that will clearly set forth the connection between their subjects and the liturgy.[1]

If any statement of the documents of the Council exposes the unfulfilled work of that Council, it is exactly this one.

---

1 *Sacrosanctum Concilium*, §16: 'Disciplina de sacra liturgia in seminariis et studiorum domibus religiosis inter disciplinas necessarias et potiores, in facultatibus autem theologicis inter disciplinas principales est habenda, et sub aspectu cum theologico et historico, tum spirituali, patorali et iuridico tradenda. Curent insuper aliarum disciplinarum magistri, imprimis theologiae dogmaticae, sacrae scripturae, theologiae spiritualis et pastoralis ita, ex intrinsecis exigentiis proprii uniuscuiusque obiecti, mysterium Christi et historiam salutis excolere, ut exinde earum connexio cum liturgia et unitas sacerdotalis institutionis aperte clarescant.'

The order indicated by the statement makes explicit its interior force: the liturgy is the *culmen et fons*, summit and source, of the very training of those to whom themselves the sacred liturgy is most entrusted: in seminaries, and in religious houses – these are the ones who, drawn from the ranks of the faithful, are those to be made most familiar with the practice of faith. To practise faith means to be a liturgical practitioner. Next in order are those most entrusted with the work of reflecting on what faith makes known: those concerned with *Sacra Doctrina*, holy teaching, the teaching that itself makes saints of those both teaching and taught.

First in rank, even before priests, seminarians, and religious, and mentioned earlier in the document, are those apostolically responsible for the Church in her very being: 'pastors of souls' – which means the bishops, the hierarchy of the Church herself – 'themselves [must] become fully imbued with the spirit and power of the liturgy and capable of giving instruction about it'.[2]

What has liturgical study actually become in the wake of the Council? Much contemporary liturgical theology is mired in 'pastoral concerns', which seems to mean at best an anodyne sense of common purpose constructed by those who seek membership of the 'parish liturgy committee', and at worst a conversion of the worship of the Church into mere social activity. Where liturgical theology escapes being 'pastoral' it is often relegated to historiography – a study of the texts and their histories (in entirely secular history departments in modern universities), but with only tangential concern (if at all) for their theological meaning. Of course we should not in the least denigrate the historical questions, indeed, we stand and exult in their fruits, but this historiographical concern is not liturgical study. Liturgical theology comprises – let me repeat *Sacrosanctum Concilium*: 'theological, historical, spiritual, pastoral, and juridical aspects', the referent of 'dogmatic theology, sacred scripture,

---

2 *Sacrosanctum Concilium*, §14: 'Sed quia, ut hoc evenire possit, nulla spes effulget nisi prius ipsi animarum pastores spiritu et virtute liturgiae penitus imbuantur in eaque efficiantur magistri, ideo pernecesse est ut institutioni liturgicae cleri apprime consulatur. Quapropter sacrosanctum concilium ea quae sequuntur statuere decrevit.'

spiritual and pastoral theology'. What this means is that the document understands the place of liturgy in theology in a way entirely consistent with the most ancient Christian theological commentators. Liturgy, and the study of the meaning of the liturgical texts, is the *inner unity* and *very possibility* of every *other* subject in the theological curriculum.[3] As yet, in no Catholic institute anywhere that I know of has this been put into practice. Liturgical theology means: theology *as such*, and *from whence* every other theological discipline must take its license, and *to which* every other theological discipline is subordinate. In this is a most important insight, taken for granted by the Fathers of Vatican II but now completely overlooked (even when lip-service is paid to it): theology which is not *prayed* by the one theologizing is not theology; it is, at best, religious studies. Prayer is not 'belief in', which simply reduces what is done to an intention. 'I believe in God' means nothing, with respect to God – even the devil can say that. But: 'I pray to God', 'I live a life of prayer in God', means 'I am available to be addressed by God': 'God makes himself known to me'.[4] All prayer is first and foremost and only liturgical: every extra-liturgical practice is dependent for its meaning on the liturgy. Even the 150 beads of the rosary represent the recitation of the 150 psalms traditionally recited in a week of the offices of the Church, as laid out in the breviary.[5] In this sense the recitation of the rosary is analogous to the recitation of the breviary by people who are not bound by their state of life (clerics and religious) to sing or recite the

---

3 Cf. Prosper of Aquitaine, *Capitula Cœlestini* 8, in *Patrologia Latina*, vol. 51, 209–10: 'obsecrationem quoque sacerdotalium sacramenta respiciamus, quæ ab apostolis tradita, in toto mundo atque in omni catholica Ecclesia uniformiter clebrantur, ut legem credendi lex statuat supplicandi': 'let us consider equally the rites of the priestly supplications which, transmitted by the apostles, are celebrated in the same manner in the entire world and in the whole catholic Church, in such a way that the law of prayer determines the law of belief'. This is often, and quite incorrectly, truncated to the tag *lex orandi: lex credendi*.

4 The more common formula in Latin for 'credo in Deum' is 'confiteor Deo' – literally, 'I am confessed to God', which retains a relic in English in the notion of making a 'confession of faith'. This grammatical structure of the deponent verb (*confiteri*) followed by the dative is best translated as 'believing in . . .'

5 The most ancient practice of monks and especially the Desert Fathers was, of course, daily recitation of the entire psalter.

offices and who do not have time because of the busyness of their lives to say the whole cursus of the offices of the Church. They imitate the *opus Dei*, the divine work of those who do have that time, and so share in it.[6] Theology requires the unity of an interior disposition with respect to what is to be learned. Theology begins in prayer, and prayer is first and foremost the prayer of the Church: the sacred liturgy. Theology has no other home.

At the same time, what does not change nevertheless does not remain the same: in seeking to understand the Roman rite we must come to a far greater understanding of its history by understanding the world in which it arose and came to fruition. This is not, however, a merely historiographical exercise, but requires a *philosophical* understanding that takes adequate account of the historical character of the being of being-human.

To the European mind until very recently it would have been self-evident not that what you do makes you what you are, but rather what you are makes possible for you to do what you do. This understanding is (philosophically) Greek in its origin. You act and are treated in a particular way because of something – some 'being' or essence – that you already *are*. This is the very opposite of Nietzsche's claim that abolishes all essences – his protestation that there is no doer to be inferred as prior to the deed, so that for him the deed

---

6 The rosary is perhaps the best example of a genuinely 'paraliturgical' practice (taking the prefix *para* here in its Greek sense of 'alongside and together with'). If the Lord discloses himself through the unfolding of the meaning of the recitation of the hours of the Church, in which the entire psalter is recited week by week, and which conforms the heart of the one praying the hours to receive God's self-disclosure, then the combination of the recitation of the prayer *ave Maria* on each bead of the rosary (each of which represents one of the psalms) with the central mysteries of redemption wrought in Christ also corresponds to the actual activity and action of the sacred liturgy on the Christian soul. The rosary is, therefore, more than a merely pious exercise in meditation (which is how it is usually explained, 'psychologically'): rather it is the pattern of prayer that an individual lay member of the faithful may share in which is exactly parallel to the religious and clerical obligation to the hours: the encounter with the mysteries of the life, passion and resurrection of Christ and the events in the exaltation of the Mother of God illuminates what the offices of the Church are also intended to do: to reveal who God is through an encounter with his divine Son and to understand what he does for mankind by understanding what was achieved in Christ's God-bearing Mother.

performs, and so produces, the doer, and that the deed *constitutes* the doer (what is now called performativity) from out of the deed.[7] How else are we to understand the ceremonies of the sacred liturgy? The priest and the sacred ministers at the altar act in the way they act because they are constituted in their respective ministries through ordination and in Christ, they act in accordance with what they already are (and so exhibit the beings that they are), because of an *essential* transformation in their being through ordination. Were I to act in an order I did not possess my actions before the altar would not be true, they could not make manifest what it is they are meant to do.

To a Christian of 1300 this would have been self-evident, and drawn from his understanding of the *world*, and so not the *Church*, he inhabited. It would be an understanding he took *to* church when he went, not one he would have to learn when he got there. Every human being was constituted by their being ordered to a wider whole – to be outside this ordering would constitute destitution, and would make of the human person something indeterminate, to the point of invisibility. Contemporary man celebrates that indeterminacy as a freedom (from which we can infer immediately the extreme poverty of the modern 'celebration' of freedom: if you know what you are you already are much freer to become something else: if you are indeterminate, and have no idea who or what you are, you come to be driven by a desperation, a drive, to become something, *anything* at all). To be anything I want to be, and in every action to *make something of myself*, is the modern mentality.

It becomes clear, by extension, that the need for a historical sense in setting out to make explicit the interior meaning of the liturgy is indispensable. However, what historical study of the liturgy has all too often overlooked is the philosophical aspect – or it has substituted the most fundamental philosophical aspect for a metaphysics or rationalism. That missing aspect is what we might call the

---

7 Nietzsche, F., *Der Wille zur Macht*, in Nietzsche, *Sämtliche Werke*, Stuttgart, Kröner, 1996 ([1901]1911, 1930), §550. (= Nietzsche, F., Colli, G. and Montinari, M. [eds], *Nachlaß 1887–1889*, in *Nietzsche*, vol. 12, Munich, de Gruyter, 1996 [1980], p. 104).

'surrounding world' – the place from out of which man emerges, needing to be redeemed. It is this surrounding world, place as such, which the liturgy addresses. The claim that the liturgy needed to be reformed and adapted came to the fore – in the Liturgical Movement and in the chaos that has succeeded the reform – in the same century that has seen the rise (and fall) of the description of and debate concerning the philosophical subject – subjectivity, the so-called 'modern man' and the 'requirements of the age'.

The confusion that arose – of who should be at the centre of that adaptation – can now exactly be seen when we take the history of philosophy from the pre-Socratics onwards as one in which a transition is made. This is a transition *from* a philosophical understanding of being (where the being in question is the being of the surrounding world) *to* the disclosure of a quite different understanding of being (where the being in question is the meaning of the being of God). This may seem a surprising thing to say, since Catholic thinking, especially since just before and then especially following Leo XIII's encyclical letter on the place of St Thomas Aquinas in the life of the Church, *Æterni Patris*,[8] has been so shaped by what has often been called 'Thomistic philosophy', which has concentrated with great fervour on questions arising from the being of God.[9] But we must not lose sight of the fact that St Thomas borrowed the language of philosophy to give form to an understanding of God which he believed was authenticated from an entirely different, and indeed higher, place. That higher place was God himself, in the form of his self-disclosure through all that is concerned with the epiphany, life, death and resurrection of his divine Son. The *place* of that self-disclosure was for St Thomas, however, not philosophy – the practice of argumentation, disputation, and the extent and limits of *human* science – but the knowledge (science) imparted by God through the liturgy itself: theology is a divinely authorized science, higher in its order and in its truth than any human science.

---

8 Leo XIII, Encyclical Letter *Æterni Patris* of 4 August 1879, in *Acta Sanctæ Sedis*, vol. XII, Rome, Propaganda Fide, 1879, pp. 95–115.

9 And also, self-evident to the medieval mind, that our being, the being of creation, flows from and is dependent on God's own being.

You will note from my earlier citation of *Sacrosanctum Concilium* that the list of the subordinate disciplines which had to be referred to the sacred liturgy did not include philosophy, despite the fact that a propensity towards philosophical rationalism was one of the motor forces of the postconciliar liturgical reform. St Thomas could *borrow* the language of philosophy so freely because all truth – the truth made available and revealed in the *cursus* of the liturgy – is consonant with divine truth; and so insofar as philosophy speaks truly, it speaks adequately but incompletely of what *in faith* has been more completely revealed in Christ to men and women. This revelation continues in our own day above all through the liturgy. Even what faith knows (and prayer – and this means the sacred liturgy – is how faith comes to know anything at all) will be completely revealed not just to faith, but directly to the intellect of the blessed at the end of time. Faith will be confirmed after the last things by certain knowledge of the truth. Faith is not faith where certainty reigns. Certainty, the goal of rationalism, is the enemy of faith. But faith triumphs, not in this life, where rationalistic certainty is sought, but following death (after all has been completed in the purification of purgatory), and after the last things, when faith is no longer needed, because it gives way to a certain knowledge imparted directly by direct participation in the divine mind.

'Thomistic philosophy', insomuch as there is such a thing (and St Thomas himself *never* said there was), is only possible because of faith: it seeks no rationalized certainty in this life. This concentration on the meaning of the being of God in all subsequent philosophy (this even lies at the roots and initial impulses of Cartesian rationalism) found its eclipse in rationalism's declaration of the death of God, and resulted in an emphasis solely on the being of the human subject, now deprived not only of his surrounding world (through Cartesian doubt), but also of his relation to the divine. In the absence of any more profound philosophical insight, this isolated figure of the modern philosophical subject, the human person revealed in his truth, was almost explosively propelled forth to become the very centre of liturgical action.

Is modern man – the man for the sake of whose requirements our liturgy came to need adaptation – the subject of the liturgy because the 'subject' is that one by whom, and against whom, everything is measured? Or is the real subject of the liturgy – the one underpinning it and making it possible, none other than Christ himself, as the tradition itself has from ancient times taught and held, in faith? In 2000, in a work translated into English as *The Spirit of the Liturgy*, the then Joseph Cardinal Ratzinger spoke of 'the boundless superiority of the subject' which characterizes contemporary liturgical life.[10] Few theologians, let alone liturgical experts, have addressed the question put here, of what unfolds – and what clash is unleashed – in the inter-relationship of modern humanity with the liturgical life of the Church and with Christological reflection: in other words, few contemporary *liturgical* theologians have thought it their business to ask what the impact of their surrounding world has been on their methods, their assumptions, and their work. Few enough theologians have been philosophically self-reflexive or self-aware.

The absence of any serious elucidation of the surrounding world – of being itself – has in part arisen because, since the Middle Ages, and since the eclipse of the ancient insight into being – 'being insofar as it is being' as Aristotle called it – thinking itself has been preoccupied with the being, not of man in his surrounding world, but of (the theistic, and in relation to the European Schools, the Christian) God. The degeneration of philosophy into both rationalism and nihilism, noted by Pope John Paul II in his encyclical letter *Fides et Ratio*, resulted in his call for a return to a 'philosophy of being'.

Without this necessary philosophical corrective, a theology which is genuinely a reflection on faith and so a genuine understanding of the liturgy will never extract itself from mere historiography to become what it should be (and what *Sacrosanctum Concilium* called for it to be): as we have seen, the very ground and centre, the very *possibility*, of theology itself.

Why should this be so, and why should we want to find ourselves so in accord with this clear and decisive implication of *Sacrosanctum*

---

10 Ratzinger, Cardinal J., *Der Geist der Liturgie: eine Einführung*, Freiburg, Herder, 2000, p. 133, 'die maßlose Übersteigerung des Subjekts'.

Concilium? Because liturgical theology, and theology in general – as St Thomas himself held – can *never* be grounded in the practices or results of any of the human sciences, but *precisely and only because* the liturgy is the means of God's continued self-disclosure of himself to the world, every other science and branch of human wisdom is itself already grounded in the meaning of the liturgy, by connections which, although trusted now in faith, will actually be revealed in their proper character not now but at the end of time. Theology is the queen of the sciences because the liturgy is the summit of human life as it is lived on earth: in death, something greater (the heavenly liturgy attested to in the book of Revelation) will be given. But what is greater already informs liturgical life as it is given even *now*: faith anticipates and is already derived from what is to come.

Before we proceed to how and from where we could elicit an adequate theology, a truly *liturgical* theology of *worship*, we need to consider one clear and important aspect of the eschatological character of the liturgy itself. It is a clear corollary from what I have already said that, when at the end of time the blessed are deified, their minds will be flooded with the divine light, insofar as God chooses to flood their minds.[11] This is what St Thomas says, both in the first section and in the supplement to his *Summa Theologiæ*, and in his *Commentary on the Sentences*. Redemption will mean that our minds will be perfected, and we will be able to see *as* God sees and see *what* God sees (insofar as God chooses).[12] Indeed, St Thomas goes so far as to say that this is the real meaning of the words from the first letter of St John, 'we shall be like to him: because we shall see him as he is'.[13] Because God has no body, St Thomas says, you will not see God, but what you do see will be seen as God himself sees.

---

11 I examined this question in detail in Hemming, L. P., 'The Experience of God: Aquinas on the Identity and Difference of Divine and Human Knowledge', in Hemming L. P. and Boeve, L. (eds), *Divinising Experience: Essays in the History of Religious Experience*, Leuven, Peeters, 2005, pp. 58–74.

12 This divine permission is how St Thomas explains the possibility of full deification of the human soul, while at the same preserving the essential difference between Creator and created beings.

13 1 John 3.2.

This is the moment at which faith ends, for all that faith has hoped for will now be confirmed in a knowledge that can be said genuinely to be certain. The most important part of this – a perspective which has been completely lost since the quest for the certainty and transparency of knowledge as such, since the triumph of what we would call rationalism – is that *first* what faith knows is incomplete and provisional, in a knowledge that is yet to be completed at the end of time; and *second*, that the knowledge itself sought is eschatological in its structure. What you know now *in faith* is constituted by the full truth which you will know with certainty at the end of time: knowing is directed not to what you can *remember* as *having been*, but to when you will perfectly know, *at the end of time*. True knowledge is from the Spirit, because the Spirit is poured out from the end-time.

This has fundamental consequences for the liturgy. For contrary to the belief that the liturgy must be immediately accessible and intelligible to all, the liturgy is the *work* of the becoming-intelligible of God. It is the *means* of intelligibility, the means by which we grow up and ahead to what we will eventually be. It is the *sacred instrument* by which God *comes to be* known. The liturgy is, both in every particular sacred action, and in the whole life of each baptized man and woman, the means by which faith increases in what it knows. A further consequence: it is not only permitted, it is *necessary* to undertake some actions, to be present at some sacred actions, whose full meaning is yet to be available. Incomprehension is part of the character of worship, which discloses the distance the soul has yet to travel in its divinely-given thirst for deification.

When we have understood this, we can begin to understand from where a genuinely liturgical theology can arise. This source is the end of time, the place from where the Holy Spirit is poured out, when we will be made perfect in Christ (and in the liturgy we are given a *present* share in that *future* perfection).

The liturgy first, foremost, and only, is oriented around the body of Christ, as the Bridegroom for whom the Temple has been made fit. In this sense its proper expression is with respect to a consecrated altar, the symbolic presence of the Lord's body in our midst. Sacramentally (which here means symbolically and mysteriously) understood, the life, death and resurrection of the Sacred Body of Our Blessed Lord is unfolded with respect to the altar. The altar authorizes and makes possible every sacred action of the liturgy, which means shows who the author and subject is of every sacred action, and the embodied means by which those sacred actions are made available to us. All sacred actions are drawn from and return to the altar. The appearing on the altar of the transubstantiated species, the blessed sacrament, is the appearing of the very life of the body whereupon it appears.

The meaning of this is disclosed for us in scripture – it is the Apostolic activity *par excellence* which is explained by St Paul in the Acts of the Apostles in the following way: 'For passing by and seeing your idols, I found an altar also, on which was written: To the Unknown God. What therefore you worship without knowing it, that I preach to you.'[14] The verb here translated as 'I preach' is in Greek *katangello*. St Paul, when he speaks of preaching, much more frequently uses the verbs *kerusso* (I proclaim), or *evangelizo* (well do I bring news). *Katangello* is a word less commonly used by the Apostle, and does not really mean preach or announce as such, but rather that the message to be laid out (*angello*) is *kata*: 'with respect to some which'. In this passage of St Paul, the 'with respect to' is the altar. The Apostles and their successors lay out the meaning of the God who is unknown to us. We are moved by the message the Apostles bring from the unknown to what of God is to be known (in faith, with respect to the altar and to what it brings, do we take knowledge that is knowledge of God). The meaning of an altar by which the unknown God is made known is through knowledge of the Sacrifice of Christ, and as it is offered on any altar now, the sacrifice of the Mass. What is sent (the *missa* of 'it has been sent out', *Ite missa est*, the concluding words of the Mass, before the blessing) effects what it signifies, exactly the theology of signification which we understand to be at work in sacramental theology, and above all in transubstantiation.

The liturgy is even more basic than scripture, since it is the means by which the Word of God is uttered, 'with respect to some which', i.e.

14 Acts 17.23.

the altar, which has the power to make available the hiddenness and give knowledge of the unknown God. Symbolically the activity of the liturgy as undertaken by the Apostles and their successors and their co-operators, the ranks of the clergy, is how the altar 'speaks' and how it enters human conversation. The conversation is double: it is the means by which the conversation between the First and Second Persons of the Divine Trinity is made available to the understanding of the baptized, and so how the baptized are inserted into the eternal conversation between the Father and the Son *through* the work of the Spirit; and it is the means by which mere human conversation is fully taken up into the divine life so that it can disclose, and so be, what it signifies. 'Speaking' here does not just mean words: it means every symbolic or ritual gesture, every silence, that the liturgy employs in its divinely authorized activity.

The altar makes available a site or place, but a place with three specificities, not one. It allows several places to become visible and be seen all at once: it is itself *not* a place in that it is what *makes places* (in this sense it exactly corresponds to Aristotle's *eschaton* and *periechon*, the altar – symbolically – has to indicate what is outermost to our world: the altar is the place where the outermost of the heavens regulates and unfolds – gives order to – the living cosmos). It makes place with respect to its origin: it gives a place to the sacrifices of the pagans and to what St Thomas calls the sacraments of the old dispensation – the sacrifices of Melchisedech and of the Aaronic or Levitical priesthood and the means by which God (in his Second Person, as Christ) manifested his hiddenness before the Incarnation; it gives *us* a place, or rather we can now find a place with respect to the altar: as sinner; as one baptized, as minister – cleric, priest or bishop; and so as one made available to the means of salvation; *and* as ones receiving from the altar the means of our salvation. Finally the altar is the goal, the *telos* of the end-time: it is the heavenly altar where the Lamb is worshipped in the New Jerusalem. As such the altar is the *centre* of the *Civitas Dei*, the New Jerusalem, the pole around which the redeemed become visible to one another in their (we hope our) entirety. It is – to paraphrase a philosophical text – the *polos*, the pole of the heavenly *polis*, the people that God has redeemed through his divine Son. The altar *establishes* these relations and lets them be known, so that the liturgy can be undertaken, both now and for all eternity. The altar therefore encompasses what is before us, what is to come, and the present (our present worship before it). The altar is a sign of how time, and so history, is to be understood. As such it represents fully the different ways in which God has approached man historically: both before, and now, and how God will accomplish the end of time.

In this, the liturgy is even more basic than the sacraments, since it is the 'means by which', the conditioning *possibility*, of the sacraments at all. Here the liturgy disappears in our consideration as some kind of a unified object (a 'thing'), and appears *only* as the form of Christ himself, since it is through the liturgy that the body of Christ becomes available to us as altar *and* in sacrament. The form of Christ is unfolded through the liturgical cycle which makes available the form in its specificities, its specific moments (the pre- and post-resurrection life of our Lord on earth), and in his eternal identity and unity as Bridegroom and High Priest.

As more basic than the sacraments themselves, the liturgy *as* the activity of Christ is – to steal the words of *Lumen Gentium* and to give them the ecclesiological significance that they really deserve – *veluti sacramentum* 'like a sacrament',[15] since the proper subject of the liturgy is Christ (who alone is the Sacrament of the Father), and insofar as we insert ourselves into the what the liturgy inserts us into, we are inserted into the body of Christ. Only with respect to the liturgy and in its activity can the Church ever be genuinely said to be in the manner of a sacrament.[16]

---

15 Vatican Council II, Dogmatic Constitution on the Church, *Lumen Gentium* (November 1964), §1.

16 This is important, lest anyone read into my remarks too much the liturgy as some kind of 'realized eschatology', or as some authors have suggested that life 'in the Church' is tantamount to being already redeemed, already in heaven. From and with respect to the altar our present being and identity is referred to the being and identity we will receive at the end of time. Who we are now will from now on be referred to who we will be; it does not bring heaven to earth *now*, but refers everything we are now to the end of time and the new earth and new heaven we hope in faith to inhabit.

The liturgy is sacred. We are not free with respect to its activity – these actions are divinely ordained and should be entrusted only to those who have both an aptitude for them and a training in their inner life, because they are the sanctifying power of God. Every sanctification takes place *with respect to the actions of the liturgy*, which means, with respect to the altar and thus to the body of Christ through the way in which its meaning becomes manifest in human life and history. Even those who have both aptitude and training for the activity of the liturgy are not adequate for it (and so must abandon themselves ever more to the mercy and grace of God), which is why the closer to the activity of the liturgy – and this means the closer to the altar – one comes the more holiness is both demanded of us and made available to us. Closeness does not mean mere proximity, but rather, closeness in understanding, spiritual closeness, sanctity itself. The saints are greater than the servants of the altar, and these servants are also called to become saints.

Abandoning oneself to the mercy of God means abandoning oneself in perfect trust and faith to the sacraments which will effect what they promise, and so make possible what they effect. In this sense is the Blessed Sacrament above all and rightly called the 'sacrament of the altar'. Here we abandon every pretence that grace is in some sense 'invisible' like radiation, as the reformers supposed or claimed, or that it is granted 'subjectively'. Grace is objectively communicated through and by means of the significatory activity of the liturgy and its sacraments, with respect to the altar. This means that *how* the sacraments are done *a*ffects, and has the capacity to alter, their *e*ffectivity. A sin of omission before the altar of God is more serious than a sin of the same rank committed in some other place. And yet even here, and above all here (before and with respect to the altar), mercy is given.

To conclude: every genuine liturgical theology begins therefore *katangellos* – announcing an understanding with respect to some which, and so 'introibo ad altare Dei . . .', 'I will go unto the altar of God'.[17]

---

17 Psalm 42.1, the psalm used in the traditional rite at the beginning of Mass at the foot of the altar.

Chapter 5

Understanding Understanding

It is a persistent feature of contemporary liturgical theology to argue that liturgical action makes God present to man. No less august a theologian and philosopher than Mgr Robert Sokolowski maintains this when he says that the Eucharist re-enacts the sacrifice of Calvary.[1] An idea that was developed extensively by Odo Casel in the course of the Liturgical Movement, it proceeds in the wrong direction. Prayer does not bring God or the divine presence to us. We have seen already that the liturgy's fundamental definition of prayer is Christ the High Priest's self-sacrifice which he pleads eternally before the Father for our sake. Rather, therefore, through prayer are *we* moved to enter the divine conspection. *We*, by uttering God's name, are *moved* to the blessing presence in which the name can be heard: this is what liturgy as *performance* and *performative* does. Most of all: by virtue of our having been moved by God's having opened our mouth to make our own the prayers of his Son, the one single sacrifice of Christ is through the Holy Eucharist (and by analogy the offices and all our other prayers and devotions) extended in its presence and effects to where we are now, and in fact to all times and all places. What this means, and what the direction of human movement is in liturgy, is what this book is really about. If it is *we* who are moved, how did it come about that we thought *we* could move the impassable *God*?

---

1 Cf. Sokolowski, R., *Eucharistic Presence: A Study in the Theology of Disclosure*, Washington DC, Catholic University of America Press, 1994, pp. 88f.

To understand understanding – this is the task of philosophy. To understand understanding is to reflect on reflection, hence where philosophy joins with theology, the reflection on faith. It is only when we are deepened in the practice and discipline of thought that we are able to understand anything: to have it lie open for us. To understand the question of the current situation of the liturgy as a question *merely about the liturgy itself* is to fail to understand at all – it is actually to lose sight of the disciplines and practices of understanding that have developed over centuries. And yet I want to argue that the process of liturgical reform began and has been so thoroughgoing (and damaging in its effects) *because* of a fundamental confusion in how understanding and faith – philosophy and theology, or faith and reason – belong together.

If we begin by disagreeing with something of Casel's, it is because in so much else that he wrote Casel recognized the importance and history of thought itself. He recapitulates well the patristic insight that the coming of Christ into the ancient world was not accidental, but was at the most opportune of times. He says, 'in concrete terms, if Christianity had appeared in the time of the Athens of Pericles or the Rome of Cato the culture of those ages would not have been ripe for a universal religion of revelation'.[2] However, he compares that to the present situation, and adds, 'because our subjectivist ways of thought have taken us so far from the ancient world and its concentration on being, it is worthwhile for us to feel our way back into that habit of mind in order the better gradually to learn the ways of thought in which revelation is at home'.[3]

Casel draws attention to the relationship between the great edifice of German scholarship on the religions and mythology of antiquity

---

2 Casel OSB, O., *Das christliche Kultmysterium*, Regensberg, 1959 (fourth edition) (1948), p. 142. 'Also, konkret gesprochen, wäre das Christentum etwa z. Zt. Des Perikles in Athen oder z. Zt. Des Cato in Rom aufgetreten, so wäre die Kultur der Zeit nicht für eine universale Offenbarungsreligion reif gewesen.'

3 Casel OSB, O., *Das christliche Kultmysterium*, p. 142. 'Sondern weil wir heute durch unser modernes subjektivistisches Denken von dem Wirklichkeitsdenken der Antiken uns so weit entfernt haben –, deshalb ist es für uns heute wertvoll, uns in dieses objektive Denken wieder hineinzufühlen, damit wir dann auch die Denkweise der Offenbarung allmählich besser verstehen lernen.'

and the significance of this work for the liturgy. He also notes, tellingly, that the Liturgical Movement (in which he became a key figure, standing in the midst of its debates), when it should have been exploring these profound and difficult questions, had in fact become preoccupied with the communal character of liturgical expression. If Casel is right, this book takes up all over again exactly the place that he identifies as the source of liturgical understanding, since contemporary liturgists are all too often still preoccupied with these issues of 'community' and 'assembly' and have not yet learned to attend to the questions he sought to draw to their attention.

At the centre of Casel's understanding of the ancient world is the figure of Walter Otto, perhaps the most important of the nineteenth- and early twentieth-century commentators on the meaning and importance of Greek cult, building on earlier authors like Erwin Rohde, in a tradition that really has its roots in the astonishing poetry of Hölderlin, and the philological investigations of antiquity undertaken by Hegel, Schleiermacher and Nietzsche, all of whom were classical philologists. The Idealism of German nineteenth-century thought is in its essence an attempt to make a return to the classical record, and not just that of Aristotle and Plato. The fundamental question for this tradition of interpretation is how to understand the connection between the Lyric and Homeric poets, the pre-Socratic thinkers, and the Athenian (and this means the Platonic, Neoplatonic and Aristotelian) intellectual tradition.

That Casel was so much in touch with this discourse and its concerns seems too often to have been overlooked, but this overlooking is hardly surprising, since the Nazi destruction of German classical pedagogy only paralleled the situation in Britain that had pertained for already fifty years at least, and in France perhaps since the Revolution, where far too few have been equipped with the languages and familiarity with the ancient world to understand or investigate the classical texts. All too little attention has been given to this interconnection between early and late antiquity, between Greek myth and Christian revelation, that forms so fundamental a part of Casel's writing, because so few are in touch with it. At the pinnacle of these interpretations is Nietzsche's declaration of the flight of the gods and the death of God, perhaps among the most misunderstood of his thoughts, while at the same time standing as his basic philosophical position. Yet this understanding of Nietzsche's is one which has been decisive for twentieth-century thought and will continue to be decisive for perhaps the full two centuries he predicted. For at the basis of this declaration, at the basis of Walter Otto's own investigations, and at the basis of this whole tradition is an enquiry into the interconnection between Christianity and the antique pagan understanding of the meaning of divinity.

Casel is intimately aware of this discussion: in this he stands in a *philosophical* tradition that also produced the fundamental (if at times misguided) polemic of Rudolf Bultmann against the supposed 'Hellenization' of the New Testament and the early Church. Casel, however, understood that the question was not what Christianity had *borrowed* from antiquity (which for Bultmann becomes a decisive question about the Hellenization, for which he meant corruption, of the record and preaching of the historical Jesus), but into what milieu Christianity itself had erupted. Casel's characterization of this milieu is not wrong: it is a milieu entirely concerned with what Aristotle calls the science of being insofar as it is being: although leaving that science *un*thematized and unresolved.[4] In what follows I want to open at least the connection between Greek philosophy and the sacred liturgy.

The theistic appropriation of antiquity undertakes a fundamental exchange in the meaning of the word 'being'. For Greek antiquity being is, insofar as it is, divine. Divine is the being of beings. In the neoplatonic Christianization of antiquity, divinity is no longer an adjectival description, no longer a characterization of being. Now being becomes a predicate of *substantive* divinity. The reasons for this are complex and span from the sometimes heretical writings of Philoponos across the Islamic schools of Baghdad to the work of Maimonides, and the intellectual ferment of the Iberian peninsula

---

4 I examined the issues that follow in far greater detail in my book Hemming, L. P., *Post-modernity's Transcending: Devaluing God*, Notre Dame, Notre Dame University Press, 2005.

before that land was recovered for Christianity, and in the astonishing synthetic achievement and spectacular baptism of many of the texts of Aristotle by St Thomas Aquinas. No longer is being divine; now *the* divinity is *first* being and cause of all else that is. Such a thought would have been unthinkable in this form in classical antiquity.

Why is this important? Because it radically transforms the way in which God is to be thought. *Philosophically*, it becomes required that God is the first cause and the ground of all being, and of every particular being in its being: God is *summum ens*, highest being. The nineteenth-century return to antiquity overturned this metaphysical settlement in ways that we are still living out today. It is *this* conception of God that Nietzsche proclaimed he discovered to have found dead. Insofar as this conception of God lives on, he does so *only* in the minds of some Christian, or at best theistic, theologians. Perhaps this above all explains the shrill imperative tone, the virulent rage, that infects some contemporary theological discourse: you *will* believe in God! Moreover, it explains the extreme moralism of much – especially supposedly entirely 'orthodox' or 'conservative' – contemporary theology, Catholic as much as Protestant. It is only by 'right thinking' and 'right living' that you can have access to God at all (which is to miss entirely the point of the Church as a school for sinners).

The thinker who has thought this through to its end, and who indicated, but only indicated in the most preliminary way, its implications for Christianity, is Martin Heidegger. Much of what has been suggested Heidegger is himself arguing with respect to Christianity has been a matter of reconstruction.[5] Heidegger was fundamentally in touch with the tradition of Hölderlin, Nietzsche, and Walter Otto, the same Otto named by Casel. Otto appears in the one set of lectures where Heidegger considers in greatest depth the meaning of the divinity in relation to the Greek gods.[6] One key part of Heidegger's

---

5 See Hemming, L. P., *Heidegger's Atheism: The Refusal of a Theological Voice*, Notre Dame, Notre Dame University Press, 2002.

6 Heidegger, M., *Parmenides*, in *Gesamtausgabe*, vol. 54, Frankfurt, Klostermann, 1982, p. 181. Heidegger refers to von Otto, W. F., *Die Götter Griechenlands: Das Bild des Göttlichen im Spiegel des Griechischen Geistes*, Frankfurt, Verlag Schulte-Bulmke, 1947.

commentary became available only very recently, his lectures on the *History of Philosophy from Thomas Aquinas to Kant*. Given in Marburg in 1927, immediately after the preparation and publication of his central work *Being and Time*,[7] they sum up in the most succinct form the position I have elsewhere reconstructed. In a section entitled 'The God-lessness of Philosophy' Heidegger has these remarks to make:

> Strongly stated nothing philosophical can be expressed concerning the eternity of God, because God is never an object of philosophy. What one uncovers with the help of the concept of God is an idol, which only has the philosophical meaning, and which becomes thereby visible, where the idea of 'summum ens' and being in general is leading. Philosophy is, if it is correctly understood, god-less.
>
> . . .
>
> If God is, he allows himself be discovered in the least possible way through philosophy. [God is] only discoverable, insofar as he himself reveals himself.[8]

Heidegger's fundamental position on this, well encapsulated here, did not, I think, change at any point in his life. He recapitulated what is said here in similar, if more delphic, words in a seminar of 1951.[9]

---

7 Heidegger, M., *Sein und Zeit*, in *Gesamtausgabe*, vol. 2, Frankfurt, Klostermann, 1977 (1927).

8 Heidegger, M., *Geschichte der Philosophie von Thomas von Aquin bis Kant*, in *Gesamtausgabe*, vol. 23, Frankfurt, Klostermann, 2006, p. 77 (*Die Gott-losigkeit der Philosophie*). 'Streng genommen kann philosophisch über die Ewigkeit Gottes nichts ausgemacht werden, weil Gott nie Gegenstand der Philosophie ist. Was man mit Hilfe des Gottesbegriffs entdeckt ist [ein] Götze, der philosophisch nur die Bedeutung hat, daß daran sichtbar wird, welche Idee von summum ens und Sein überhaupt leitend ist. Philosophie ist, wenn si recht versteht, gott-los . . . Wenn Gott ist, läßt er sich am allerwenigsten durch Philosophie entdecken. Nur entdeckbar, sofern er sich selbst offenbart.'

9 Cf. Heidegger, M., *Seminare*, in *Gesamtausgabe*, vol. 15, Frankfurt, Klostermann, 1986, pp. 437–9.

Philosophy provides no access to God because God is not an object of philosophy. This is an astonishing statement from a formerly 'Catholic' philosopher. This does not mean that philosophy cannot discuss God or the gods – Heidegger's own work is a case in point – Nietzsche's another. They both, in very different ways, discuss divinity from the negative position of showing the limits of what can be said of God in what is said *philosophically*. This is critically important. What is said philosophically is human speaking – philosophy is a wisdom concerning the being of being *human* – it concerns human self-transparency, human self-presence. Philosophy has since late antiquity, and above all in the medieval period, become a discussion governed by the attempt to describe the divine essence, and the relation of human being to the divine essence (even when it discusses it in negative terms, in terms of what *cannot* be said or asserted). In this sense a philosophical construction has been placed upon the kind of *theological* claim made by St Thomas Aquinas, for instance, that only God is transparent to God. Because God is construed as the plenitude of self-presence to self, and so the plenitude of presence *as such*, God as *pure* presence is understood as the abolition of all nothingness, all privation. Privation, nothingness, absence, are given an explicitly moral construction – by St Augustine, and above all by St Thomas Aquinas himself.

There is a second consequence, one which Heidegger examines in some depth and which will have consequences that I hope to demonstrate. Heidegger takes up the question of Aquinas from his compilation of questions entitled *De veritiate*, the 'disputed questions' on Truth, *utrum omnis veritas sit a veritate prima* – whether all truths are from first truth.[10] The question asks about two things – one obvious, the other concealed. The obvious is the unity of truth *as* the unity of being in itself. The concealed question, however is concerned with time. For every *particular* truth has a place and time. Aquinas notes that 'the truth of existing things includes their beingness in their intelligible character, adding to this a relation of conformity to the

---

10 Aquinas, *Quæstiones disputate de veritate*, Question 1, article 8.

human or divine intellect'.[11] What this means is that the unity of being, as the unity of what manifests itself (what manifests itself is what is *true* in the sense in which Aquinas is speaking here), subsists in God.

Even knowledge of evil in this sense is knowledge from God. The example Aquinas gives of this is an important one. Fornication, he notes is true.[12] But he adds 'when we say fornicating is true, we do not imply that the defect involved in the act of fornication is included in the notion of truth. "True" predicates merely the conformity of that act to an intellect'. Aquinas' point here is that while an act of fornication is 'true', its truth does not come from God, but rather *knowledge* that it is true, and this means also knowledge that fornication is evil, comes from God. In this sense the unity of truth, including the truth of evil and privation, is held in the unity of the truth of God. However, this unity of truth is at the same time a unity of divine presence, and a unity which is eternal. Every particular contingent truth, every being in its particularity, is held and understood in the single, eternal, intellectual unity of the single truth of God's self-presence to his self. Moreover *only* the unity of truth that God is, first truth, is eternal. God's own act of knowing 'does not involve time, since it is measured by eternity, which abstracts from all time inasmuch as it embraces all. It remains, therefore, that there are not many truths from eternity, but one.'[13]

Now it should be said (and this is a point often misunderstood in St Thomas) that St Thomas himself, in developing what appears to be a strongly philosophical and rationalistic conception of the being of God, is in fact defending what he understands to be an essentially scriptural understanding. He is, in this sense, showing the conformity of reason to scripture (an essentially theological task): what reason knows is, in the cosmic order, *dependent* on what is more

---

11 Aquinas, *De veritate*, Question1, article 8, corpus. 'Unde veritas rerum existentium includit in sui ratione entitatem earum, et superaddit habitudinem adæquationis ad intellectum humanum vel divinum.'

12 Aquinas, *De veritate*, Question 1, article 8, corpus ad 1.

13 Aquinas, *De veritate*, Question 1, article 5, corpus. 'Similiter eius cognitio non concernit aliquod tempus, cum æternitate mensuretur, quae abstrahit ab omni tempore, omne tempus continens.'

eminently revealed in scripture. He relates this understanding to an explicitly Christological verse from the letters of St Paul. This verse says: 'Wherefore, I give you to understand that no man, speaking by the Spirit of God, saith Anathema to Jesus. And no man can say "The Lord Jesus", but by the Holy Ghost.'[14]

The significance of this cannot be underestimated: the meaning of the whole question that St Thomas is asking about is therefore founded *not* in a rational, speculative argument, *nor even* in the revealed word of God in scripture, *but in the specific and actual person of Christ and of what through Christ alone comes to be known.* Even scripture depends on Christ and what is revealed by the Spirit. St Thomas adds by noting 'Every true thing, no matter who says it, is from the Holy Spirit.'[15] In this sense everything that St Thomas has had to say would have to be understood within the very context of the meaning of prayer that I have argued is the true understanding of prayer in the first chapter. The coming of Christ, High Priest and Bridegroom, transforms not *what* is known, but *in whom* it is known. We who know Christ know that even what the unbelievers know to be true, they know only because of Christ. We know to be true what they know to be true, and we know more eminently than they do the meaning of what they know, because what they only know by means of the mind we know in the Spirit and the fullness of God's inner life. We have here in microcosm how the divine liturgy, how sacramental signification, fulfils and completes all human signification in its truth, and lifts it to the heights and depths of the heavens *through the activity of understanding itself, but an understanding that is of the Spirit, of the end-time, and not from out of our own thinking or 'reason'.* Nothing appears changed in the real physical world; everything is seen in a higher light in virtue of what is known by the gift of faith, a gift that comes from beyond, through the Spirit.

This is what St Thomas relies upon to make intelligible the doctrine of transubstantiation when he says: 'the true body and blood of

---

14 1 Corinthians 12.3.
15 Aquinas, *De veritate*, Question 1 article 8 *sed contra* 1. 'Supra illud, Nemo potest dicere, Dominus Iesus etc., dicit Ambrosius: omne verum, a quocumque dicatur, a Spiritu sancto est.'

Christ in this sacrament are able to be detected not by the senses, but alone by faith'.[16] All too frequently transubstantiation, with its talk (in St Thomas's formulation of it) of 'substance' and 'accidents' – the categories of thirteenth-century thought, derived from neoplatonism and from Aristotle – is criticized for attempting to describe a kind of 'Eucharistic physics'. It does nothing of the sort.

St Thomas rightly says that the miraculous conversion in the holy Eucharist of the whole of the substances of the bread and wine into the substances of the body and blood of our blessed Lord and saviour takes place '*per [Dei] infinitam virtutem*', that is 'through the infinite power of God' and by no other means.[17] Moreover, although the transformation is wholly and entirely objective, and is perceived intellectually, it is known through faith and by no other means. Transubstantiation has nothing to do with physics, and everything to do with faith. The extraordinary aspect, however, is that what God makes manifest in our midst can at one and the same time be known for what it really is – the body of Christ – and overlooked entirely (by the unbeliever) and so mistaken for mere bread and wine.

The doctrine of transubstantiation as St Thomas describes it, however, turns out to be a local (and highest) instance of a more general theology of liturgical and sacramental signification, by showing that the truth that is disclosed through the liturgy is the truth known and understood through faith (in virtue of Baptism), not any kind of truth that is rationally demonstrable.

However, what St Thomas says comes to be taken over by other commentators and transformed into a metaphysical discourse *without* the Christological reference (indicated by St Paul), and is understood to be a way of explaining the being of God, not in the light of revelation (the very light Heidegger insists is the only basis on which God can be understood to be self-revealing: theologically), but *philosophically*, as if what is said here is reached *by the light of reason*

---

16 Aquinas, *Summa Theologiæ*, IIIa, Question 75, article 1, corpus. 'Respondeo dicendum quod verum corpus Christi et sanguinem esse in hoc sacramento, non sensu deprehendi potest, sed sola fide.'

17 Aquinas, *Summa Theologiae*, IIIa, Question 77, article 1, corpus.

alone. It becomes clear, therefore, how ambiguous metaphysics is, and how ambiguous a work St Thomas' synthesis came to be. The very precious priority given to the work of the Spirit is reversed: whereas the Spirit is the foundation of what is known by the mind to be true, now reason becomes the foundation as such – all reference to the founding event of Christ is lost.

Chapter 6

Sacred Scripture

What of sacred scripture, and surely shouldn't scripture itself ground the liturgy? The vexed and contested status of sacred scripture has, since the Reformation and the Enlightenment, perhaps troubled the understanding of the liturgy more than anything. If the traditional and Catholic understanding, certainly since St Thomas Aquinas but even long before, is that the results and understanding of philosophy, wherever it is true, is confirmed through God's higher self-disclosure of himself, the contemporary instinct is to assert the opposite. For St Thomas, philosophy is consonant with scripture, even if separately grounded, because both are concerned with truth. However this very tying together at the point of truth led philosophy to predominate over scripture, and for strange reasons. The Reformation introduced the idea that everything Christian must be grounded in the written word of scripture (which itself had become canonically fixed only three hundred years before), and in what we now call the 'Hebrew scriptures' rather than the Septuagint. The Septuagint is the Greek translation of the Old Testament, and was the version of the Old Testament that was available to the Gospel writers and the early Church (we should not lose sight of the fact that, whatever else their origins, all the books of the New Testament also came to us in Greek). The Septuagint contains many of the important prophecies which the early Church interpreted as corroborating and explaining the meaning of the life of Jesus and his status as the Christ, especially with reference to the priesthood of Melchisedech.

The current Hebrew scriptures, themselves not settled on until after 200AD, excised or did not contain this material.[1]

The Renaissance Church, developing a belief found in St Thomas Aquinas that natural reason and scripture *must be* consonant, became preoccupied with *actually* reconciling natural science and scripture. At the same time (in marked contrast to medieval theologians like St Bonaventure), the Church came increasingly to interpret divine self-disclosure as *identical* with scripture itself, a tendency toward which it was pushed in order to answer the Reformers' emphasis on *sola scriptura*, 'by scripture alone'. These tendencies meant that when the late medieval interpretation of Aristotle's understanding of the cosmos, which after a long period of modification (as part of this process) had been declared by the Church to be consonant with scripture, was exploded by Galileo and others, it was scripture and not scientific knowledge that was put into doubt. Scientific knowledge was demonstrable, and a matter of fact: scripture, or the interpretation of it that had come to prevail, was forced to give way. The eclipse of this 'Aristotelian' interpretation was used as the pretext to throw into question the basis and veracity of scripture itself. The problems are dense and complex, and there is not the space to deal with them in full. Part of the problem was that whereas in earlier centuries scripture and divine revelation had not previously been understood to be the same thing, after the Reformation they came increasingly to be thought as identical. One place where I have touched on this issue is in Benedict XVI's own description of divine revelation which he undertook in his *Habilitation* study of St Bonaventure in the 1950s.[2] Here it becomes clear that for the medievals at least, the liturgy's mediation of scripture becomes the *context* for God's self-disclosure but is not identical with it.

Scripture itself has to be interpreted, and a fundamental aspect of that interpretation is the oral tradition which from the very first is

1 This is dealt with in much greater detail by Barker, M., *The Great High Priest: The Temple Roots of Christian Liturgy*, London, Continuum, 2003, pp. 294–315.

2 See Hemming, L. P., *Benedict XVI Fellow Worker for the Truth: An Introduction to his Life and Thought*, London, Continuum, 2005, pp. 143–50.

mediated in the liturgy itself. The fundamentally protestant view that scripture contains its own interpretation is absolutely foreign to the Catholicism of the West, and no less foreign to the Eastern and Oriental Orthodox Churches. The exegete Margaret Barker has shown how the Christian interpretation of the Old Testament especially was derived directly from the early Fathers' understanding of what they believed Christ had (secretly) revealed to the Apostles in a tradition which came to be preserved above all liturgically.[3]

This reaffirms a truth unsurprising to Catholics, that the liturgy is the proper ground of scripture (and not the other way round, i.e. the false view that the liturgy *derives* from scripture!),[4] as well as pointing up that scripture has lost its ground. This loss of its liturgical basis coincided with the attempt to provide a philosophical ground for scripture. Early attempts to 'justify' scripture philosophically (Lessing comes immediately to mind) quickly led to (for instance) the denial of the miraculous because it is philosophically impossible to describe. Philosophy and science after the Enlightenment look for regularities, for patterns of behaviour that allow for prediction and system. The miraculous *cannot* be predicted, by definition: miracles are exceptions to the ordinary and predictable. In a world explained only by scientific knowledge, miracles have either to be disbarred, or to be accounted for as 'natural' occurrences (and so again, not miraculous exceptions). Philosophical attempts to justify the events of scripture – especially the Gospels – become subordinated not even to questions of 'natural' possibility, but, coincidental with the effects of Descartes' *cogito* that philosophy itself becomes essentially a *psychology*,[5] to questions of psychological possibility.

---

3 See Barker, M., *The Great High Priest: The Temple Roots of Christian Liturgy*, especially pp. 1–33 and 73–102.

4 This view manifested itself especially in multiple attempts from the seventeenth and eighteenth century onward to reform the liturgy by restricting its texts solely to ones derived from scripture. Perhaps the first of these attempts was Cardinal Quiñones' revision of the Breviary, first published in 1535 and revised in 1536. Many 'neo-Gallican' versions of this and other reforms appeared in dioceses in France in the sixteenth to the eighteenth centuries.

5 This possibility is already present in Wolf and Baumgarten (Baumgarten, A. G., *Metaphysica*, Halæ Magdeburgicæ, Magdeburg, 1743 [1738], §1) with the division of

In short, the inability to ground the Gospels in the actual being or psychology of Christ comes gradually to be the central interpretative question for the whole of scripture as far as Christians – even Catholics – are concerned, especially from the outset of the twentieth century onward. Put very simply, and cutting the story (very) short, contemporary exegesis takes for granted, and on psychological grounds, that this man Jesus could not possibly have thought he were God – it must have been his disciples who came to this conclusion. This understanding has had a profound effect on the liturgy, and on the motors of liturgical reform. First, as I have already hinted, liturgy has been subordinated to scripture; but second, subordinated to an understanding of scripture that is itself driven by, and believed to be grounded in, philosophical presuppositions that deprive scripture of its revelatory capacity.

The Jesuit John McDade has concluded in a discussion of Barker's and others' work that 'Jesus himself is the first and best Christologian and . . . it is possible to uncover the main features of his self-interpretation in a way that makes later Christian doctrinal teaching about him both credible and necessary'.[6] The renewed tradition of interpretation that McDade and Barker (with the biblical scholar and exegete Robert Murray powerfully in the background) point to is one that has the potential to transform biblical studies in the next years. What Barker and Murray in particular have pointed to is the astonishing way that the Qumran discoveries, beginning in

---

philosophy into *metaphysica generalis* (ontology, being in general) and *metaphysica specialis* (in the three divisions of theology, cosmology and psychology). In Kant these latter three become the problems of *der Gott, der Mensch, die Welt* (cf. Kant, Immanuel [Adickes, E. ed. and arr.], *Opus Postumum*, Berlin, Kantstudien Ergänzung, 1920, §21).

6 McDade SJ, J, 'Jesus: Son and Priestly Companion of God's Throne', an unpublished paper presented at the Maryvale Institute in 2005. McDade quotes Hengel, M., *Studies in Early Christology*, Edinburgh, T&T Clark (Continuum), 1995; Meyer, B. F., *The Aims of Jesus*, SCM Press, London, 1979 and, as well as the text of Barker's I have cited myself, Barker, M., *The Risen Lord: The Jesus of History as the Christ of Faith*, Edinburgh, T&T Clark (Continuum), 1996. McDade has made similar arguments in other recent articles and lectures. See 'A Promise Fulfilled, A Ransom Paid', in *The Tablet*, 8 October 2005, pp. 6–7, an edited version of his lecture on *Catholicity* given to the Margaret Beaufort Institute of Theology in Cambridge on the same date.

1948, have corroborated and authenticated a biblical interpretation – especially of the Old Testament (but here we must note, the Septuagint and *not* the Hebrew scriptures), which also undergirded and was implicit in the Church's sacred liturgy until 1970 (and remains so in the liturgies of the East and the Orient).

This interpretation substantially minimizes the emphasis on the Pentateuch in favour of what Barker calls the priestly, Enochic and wisdom traditions, and the identification of the figure of the Messiah with the priestly figure of Melchisedech (almost erased from the non-Septuagint texts). Barker in particular argues that Jesus' self-understanding is developed out of the idea that Melchisedech is the Messiah, and Jesus understands himself to be the return of the messianic priestly figure of Melchisedech. Barker especially emphasizes in all of this the roots of the Holy Eucharist in the First Temple, a temple in which there is no tradition of animal sacrifice, and in Melchisedech's offerings of bread and wine. She has developed this argument still further in relation to the ritual of the atonement.[7] Paradoxically this reinforces the Jewish tradition of God having prevented Abraham from sacrificing his son Isaac not as a prefiguring of the Exodus typology of the sacrifice of the first-born, but of the bringing to an end of the pagan and non-covenantal tradition of animal (and human) sacrifice.

McDade draws out the conclusions for this starkly. There has been a failure to emphasize that the meaning of the Eucharist is atonement: he notes that recent theology (he cites the Dominican Eduard Schillebeeckx) 'is unable to bring himself to say that Jesus saw his death as an offering for sins', and concludes 'Schillebeeckx may be the characteristic post-Vatican II theologian, but he is simply not good on Jesus'.[8] McDade proceeds to show that the real solution to the riddle of Jesus from the Gospels – 'destroy this temple and in three days I will rebuild it'[9] is (quoting Ben Meyer) 'for the temple cult Jesus would substitute, climactically, the expiatory and covenantal

---

7 Barker, *Temple Themes in Christian Worship*, pp. 173–80.
8 McDade SJ, J., 'Jesus: Son and Priestly Companion of God's Throne'.
9 Cf. Matthew 26.61 (27.40); Mark 14.58 (15.29); John 2.19–20.

offering of his own body and blood'.[10] The consequences for contemporary liturgical study are immense, and he does not fail to spell them out:

That the core of Eucharistic theology is 'expiatory and covenantal' has implications, of course, for how we think of the Eucharist; in recent years we have so focused on the aspect of the Eucharist as a sacred meal that we have forgotten that Eucharistic theology is atonement theology because it centres on the priestly Lord offering himself for sins. You cannot get to the notion of atonement for sins from what is contained in Passover theology: Eucharistic theology comes from the Day of Atonement, not from Passover.[11]

The consistent attempts to explain the Eucharist through the Passover rituals, 'Haggadah' as the record of the liberation from Egypt, and its connection with the *chabûrah* meal look decidedly shaky in light of this recent analysis.[12] This has particular significance for the change in the Catholic 1969 Order of Mass to the rites of preparation of the gifts at the altar, and the insertion of the two

---

10 McDade SJ, J., 'Jesus: Son and Priestly Companion of God's Throne'. Cf. Mayer, B. F., 'The Early Christians: Their World Mission and Self-Discovery', in *Good News Studies*, vol. 16, Wilmington, Michael Glazier, 1986, p. 64.

11 McDade SJ, J., 'Jesus: Son and Priestly Companion of God's Throne', p. 14. He adds a reference to Barker, in a note (40) on this passage just quoted: Margaret Barker, *The Great High Priest*, pp. 56ff.

    There are immediate and obvious problems trying to link the Eucharist with Passover as we recognize it: the Passover was the only sacrifice not offered by a priest and the essential element was that the offering was whole (Exodus 12.46), whereas the descriptions of the Last Supper in their various forms emphasize that the bread was broken. Further, the cup at the Last Supper is linked to the covenant . . . and the Letter to the Hebrews links the death of Jesus to the covenant renewed in the Day of Atonement. (Hebrews 9.11–15)

12 See, for an example of this, Dix, G., *The Shape of the Liturgy*, London, A&C Black, 1978 (1943), pp. 50ff. Although Dix favours the Johannine interpretation (see note 1 on p. 50), that the Last Supper was specifically not the Passover but a meal that took place the night before, he still connects the origins of the Eucharist with the *chabûroth* meals which derive in their significance from the *non*-priestly tradition of domestic offering associated with ritual derived from Passover.

berakah or (domestic) blessing prayers over the gifts which even Josef Ratzinger had defended on the basis of their origin in domestic Jewish life, noting with approval that the newly inserted prayers 'are in the main taken from the table prayers of Israel',[13] and have their origins in Haggadah,[14] as justification for their connection with the Eucharist. Although Ratzinger is right to note that the offertory prayers that they replaced, with their strong emphasis on sacrifice, did not appear (in written form, at least) in the Roman rite until the ninth century, nevertheless these prayers are indications of the human desire to make sacrifice, even though that attempt can only ever fail before God. Here we find just one example of the way in which the interpretation of scripture has had the capacity to drive alterations to the shape of the liturgy, when classically the direction of influence has been the other way around. The real point of the older offertory prayers is that the ambiguous character of the sacrificial attempt (also expressed in the theologically difficult invitation '*orate fratres*', 'pray brethren that this my sacrifice and yours . . .') can *only* be completed by the action of Christ as the one truly human who is (as truly divine) alone able to make sacrifice before God. The prayers all therefore make mention of the atonement for sins of the living and the dead so that the transformation to be wrought in the bread and wine prefigures the transformation to be wrought (deification) in the ones for whom the offering is made – in the case of the prayer over the chalice, the implicit reference is the miracle of the wedding at Cana.

It becomes clear why Psalm 109 is by long tradition *the* Vesper psalm in the Roman rite. Because it extended (with its mention of Melchisedech) the priestly, sacrificial meaning of the Eucharist into the most important of the liturgical offices (Vespers, the office with its profound association with the baptistry on Easter Day, an association preserved especially in the Milanese or Ambrosian rite even

---

13 Ratzinger, Cardinal J., *Gott ist uns nah. Eucharistie: Mitte des Lebens*, Augsburg, Sankt Ulrich Verlag, 2001, pp. 67f. 'Sind im Großen ihrer Gestalt aus den Tischgebeten Israels genommen.'
14 Ratzinger, Cardinal J., *Gott ist uns nah. Eucharistie: Mitte des Lebens*, pp. 48–9.

now, but equally prominent in the Old Roman or papal rite), it indicates the fundamental connection between the sacrificial character of the Mass and the liturgy of the hours.

McDade's conclusions show what liturgical theology must recover in future years, and at the same time they call into question the prominence and emphasis given in the revised rites to the relation between the events of the Exodus and the Passover during Lent as preparatory to the Sacred Triduum.[15] There would be scope to say much more about the way in which Barker and others have begun to indicate how the specific ritual forms of the liturgy are rooted in the oral tradition of interpretation that surrounds the scriptural texts. If, as Barker argues but tantalizingly does not always substantiate (because of the sheer scale of study that would be required, and because we simply do not always know), many ritual actions are designed to indicate meanings derived from the oral tradition, then ritual forms (and architectural forms – she notes, as I have in Chapter 1, that the place of the altar and the structure of churches up until the Renaissance was specifically an indication of the relation of Christ's body to the physical structure of the Temple) should be far less plastic and malleable than we have taught ourselves to believe they can be in contemporary (especially postconciliar) thought. We must learn to corroborate scripture, the patristic witness and actual practices we have received historically much better than we have.

More seriously there is so much we don't know about the origins of the sacred liturgy that we need to exercise far more caution than has been apt in what has been a period of dramatic, not to say revolutionary, liturgical reform. In particular, much that we have presumed was simply 'custom' or human invention turns out to have an

---

15 Martimort, in discussing these changes of emphasis, justifies them with the claim that 'the origins of [the] paschal celebration go back to the initial establishment of God's people at the Exodus and the covenant on Sinaï'. Martimort, A. G., *et al.*, *The Church at Prayer*, 4 vols, *Principles of the Liturgy*, vol. 1, p. 261. There is not much emphasis on themes derived from Exodus literature in the readings at Mass and in the hours in the preconciliar rites, and much more emphasis on the wisdom literature, Hebrews, and the meaning of Jesus' ascent to Jerusalem – in other words to the priestly and sacrificial meaning of the preparatory season of Lent.

origin that was believed to have been divinely commanded, or a signification derived from a Dominical tradition (something given in
secret by Christ himself to his Apostles). In his 1917 *Preface* to Fr
Adrian Fortescue's *Ceremonies of the Roman Rite Described*, Cardinal
Bourne began by saying that:

> The Catholic Church has surrounded all the acts of Divine
> Worship with a definite ceremonial to ensure on the one hand
> their due accomplishment, and on the other to safeguard the
> external reverence that should accompany them. She never
> employs ceremonial for the sake of ceremony itself. Each
> separate rite has grown out of the twofold object that we have
> enunciated, even though in the process of time the origin, and
> the history of the development, of such rite may long have been
> forgotten.[16]

There is here both a caution, an acknowledgement of provenance,
and a *faith* that many liturgists working more recently perhaps too
often disdained. Often the liturgy has been treated as a set of actions
to be manipulated or controlled for specific outcomes or effects with
a degree of contempt for the deference to the *sacredness* of the liturgy
that Cardinal Bourne so carefully calls us to respect. The meaning of
the liturgy is not something at our disposal; it is something into
which we have to grow as we advance in understanding and faith. Its
meaning is *primarily* for God, only *secondarily* for us.

---

16 Bourne, Cardinal F., 'Preface', in Fortescue, A., *The Ceremonies of the Roman Rite
Described*, London, Burns & Oates, 1918, p. xi.

Chapter 7

Liturgy as a Cause

In her book *After Writing*, Catherine Pickstock, in the context of discussing the liturgical theology of Henri de Lubac's book *Corpus Mysticum* ('The Mystical Body'),[1] speaks of 'liturgy as the "site" where the visible community (*laos*) and the mysterious work (*ergon*) combined'.[2] Here Pickstock, whatever else she is resisting in current liturgical theology, falls in entirely with the contemporary interpretations of this word. For her etymology of the word *leitourgia* in fact reverses its real meaning.[3] If liturgy is the 'work' of the 'people' (to give it its most naked and basic reading), the *laos* is not ever the *visible* people or 'community', but rather the invisible *stem* and root, the tribe or nation, implied and made manifest by *this one here*, this man or woman who is variously, perhaps, a Briton, a Catholic, and so forth. The members of the *laos* are the ones who represent and bring to visibility the *laos* as such and in itself, but they are not, even in their entirety, the entirety of the *laos*. The *laos* has a past and a future – a mission and a destiny: it is never *reducible* to any exemplar, any merely visible form. The word *laos*, properly understood, is precisely the *opposite* of the definition given by Pickstock. What of the *ergon*, which she interprets as 'mystical work'? Here again confusion reigns. In every case in Greek, the word *ergon* relates to that which is *done* and so is a present, visible, or recordable *deed* – it has this meaning

---

1 De Lubac, Cardinal H., *Corpus Mysticum*, Paris, Aubier, 1948 (1944).

2 Pickstock, C., *After Writing*, Oxford, Blackwell, 1998, p. 159.

3 We should not lose sight of the fact that *leitourgia* and its cognates is a scriptural term found in the Septuagint in the 'liturgical' books of Chronicles, Numbers and Deuteronomy, and in the New Testament in the Letter to the Hebrews.

even in its dependent sense of 'the work of thinking' (where the work done is done in a specific place and time). The *ergon* is in each case, whilst potentially significatory, signifying from out of what is done *here* and *now*, at a specified point. If we take the most common rendering of *leitourgia* as 'public service due from an individual' (either in its pagan or scriptural use) then we see it is *that* visible and required work or works which signifies, and arises on the basis of, membership of the *laos, invisible in its essence*: the city, tribe, and nation. To undertake *leitourgia* is to make a public manifestation, through visible works, of the invisible (and so mystical) meaning and destiny of the *laos*. The word liturgy means the opposite of what Pickstock makes it mean.

In the specific question of the mystical character of *leitourgia*, the mystical pertains to the body as people, nation and city – and not to the work to be done. The visible and so not-mystical deed brings to visibility the significatory, the *sacramentum*, the real meaning and being of the *laos*. There is a final indication from the word *laos* that we must not overlook. For the *laos* are those inscribed into a head – formerly a prince, or leader of the people, or even of a god (although here there is confusion since in pagan Greece the prince, hero, or leader can often make a claim to divine lineage); more latterly, perhaps, a city, or a land, but these are also more often than not divinely apportioned in the pagan texts.[4] Membership of a *laos* therefore has a divine reference and suggests the making manifest of the unseenness of the god in the visible work done. Not for nothing had the word *leitourgia* religious significance for the pagans: not for nothing does it appear in the most liturgical passages of scripture; not for nothing was it selected as a word describing the Christian rites and mysteries. What is signified in every Christian case is the invisible meaning and subject of the visible deed: the person of the Christ in his relation to the Father.

Yet Pickstock can be forgiven for the confusion her etymology exhibits, for she exactly, one might say, *accidentally*, follows the contours of the preoccupations of the debates surrounding the sacred liturgy in the post-war period. But the slippage in the use of this term

---

4 Just for one example, the allotment of Rhodes to the god Helios (cf. Pindar, *Seventh Olympian Ode*), let alone Athena's possession of Athens herself.

'mystical' is critical, for it demonstrates that what is often read back into de Lubac's understanding of the liturgy is the visibility of the assembled community, the *ecclesia*, whilst at the same time accomplishing an enforcement of the visibility of the work done in the liturgy as mystical. In fact the *ecclesia* appears from out of the work done, and *mystically* signifies the body in question. The *ecclesia* does not assemble to do the work; the work only shows the *ecclesia* to have been *already* assembled, and as assembled, to belong to something mystically and invisibly wider than itself. The true scope and meaning of the *ecclesia* is *precisely* what is *unseen* in what is *seen*. Moreover, inasmuch as Pickstock's interpretative key shifts the emphasis *from* the work *to* the assembly, so it loses the essential point that the work done is also the work of Christ and not a deed or set of practices undertaken by the assembly. De Lubac seems well aware of the significance and the direction implied here by the work done: the result of the work done is, he notes: 'He himself is the body whose food those who eat it become'.[5]

How does the liturgy make possible the work it undertakes? The causality of the liturgy has traditionally been considered in relation to the phrase developed dogmatically (originating with Peter of Poitiers) and formally adopted by the Council of Trent, *ex opere operato*. This phrase literally means 'from out of the work done'. Canon eight of the decree *On The Sacraments in General* of the seventh session of the Council of Trent asserts: 'if anyone says that grace is not conferred by the sacraments of the new law through the sacramental action itself, but that faith in the divine promise is by itself sufficient for obtaining the grace: let him be anathema'.[6] This canon was aimed at overcoming what was understood to be the reformers' emphasis on the *opus operantis* (the one doing the work) that is to say the worthiness of the minister in the activity of effecting the sacraments.

---

5 De Lubac, Cardinal H., *Corpus Mysticum*, p. 201. 'Est lui-même le corps dont ceux qui le mangent deviennent l'aliment.'

6 Council of Trent, Session 7, *De sacramentis in genere*, in Tanner, N. (ed.), *Decrees of the Ecumenical Councils*, London, Sheed & Ward, 1990, vol. 2, pp. 684f. 'Si quis dixerit, per ipsa novæ legis sacramenta ex opere operato non conferri gratiam, sed solam fidem divinæ promissionis ad gratiam consequendam sufficere: anathema sit.'

In the distinction *operatus/operans* (the work done/the one doing the work) an entirely different understanding of causality emerges, almost without being noticed, which subsequent dogmatic treatments struggle both to admit the exigencies of, and overcome. The emphasis on the 'work done' on the one hand overemphasizes the brute fact of what the commentators then repeatedly refer to as the 'instrumental efficacy' of 'the liturgical sign in each of the seven sacraments'. Thus there is a complete overemphasis on the 'whatness' of the sign in each case. At the same time the question of the *operans* becomes either on the one hand a question of mere discipline, or becomes radically subjectivized to the extent that the character and status of the minister is effaced altogether (it doesn't matter, although he will have to face judgement for himself if he is not worthy), or – the inverse but in fact identical resolution – *all* of us are *operantes* and so the individuality of the minister is subsumed under the common intention of a specified group, come together to 'effect' (make, produce, transsignify) a sacramental sign. To argue that the Church herself is the *operans* (the one doing the work) does not clarify the question at all, as we shall see. Dogmatically the phrase *ex opere operantis Ecclesiae* (from out of the work of the Church) does not resolve the question as the reformers raised it, because the *operans* (one doing) in this case was specified to refer to what is instituted and effected by the Church for the sake of the liturgical signs – the sacraments – as such: 'prayer and sacred ceremonies . . . "sacramentals" and the other rites instituted by the hierarchy of the Church', a specification given formal status by Pius XII in the 1947 encyclical letter on the sacred liturgy *Mediator Dei*.[7] In this sense it reflects the intrusion into dogmatic resolution of the pair *operatus/operans* of the question of the relation of liturgical actions to historical time that Odo Casel had attempted to resolve with his *Mysterienlehre* (doctrine of the mysteries) and notion of *Mysteriengegenwart* ('presence in mystery') such that, as he says, 'the

---

7 Pius XII, *Mediator Dei*, 1947, p. 532. '. . . precibus sacrisque cærimoniis . . . de "Sacramentalibus" ac de ceteris ritibus . . . quæ ab Ecclesiastica insituta sunt Hierarchia'.

Christian mystery is a remembrance of such a fullness of reality, that it makes the holy action present . . . God is presence.'[8]

In fact the pair *operatus/operans* comes apart precisely where its unity really matters (and takes real material form), in the person of Christ himself. The work done is, properly understood, identical with the one doing, but this is in each and every case Christ. Immediately it becomes possible to resolve the question of the particular 'one doing' (the priest or minister of the sacrament as *operans*), because inasmuch as the work done will be determinative for his salvation, so will it at the same time and in the same way be determinative for all those for whom and to whom the sign is addressed. The one(s) 'producing' the sign (in the specific, restricted, technical sense of undertaking the work that lets it appear) do what they do in order to make possible the co-participation of all those receiving the sign. *All* who receive the sign receive it in the same way and to the same *possible* end: *not all* who receive the sign participate in the activity of its being-given in the same way.

This is tantamount to saying that in the giving of every liturgical sign, the question of salvation is posed, *here*, in the *giving* of the sign. At the same time, every time the question of salvation is posed, the person of the Christ is both the one posing, and the one giving, and the one effecting. If the minister has a more complex immediate relation of bringing himself into proximity with the given sign (because of his responsibility with respect to the actual letting-be-apparent of the sign), at the same time no less than anyone else's, and no more, is his salvation *also* at issue in the sign's being-given. In this the minister of the sacrament is the one who does not so much give the sign as let it be given (causes it in a strictly secondary sense) – inasmuch as he lets it be given, he is also the recipient of what he has let occur.

What is posed in the giving of every liturgical sign is therefore the eschaton, as the 'outermost' and end-time, as such. Every liturgical sign actually signifies only in the sense that it produces *here* a

---

8 Casel OSB, O., *Das christliche Kultmysterium*, Regensberg, 1959, p. 173. 'Das christliche Mysterium ist Gedächtnis von einer solchen Wirklichkeitsfülle, daß es die Heilstat gegenwärtig macht . . . Gott ist Gegenwart.'

meaning that is in full yet to come, but which through faith can already be understood. When St Thomas Aquinas says, 'thus we hold by faith the ultimate purpose of the human to be the vision of God',[9] this discloses what faith is – faith makes possible the having here in occluded (significatory, sacramental) form what we will ultimately ('eschatically') have actually. The sacraments are given in, and through, faith. Faith here is to be understood as nothing like the 'intention' of the believer – a 'directedness towards' the sign that somehow makes it what it is – but rather what has been *formed in* the one-believing (in a gift, given by the Spirit) *that he might believe,* and, as believing, understand the sign for what it really is. Faith in this sense is the activity of the Spirit, it is not the believer's intentionality. It is for this reason that only those sealed in the Spirit (baptized, confirmed) can receive a liturgical sign spiritually (i.e. more than sacramentally, more than just in its bare capacity to be a sign).

Only for the one sealed in the Spirit can both the meaning, and the effect of the meaning, be given. Those to whom the Spirit is given, both in Baptism, Confirmation, and in Orders, live in the 'here'-character of the immediate sign from out of the end of time. They recognize the meaning of the sign, not because they *already* know what it means (which is how I recognize the things I know ordinarily) but because the Spirit gives them to know *now,* in faith, what they will *perfectly* know at the end of time.

To receive the sign spiritually is to receive it in the effect it has for salvation, and not just, as St Thomas says, 'sacramentally', that is, as a 'mere' sign. Therefore any understanding of what I have here entitled causality is not a 'theory of signification' nor as such can it ever be resolved *merely* philosophically. The sacrament or sign depends for its understanding on the promise of the future salvation which it now offers, and on the faith given for that signification to have spiritual effect. Only those to whom the Spirit has been given for the (ordained) purpose can bring about the giving of a liturgical sign. When the people respond to the priest *Et cum spiritu tuo,* they

---

9 Aquinas, *Summa Theologiæ,* Supplement, Question 92, article 1, corpus. 'Sicut secundum fidem ponimus finem ultimum humanæ vitæ esse visionem Dei.'

acknowledge this liturgically – he is the one to whom the Spirit has been given (in ordination) to make possible, and so effect, what is to be done.

The phrase *ex opere operato* has in the recent period either been treated as an essentially rational and philosophical formulation, which makes the meaning of the liturgy available because it is susceptible of discrimination by human reason, or it has been abandoned altogether because it is thought somehow to be inadequate to postconciliar sacramental theology. In each case this represents the formal historical situation arising from the radical subjectivization mentioned earlier, which both fails to understand *ex opere operato* as a response to a historical situation, and fails to see what is actually posed in its appearance as a term.

Cipriano Vagaggini betrays this rationalism when he notes, in relation to the *opus operatum* (and in his critique of Odo Casel) that Casel's understanding of the *Mysterienlehre* or 'mysteries doctrine' is to be rejected, not because the liturgy itself speaks against what Casel claims, but because 'first, to deny the demands of conceptual reason and of metaphysical reasoning is not to resolve the questions which they inevitably pose; and secondly because this would mean putting into question fundamental principles of philosophy without which faith itself and theology as such are not able to subsist'.[10] Yet neither faith nor theology 'subsist' in either conceptual reason or metaphysical reasoning: theologically the reverse is the case – as we have seen already, reason and metaphysics (everything the human mind can work out for itself) 'subsist in' and are most fully explained by what faith knows *more eminently*. From the perspective of what faith knows, *both* conceptual reason *and* metaphysical reasoning are themselves only *fully* and *finally* explained by the truth of the divine self-disclosure which completes and shows how each can be understood

---

10 Vagaggini OSB, C., *Il senso teologico della liturgia*, Rome, Edizione Paoline, 1965 (1957), p. 119. 'Primo, perché negare le esigenze della ragione concettuale e del ragionamento metafisico non è risolvere le questioni che esso inevitabilmente pone, e, secondo, perché ciò significherebbe mettere in questione principi fondamentali di filosofia fuori dei quali la fede stessa e la teologia come tale non possono sussistere.'

to be established in the divine. Understood from the perspective of faith itself, what thinking thinks with respect to God is only because God gives it to be. This means that any understanding of causality in the liturgy must first show itself to be grounded, not in thinking as such, or in what thinking is capable of thinking for itself, but in what God offers thinking to think. What the liturgy causes and does is both initiated by, and dependent on, God.

It is not accidental that Vagaggini's description of the *opus operatum* coincides with his critique of Casel. If we take aside the specific issues raised by Casel's *Mysterienlehre* we should see that Casel himself had entirely correctly understood that in the course of time the understanding of the *opus operatum* had failed adequately to account for the way in which the liturgy was able to relate the end-time with the time of Jesus' own life and the present. We see immediately that the pair *operatus/operans* itself is insufficient to account for *three* temporalities. If Casel, and following him Vagaggini (especially after Vatican II), draw attention to the true *operans* as Christ, this leaves out exactly that moment which the *opus operatus* was meant to resolve – the objectivity of the given sign in the present – that is to say in the temporal Church.

This is exactly the vexed point of the whole of what the liturgy is able to do or cause (and so liturgical causality as such) – how does the present moment enter into *both* the historical event of the passion and resurrection (the *Triduum Sacrum* as such) and at the same time the liturgy of the last times, and so of the heavenly Jerusalem? If I have succeeded in sketching an understanding of the possibility of how the liturgical signs indicate and signify through what contemporary dogmaticians would call a 'pneumatology' (a theology grounded in the activity of the Spirit), then, we must ask, what is meant by 'causality' here?

Vagaggini gives us a classical dogmatic definition when he says:

> When we say that the sacraments confer grace we mean, of course, that God confers it as principal cause, but in connection with and having regard to the sacramental rite. The Council of Trent says 'by means of these sacraments'. The same council

explicitly defines for Baptism that the 'by means of' signifies the instrumental cause. There is no reason for doubting that the council considered all the other sacraments also as instrumental causes which God uses to confer grace. Hence this is the doctrine admitted today by all theologians.[11]

Vagaggini repeats here what a certain kind of theologian takes for granted and bandies around without checking his sources. The relevant decree of the Council of Trent (*On Justification*) has been transposed by 'all theologians' of 'today' into an essentially philosophical account of causation. Sacraments 'cause' something: grace, worship, and so forth – on how this instrumentality works 'there is still a diversity of opinion'.[12] Careful scrutiny of the Tridentine decree shows that there is little justification for claiming that the instrumental causality discussed there is identical in all the sacraments.[13] The decree speaks of a variety of causes, and twice of an instrumental cause. In the first case the instrumental cause (of justification itself) is 'the God of mercy, who gratuitously washes and sanctifies, signing and anointing *with the promised Holy Spirit who is the guarantee of our inheritance*'.[14] The reference here is clearly to Baptism

11 Vagaggini, *Il senso teologico della liturgia*, pp. 110f. 'Quando si dice che i sacramenti conferiscono la grazia s'intende, come detto, che Dio la conferisce, come causa principale, ma in connessione e avuto riguardo al rito sacramentale. Il concilio di Trento dice: "per mezzo di questi sacramenti". Lo stesso concilio definisce esplicitamente per ill battesimo che quel "per mezzo" significa la causa strumentale. Che anche per tutti gli altri sacramenti si tratti, nelle intenzioni del concilio, di cause strumentali delle quali Dio si serve per conferire la grazia, non c'è nessun motivo di dubitarne ed è perciò dottrina oggi ammessa da tutti i teologi.' Cf. Council of Trent: 7th Session, *Decrees on the Sacraments, Canons on the sacraments in general*, §§6–8; 6th Session, *Decree on Justification*, Chapter 7, *What the justification of the sinner might be, and what are its causes.*

12 Vagaggini, *Il senso teologico della liturgia*, p. 111. 'È anche oggi diversità d'opinioni.'

13 Although this is clearly Aquinas' eventual view: cf. *Summa Theologiæ*, IIIa, Q. 62, art. 1, corp. Vagaggini is repeating the common assumption of the commentators contemporary to him that the decisions of the Council of Trent is to be interpreted through St Thomas Aquinas's *Summa Theologiæ*. Trent made much use of St Thomas, but also modified and nuanced what it received from him, while at the same time drawing on other sources as well.

14 Council of Trent: 7th Session, Chapter 7. 'Efficiens vero misericors Deus, qui gratuito abluit et sanctificat, signans et ungens *Spiritu promissionis sancto, qui est pignus hæreditatis nostro*' (emphasis in original).

alone (or at the most Baptism together with Confirmation, as the completion of the sacraments of Christian initiation), but the second reference is yet stronger: 'likewise of instrumental Baptism, which is the sacrament of faith'.[15] The final cause is specifically the glory of God and eternal life: the formal cause is the justness of God (here we would have to understand the sacrifice of Christ as in conformity with the formal cause – it is how this cause actually manifests itself and can be seen). One other cause is mentioned, specifically outside the very pseudo-Aristotelian language (of the 'four causes') so far employed, which shows this discourse to be relying on philosophical language but actually theological in its import: Christ is the 'meritorious' cause because he 'made satisfaction for us to God the Father'.[16] Moreover, the instrumental cause of justification (and not, therefore, 'of the sacraments' or 'of what the sacraments themselves produce') is here rightly and primarily (even if the sacrament of Confirmation is also being alluded to): Baptism.

Instrumental causality as laid out in the decrees of the Council of Trent and in relation to the sacraments is a significant development of the understanding of causality even as it is developed philosophically using neo-Aristotelian categories from Avicenna, Averroes and then (abandoning these categories) christologically (and soteriologically) from Aquinas' encounter with the Greek patristic writings and his thoroughgoing return to the scriptural sources.[17]

The Dominican theologian Berhard Blankenhorn notes that Aquinas is forced to abandon the neo-Aristotelian language of middle scholasticism in its engagement with earlier Arab philosophers in order to arrive at the view that 'if Christ is an instrumental cause of salvation in the unrestricted sense of direct or perfecting

---

15 Council of Trent: 7th Session, Chapter 7. 'Instrumentalis item sacramentum baptismi, quod est sacramentum fidei.'

16 Council of Trent: 7th Session, Chapter 7. 'Pro nobis Deo Patri satisfecit.'

17 For a discussion of this, and of the way in which Aquinas resolves the question of instrumental causality (in such a way that it is the background to the Tridentine decrees) see Blankenhorn OP, B., 'The Instrumental Causality of the Sacraments: Thomas Aquinas and Louis-Marie Chauvet', in *Nova et Vetera*, vol. 4 (2006), pp. 255–93: see esp. pp. 282f.

efficient causality, then the sacraments *can* be as well. [The later] Thomas seems convinced that the sacraments *must* be such perfecting causes because the universal cause of grace has ascended into heaven, and grace needs to be applied to us by particular causes.'[18] Blankenhorn adds that 'the early Thomas followed many of his contemporaries by adopting a still unrefined metaphysics while allowing the development of his theological positions to remain fairly detached from Scripture . . . [the late] Thomas could return to Scripture and make sense of its realistic language'.[19] These two perspectives are entirely consistent with, and confirm in an abstract way, the dogmatic argument I will develop in the next chapter from out of the texts of the sacred liturgy itself.

The instrumentality at issue is the ability of the sacraments to be particular, local, 'causes' of the salvation offered to man that is revealed in Christ. In this there is a sacramental *order* – first in the order of these is Baptism, since it makes the possible activity of all the other sacraments actual; pre-eminent among all of these is the holy Eucharist, for it is the sacrament of the passion and has a special relation to the Incarnation of the Lord.

The dogmatic intention behind taking over the word 'cause' from philosophy to theology is in order to explain why the worship of the Church is efficacious. In this Vagaggini's almost careless use of the word 'cause', typical of so much recent theological use, and its restriction to the question of 'what produces what', so much does not get beyond the merely philosophical employment of the term to explain its theological meaning that it does not *even* touch what the philosophers intended in their original development of the term at all. The word 'cause' and the thinking of causality derives from Latin *causa*, *causalitas*, itself a translation of the Greek term *aitia*.

Originally *aitia* was a legal term meaning 'that for which something can be blamed' or said to be responsible for. In the endless distinctions cut by the Schoolsmen, the original reason for taking up

---

18 Blankenhorn OP, B., 'The Instrumental Causality of the Sacraments', p. 284 (author's emphases).

19 Blankenhorn OP, B., 'The Instrumental Causality of the Sacraments', p. 288.

the word *aitia* at all is lost and covered over. It is significant that St Thomas's development of an adequate theology of sacramental instrumental causality is forced to abandon the language of Aristotelianism and the medieval schools with their dependence on the Arab interpreters, in order to explain the actual meaning of how our salvation can be caused by God in the life and work of the Church. In this he also undermines any employment of the later distinction deployed by Pius XII in *Mediator Dei*, of *ex opere operato*, and *ex opere operantis Ecclesiæ*. In doing so he both returns the notion of causality to its proper home, and shows how faith completes and surpasses this original meaning for the sake of human salvation in Christ.

In attempting to understand what is meant by 'causes', Catholic theologians have either trotted out various accounts of Aristotle's 'four causes' or attempted to abandon language of causality altogether. If recourse is made to the first move, it should be noted that neither the 'instrumental cause' nor the 'meritorious cause' mentioned in the Tridentine decree is to be found among any causes defined by Aristotle.[20] On the other hand, Louis-Marie Chauvet is a good example of a theologian who wishes to do away with all language of causality because he reads it as 'mere' metaphysics. Thus Chauvet says: 'Metaphysics: a causalist onto-theo-logic'.[21] This has, he claims, the effect of producing grace as a 'thing', 'in the manner of an "object" or "finished product", even if it is a "spiritual" one. Grace must be treated beyond value, according to the symbolic mode of communication, and in the first place communication of the word'.[22] In denouncing causal language as 'ontotheological' Chauvet is

---

20 Blankenhorn notes, quite correctly, that actual references to anything like instrumental causality in Aristotle are, to say the least 'sparse'. Blankenhorn OP, 'The Instrumental Causality of the Sacraments', p. 276.

21 Chauvet, L.-M., *Symbole et sacrement*, Paris, Éditions du Cerf, 1987, p. 30. 'La métaphysique: une onto-theo-logique causaliste.'

22 Chauvet, L.-M., *Symbole et sacrement*, p. 30. 'Sur le mode de l'"objet" ou du "produit fini", si "spirituel" qui soit celui-ci. Elle requiert d'être traitée hors-valeur, sur le mode symbolique de la communication, et prioritairement de la communication de parole.'

making appeal to Martin Heidegger's notion of the 'overcoming of metaphysics'.[23]

Although Chauvet is right to be concerned that grace not be understood as a thing,[24] and that what is to the fore in any understanding of grace is communication, he is not right (nor are any of the other theologians who would share his viewpoint) to eschew the notion of causality. Chauvet's nervousness towards causality betrays the inadequate way he has appropriated the critique of metaphysics. For Heidegger the critique of causality in metaphysics turns on the way in which God as 'first cause' had, in the Christianization of philosophy, become an axiom of philosophical truth, and so had become determinative for any philosophical understanding of truth at all (preventing access to understanding truth as ἀ–λήθεια, disclosure). This does not at all mean that 'In the beginning God created the heavens and the earth'[25] cannot be given in faith and so believed *in faith*. *Nor* does it mean that all causal language is to be abandoned, a move which thereby reduces philosophy to trivialities and absurdity. For Heidegger, as for anyone seeking to speak of the completion and overcoming of metaphysics, the *philosophical* tying together of man and God through a 'causal bond' ('createdness') *has already*

---

23 Specifically Chauvet is referring to the discussion of ontotheology in the 1956/57 lecture *Die onto-theo-logische Verfassung der Metaphysik* (published in Heidegger, M., *Identität und Differenz*, in *Gesamtausgabe* vol. 11, Frankfurt, Klostermann, 2006 [1957], cf. pp. 51–79). Heidegger began using the term ontotheology (in relation to Hegel) from 1930. See for a full discussion of the origins of this term Hemming, L. P., *Heidegger's Atheism: The Refusal of a Theological Voice*, pp. 106–10, esp. 109. Heidegger in fact employs two phrases repeatedly through his later work: 'Überwindung der Metaphysik', by which he means metaphysics' own self-demise as a basis for thinking in the wake of Nietzsche, and 'Vollendung der Metaphysik', as the 'completion' and triumph of metaphysics in the work of both Hegel and Nietzsche. The point is that because metaphysics is, as a basis for thinking, exhausted, we cannot simply return to metaphysical thinking as if the nineteenth century had never happened, claiming that all is well in 'Christian' philosophy because Nietzsche (and for that matter Hegel) are neither to our taste nor 'true'. No more than could Nietzsche, are we able to 'choose' what will and won't be true, which is the effect of any claim of this kind.

24 Blankenhorn does a fine job in showing (and against Chauvet) that grace is in no way understood as a thing or object in St Thomas, and that intrinsic to any understanding of grace is that grace communicates salvation. Cf. Blankenhorn OP, 'The Instrumental Causality of the Sacraments', p. 291.

25 Cf. Genesis 1.1.

been overcome in Nietzsche's (and Hegel's) unfolding of the description of the *situation* of the death of God – a situation in which even the faithful have to take their place (because we who believe have to live in a world which expects us, even as believers, to believe privately and publicly to behave *as if* God were dead), irrespective of the entire liveliness of the God in whom we faithfully trust.

What then of language of causes? Aristotle, in clarifying the philosophical meaning of the term *aitia*, says that 'we only think to be understanding inasmuch as we recognise the causes'.[26] Causes, for Aristotle, are a means by which understanding and recognition can take place. Again, for Aristotle, what Chauvet names as 'communication' is intrinsic to causes. What this means is that for Aristotle 'the' causes are not concerned with 'what produces what' but are concerned with how in each case any particular phenomenon in its appearing is available to understanding. Causes are simply a thematic way of describing how the understanding *understands*, and knows *in* its knowing.

For Aristotle what is at issue is the perfection (completion) of the intellect, such that, in knowing what it knows, the world is disclosed to it and continually made available to it. What Aristotle omits in the description of causes is that everything whose cause is to be determined is determined *with respect to* world, in which it appears (this omission is because Aristotle takes it for granted this is how causes will be understood). The causes, and causality as such, do not produce the world, they take the already being-in-place of world for granted. The only cause where this appears 'formally' or at all thematically is in the so-called 'formal' cause, the *to ti ēn einai*. The meaning of this phrase is extremely difficult to translate. The word *ēn* is the imperfect form of the verb 'to be'. The imperfect in Greek is, however, a form not of the past tense (it was), but of the present (it *is* such that it *was already* and *goes on* being). However the persistence – the 'what is (was, and goes on being) in advance of, and lets happen

---

26　*Posterior Analytics* 94 a 20 ''Επεὶ δὲ ἐπίστασθαι οἰόμεθα ὅταν εἰδῶμεν τὴν αἰτίαν'. It is only after this that Aristotle adds 'αἰτίαι δὲ τέτταρες' ('causes of which there are four'), and then proceeds to enumerate them.

this particular what' has become an aspect of the *thing* (the 'quiddity' or 'whatness' of the thing to be enquired about) instead of being the 'wherein' for the thing's appearing (world). It is the disappearance of the world-character wherein any 'thing' appears from Aristotle's description of the meaning of causes that impairs Aquinas from being able to derive from Aristotelian causality the understanding he needs for a genuine sacramental causality. When Aquinas attains an adequate description, not with respect to the facticity or givenness of world as such, but with respect to the salvation-world within which the liturgical sign is always given – he quite correctly derives it from the character of the sacramental sign itself.

The sacramental sign indicates, not the givenness of the 'natural' world (because it only appears provisionally and problematically in this world, with respect to faith), but the world the sign has been given within, the salvation-world *constituted* by its appearing liturgically, the world which God has disposed and allotted for the sign's appearing through the action and revelation of his divine Son.[27]

The replication of every liturgical sign – sacrament *and* sacramental (and so including the sacred ceremonies of the liturgy) – must be presupposed as having been ordained and revealed by Christ himself in the name of the Father, so that Christ, as the Second Person of the Divine Trinity and the one who both appears in the world and orders the world towards the First Person, chooses each sign, and orders it, and decides in advance what it would mean. This is especially true of the situation where Christ, and in his name, Christianity, takes over and transforms the meaning of the former worship of Israel in the worship of the covenant between God and man as it is now renewed in Christ. Here we would think especially of the psalms, not just in themselves, but also in their ordering and structure; the Baptism of the Lord would be another example, where the baptismal practices of

---

27 The 'problematic' character is not a deficiency in the sign, but rather in its reception, a problematic character that exactly reflects the problematic character of the appearance of the Christ in the ordinary world himself. There are those who, by God's grace and so through faith, recognize instantly the Son of God and respond accordingly, and those who encounter a mere man, and therefore, because of what others encounter in him, a blasphemer at that.

Israel are taken over and transformed *because* Christ himself, in being baptized, transforms their meaning.

This is why it is inadequate to make the distinction between the *ex opere operato* and the *ex operere operantis Ecclesiæ*, because the suggestion in *Mediator Dei* is that the signification implicit in it is in the hands of, and at the disposal of, the hierarchy, who can choose how the signification can manifest itself. In fact, however, the signification must *also* be divinely instituted, and be presumed to be the temporal manifestation of the liturgy of the end-times, the heavenly liturgy. In this case, therefore, the Church is only guardian of the work in question, and not its arbiter, since if the work were founded in anything *other* than the liturgy of the end-time it could not be a work of, and for, Christ (it could not signify, it would itself be deprived of its instrumentality, and it would impair the instrumentality of every other sign). It is for this reason that every reform in the liturgy must not only be 'organic' in the sense of genuinely successive to what went before, but also *eschatic*, that is, capable of signifying the meaning of the end-times. It must in each case be the work of the Spirit and inspired *by* the Spirit.

Finally, therefore, all liturgical signification presumes the sanctified place which indicates the liturgy of the end-times: the altar and the sanctuary as the body of Christ and the 'holy of holies' of the Temple of the New Jerusalem, that alone has the potency to bring man into the precinct of the eschaton. All liturgy has its home in Church, and in *a* church as the place which makes visible the New Jerusalem.[28]

Although the capacity to understand a sacrament is grounded in the being of being human, nevertheless, even if the *capacity* for the sign is such, the *meaning* of the sign is not, nor is it ever given in advance or able to be worked out in advance of its appearing by mere human reason. A genuine disclosure of God (a real miracle) is not something we can predict or recognize for ourselves, except that we

---

28 Even when it does not take place in *a* church, a minimal level of significatory elements are necessary to let the sanctuary be present – a cross, appropriate liturgical dress, lights, etc.

have been taught by God's own informing us of the meaning of what it is by means of what God says about himself. For this reason, Aquinas says, it is not by any rational(istic) means, nor by any human power that a sacrament is what it is, but, as we have seen, *per infinitam virtutem Dei*, by the infinite power of God. In each case what discloses the meaning of a sacrament is Christ himself, who is fully present in the meaning that the sacrament is. Strictly speaking the sacraments can be understood therefore fully to be instrumental causes in Aquinas' formal dogmatic definition of them, because they both contain and communicate fully what they at the same time are causes *of*.

In each case a sacrament is what it signifies, and in each case it signifies a formal aspect of the presence and being of Christ. The question therefore is the character of the disclosure of the meaning. The sacred liturgy is the 'means by which', it is the 'instrumental' world in which the meaning of the formal instrumental cause can be read-off. Here is the very reason both for the *complexity* and the poly-form *character* of the cursus of the sacred liturgy. The sacred liturgy taken in its entirety – above all the office and its intimate interconnectedness with the liturgy of the Mass (the Gradual, the Ordinary and the Common), but the adjunct rites as well – is the unfolding of the world within which the full significatory meaning, the *capacity to communicate* of the *instruments of divine self-communication* are disclosed. At the same time *every divine self-communication, because it is inherently ordered to intelligibility, is at the same time inherently ordered to an appropriation which at the same time transforms, and so prepares for deification, the soul attuned to, and receptive of, what is communicated.*

'Ordered to intelligibility' does not mean capable of being immediately appropriated, so that its meaning is recognized or given in a flash of understanding: but rather, is *mediate* and *mediating*, and so causes understanding to grow over time. Formally, the individual sacraments are inseparable from the world from out of which they are communicated: that world is at the same time a unity, even though it is comprised of parts. The liturgy constantly *moves* the intellect that responds to it, from incomprehension to understanding. By means of familiarity and the repetition of what becomes familiar, the liturgy is able to introduce and cause understanding with respect to the unfamiliar. The liturgically exceptional always occurs within the context of the familiar, at the same time exposing the familiar to a transformation and deepening in itself.

In each case in sacramental and liturgical causality the issue is not that something causes another or produces another, but that the sacramental sign *is* the capacity to produce a divine effect, the effect of uniting a present time with, and relating it (literally, carrying it) to, the end-time, making present time present to the end-time. This is a kind of *analogia temporalis*, given not metaphysically, but in faith, because it is the effect of what the faithful know God has decided will pertain (*per inifinitam virtutem Dei*). The *virtutem Dei* or power of God is, historically speaking, Christ himself, that one who enters human history. It is because Christ has entered human history and revealed how it is to be understood by *being* the means of divine signification and so *establishing* the meaning of every divine sign that this power is at work. And at the same time the *virtutem Dei* is the power of the Spirit who establishes and makes possible the relationship between the *eschaton* and the glorified Christ with the passion and sacrifice and resurrection of the earthly Christ. Establishes here means 'establishes in human minds'.

The sacraments *are*, as aspects of Christ, at the same time what they *cause to come into being*. In each case, therefore, they require both divine initiation and the (human) capacity for their reception. Capacity is, again, in each case, not in virtue of human initiative, but only in consequence of human cooperation with the divine initiative. The sacraments have the unique attribute that they are at the same time the grace that they cause and effect: in each case something is communicated *of* the Second Person of the Divine Trinity *through* the power of the Third Person *for the sake of* the disclosure of, and so union with, the First. There is no 'rational' account of this inclusion into the divine life which does not at the same time presume the implicit and interior perfection of the very one capable of receiving, and so thinking (we may, perhaps, say: acquiring by reasonable means) what he receives. To put it another way, we return to the basic patristic insight that the human being is perfected through union of the human intellect with the divine intellect. This insight is above all clarified by St Thomas Aquinas in his discussion of deiformity. The soul is to be made deiform: *inasmuch as it is* made deiform, by grace it knows and comes to understand what God *already* knows, insofar as, and to the extent that, God chooses to flood the human mind with the light of the divine intellect.[29]

---

29 Cf. Aquinas, *Summa Theologiæ*, Ia, Q. 12, art. 7 resp. 'Nullus autem intellectus creatum potest Deum infinite cognoscere. Instantum enim intellectus creatus divinam essentiam perfectius vel minus perfecte cognoscit, inquantum maiori vel minori lumine gloriæ perfunditur.' ('In no way therefore is the created intellect able to know God infinitely. In that way indeed will the created intellect know the divine essence more perfectly or less perfectly, to the extent of the greater or lesser light of glory poured into it.')

Chapter 8

Meaning Liturgy

Christ has come, by the divine initiative both of his having come among us and because God longs for us to know his Son and so prompts us to greet him, as one who *has* come, and for this reason the soul goes out to greet its Redeemer, the Bridegroom, the great High Priest. The model and figure of this 'going out' is communicated in the liturgy of Palm Sunday.[1] The liturgy for this day makes constant reference to the fact that Holy Week begins with the spreading of palm and olive branches before the Lord. The collects (of which there were originally seven) for the blessing of the palms emphasize something that is often overlooked in modern considerations of the rites of Holy Week – that just as the strewing of olive branches on the Lord's entry into Jerusalem was Israel's figurative going out to greet the Lord who is their messiah, 'so may we carrying palms and branches of olive, with (these) good works go forth to meet Christ'.[2] The 'works' in question are also the spiritual works of prayers made. The implication is that we are to be prepared for the end of time, for the final consummation of all things.

The opening collect for Palm Sunday in the Dominican Rite makes the connection that all of this is to prepare us, not only to understand the Lord's entry into Jerusalem and his passion, but at the same time make us fit to go out again to greet His second coming, that we may

---

1 Reference is made here to the unreformed (pre-1955) rite for Palm Sunday.
2 First collect of blessing (before the Preface). 'Ita nos portantes palmas, et ramos olivarum, bonis actibus occurramus obviam Christo.'

be worthy to be ones rejoicing with the palms of (final) victory.³ Significantly, both in the Roman and Dominican rites, mention is made in the prayers of benediction of (in the words of the first Roman prayer) the 'figure of the Church' represented in the ancient covenant being fulfilled in this central moment of the unfolding of the meaning of the *same* covenant's renewal.

We are not passive therefore – this being led through the passion is for a purpose – to make us in the world what one of the Fathers calls 'the hands, the feet, the eyes, the ears, the very mouths of Christ himself' – for every good work that we might do is a work for the salvation of the world – it is a work of Christ (the subjective and objective genitives are both essential here) which we perform in his name. We modern people are accustomed to making a separation between what we believe and what we do, between mind and body. Here again, however, is that deeper wisdom of the liturgy itself, constraining us to abandon the separation of mind and body. One of the collects for the procession of Palm Sunday reminds us: 'that what thy people this day bodily perform for thy veneration, this they may with highest devotion perfect spiritually'.⁴ The ways in which we dispose our bodies determines what happens to our souls and has an effect upon them. This action is in response to the faithful understanding 'what is mystically signified in deed' when the multitude 'on this day inspired by a heavenly illumination' took up palms to greet the Lord: 'the branches of palms, therefore, signify his triumphs over the prince of death; and the branches of olive proclaim, in a manner, the coming of a spiritual unction'.⁵

Because the liturgy makes this connection of bodily disposition *before* the event of the passion, but make clear that this disposition is

---

3 *Missale S. Ordinis Prædicatorum* (1933), Dominica in Ramis Palmorum, prayer of blessing of the palms: 'et sicut illi processerunt obviam tibi cum arboreis frondibus egressi, ita nos, te redeunte in secundo adventu, cum palmis victoriæ læti mereamur occurrere'.

4 Sixth collect of the blessing of palms. 'Ut quod populus tuus in tui venerationem hodierna die corporaliter agit, hoc spiritualiter summa devotione perficiat.'

5 Fifth collect of the blessing of palms. 'Quid mystice designet in facto quod hodie coelesti lumine afflata ... Palmarum igitur rami de mortis principe triumphos exspectant; surculi vero olivarum, spiritualem unctionem advenisse quodammodo clamant.'

itself in consequence of a divine prompting and inspiration, let us turn, by reference to a prayer that might overarch our next investigations, to the consummation of that preparation, from out of which the meaning of the preparation itself can flow:

Deus, cuius Filius in alta cælorum potenter ascendens captivitatem nostram sua duxit virtute captivam; tribue, quæsumus, ut dona, quæ suis participibus contulit, largiatur et nobis: Jesus Christus Filius tuus Dominus noster qui tecum vivit, et regnat per omnia sæcula sæculorum. Amen.[6]	O God, whose Son into the heights of the heavens powerfully ascending has taken our captivity captive, grant we beseech you, that the gifts which were bestowed on his companions be extended to us: Jesus Christ your Son our Lord, who lives and reigns with you, throughout all ages. Amen.

A central moment of the Easter cycle is the feast of the Ascension and its relation, through its (original) extended octave, to the liturgy for Pentecost. Formerly the celebrations of the Ascension and Pentecost were kept together on the same day, but came to be separated over time. The day of the Ascension indicates a parallelism between the forty days of Lent and the forty days following Easter day during which (according to St Luke) the risen Lord appeared and taught the disciples the meaning of his resurrection and its significance for the kingdom yet to come.[7] This period, says St Luke, culminates with the Ascension. Liturgically the Ascension is followed by an octave of eight days which includes texts for the Sunday of the octave (in common with many octaves whose days are not presumed always –

---

6 *Processionarium Iuxta Ritum S. Ordinis Prædicatorum*, Prayer at the entry into the church in conclusion for the procession after Terce on the feast of the Ascension.

7 Acts 1.1–5. In particular: 'To [the apostles] he showed himself alive after his passion by many proofs, during forty days appearing to them and speaking of the kingdom of God.'

or in this case ever – to fall on a Sunday) and additional texts specific to the eighth, or octave, day.[8]

This period is unusual because the liturgy for the Sunday is repeated after the octave, on the ninth day (the second Friday after the feast), and then (on Saturday) the liturgy moves into the Vigil for Pentecost. A further feature of this period is that the Vigil, whose Mass, like that of the vigil liturgy of Easter before 1955,[9] is celebrated on the Saturday morning before Pentecost, and begins in purple vestments (in parallel with the Easter liturgy, with, again as at Easter, folded chasubles for the sacred ministers), repeats six of the twelve prophecies from the Easter vigil liturgy, and likewise the litany of the saints and blessing of the baptismal font, before the liturgy of the Mass transfers to red vestments (rather than the white or gold of Easter). Matins for the octave of Pentecost, having begun in the vigil with three nocturns, has for the entire week up until the feast of the Holy Trinity, in a parallel with the Octave of Easter, but unlike any of the other octaves, only one nocturn in each day of the octave.

If we have become accustomed to thinking of Pentecost as the 'birthday of the Church', in fact the whole of the liturgy for Eastertide is a pedagogy on the meaning and establishment of the Church itself, grounded in the liturgy of Passiontide, and especially from Palm Sunday onwards. The entire liturgy of Eastertide is ecclesiology from beginning to end. Not only does the Gospel for the feast of Pentecost itself report the establishment of the Church in the Holy Spirit, but from the most ancient times the Gospel for the octave day of Easter

---

8 This structure remained largely intact after the 1911 reforms to the Missal, Calendar, and Breviary. It was impaired by the reforms of 1955, transforming the Vigil liturgy for Pentecost into a merely festal Mass removing all the penitential aspects, the prophecies, blessing of the font and transition of liturgical colour from purple to red. Although the octave was suppressed (together with most of the octaves and most of the vigils of feasts) in the reforms of 1955, the textual structure was left intact. The entire liturgy for the period from Ascension to Pentecost was recast in the reforms of the Breviary in 1961 and those of the Missal in 1962 so that the intimate interconnections between the two feasts, with their theological consequences and meaning, are all but atomized or erased even before the postconciliar reforms.

9 Until the permission given in 1951 to celebrate the vigil liturgy in the night hours, and then the reforms of the rite of the vigil and requirement to celebrate it at night from 1955 onward.

– Low Sunday – also contains the words from the risen Christ who appears in the midst of the terrified disciples to say 'receive the Holy Spirit'.[10] As we encountered in the discussion in Chapter 1, It is clear that the Gospel for this day is at the same time *the* primary Eucharistic text of St John's Gospel: the disciples are assembled on the *eighth* day which is the recapitulation of the *first* day. This establishes the pattern for Easter that it is a sequence of reduplications, each modifying and amplifying the understanding of the *singular* event of the triumph of the passion in the truth of the resurrection.

The alleluia chant for the octave day of Easter prepares us for this: 'after eight days, the doors having been shut, Jesus stood in the midst of his disciples and spoke'.[11] St Thomas is able to touch the wounds of Christ because he is joined to them in and through the Holy Eucharist. We should recall here that this follows on immediately after the Lord's injunction to cease touching him, made only lines earlier in the same Gospel, to St Mary Magdalene, because 'I have not yet ascended to my Father'. It is behind closed doors – the closed doors of liturgical signification – that the Lord may properly be touched, in a possibility that only becomes fully realized after he has ascended to the Father, as we shall see.

The Ascension is a further liturgical reflection on the meaning of the Church. The event presupposes that the assembly has been assembled – exactly as on the eighth day. This time, however, the assembly gathers on the fortieth day. The first forty days of Easter are explicitly a pedagogy on the eschaton as the inception of the Kingdom itself. The liturgy reflects this in its alleluia chant from Psalm 67 (which, as we shall see, is *the* explanatory psalm for this entire liturgical period from Ascension to the end of the octave of Pentecost): 'Dominus in Sinaï in sancto': 'the Lord is in Sinaï in the holy place'. The indication is that Sinaï *itself* has been transformed from one thing to another because the Lord is there in triumph. The desert is no longer a desert; it has been transformed into the

10 John 20.22.
11 *Missale Romanum* (1884), Mass for Low Sunday. 'Post dies octo, januis clausis, stetit Jesus in medio discipulorum suorum et dixit.'

kingdom yet to come: the mountain, as the original holy of holies; and the place where Moses builds an altar to the Lord, has become the *sacramentum* of the new and eternal (and so ancient and ever-new) covenant – which is nothing less than the Temple of the New Jerusalem itself.

The entire mood of the liturgy of the Mass of Ascension is one of triumph, of God (in the person of Christ) taking possession of what is rightly his (of God's presence and majesty filling the house).[12] At the same time in the Ascension the liturgy indicates that an important exchange takes place – the physical, bodily, presence of the Lord is withdrawn from the world: but this is not a taking away, it is a transformation in how we are to understand Jesus' own being-located. It is not to be resolved as a departure. The third antiphon at Lauds and Vespers emphasizes this, from St Luke 24.50, 51 – in the rising-up of the Lord, a blessing is bestowed: 'His hands being lifted, he blessed them, and was carried into heaven'.[13] The disciples are consoled by angels, which signifies that, through the effects of Jesus' Ascension to the Father, the disciples can now enter the company of angels. This is directly parallel to the consolation received by St Mary Magdalene on the day of the resurrection, from an angel. The Ascension amplifies what is already made true at the empty tomb. *This* is what it means to be able to touch the Lord: to enter into the company of those who surround him and have constant communication with him. They touch by knowing and understanding.

The French theologian Jean Corbon notes that the Ascension is 'above all the inauguration of a relation of faith, entirely new, to a new time: the Liturgy of the end times'.[14] The liturgy of the last times does not receive its inception here, however, but rather, it receives its possibility of visibility, its possibility of being understood. As we shall see in the last chapter, the inception of this liturgy begins in Christ's heavenly birth. The exchange that takes place is not the removal of

---

12 Cf. Matins of dedication of a Church, p. 7 above.
13 'Elevatis manibus, benedixit eis, et ferebatur in cœlum.'
14 Corbon, J., *Liturgie de source*, Paris, Éditions du Cerf, 1980, p. 44. 'Surtout l'inauguration d'une relation de foi, toute nouvelle, d'un temps nouveau: la Liturgie des derniers temps.'

Christ from the world, but that from now on he is to be seen in another way, a way which is a blessing for us, and so the communication of confirmatory grace. It is for this reason that the Paschal Candle is extinguished after the Gospel on this day, and removed from its place in the sanctuary: the one light of Christ, once singularly located by a physical body in a physical location (signified liturgically by the chanting of the words of the Lord himself in the Gospel), is now manifest by other, multiple, means, which are themselves capable of the same blessing that his singular presence had hitherto bestowed. The Bridegroom and High Priest is present in every sanctuary, every place from wherein 'I see' the descending of the New Jerusalem, the actual, physical location of the presence, on the earth.

The whole symbolic, and this means sacramental, order of the Church (as the fulfilment of the meaning of the Jerusalem Temple) becomes possible on this day, or rather, every sacramental sign, every ritual gesture and prayer, the Church herself *as* an order of sacred signification, comes to be understood in its possibility on this day. This is the day of the *replacement* of the one Temple with the possibility of many temples, and so of many sites of sanctification, many churches. Once again the connection with Pentecost is intrinsic, and intrinsically related to the character of the possibility of the manifold appearing of the meaning of the possibility of *one, unique and eternal* sacrifice on many altars.

It is not that on this day for the first time sacramental signification becomes possible, but rather this day uniquely reveals what sacramental signification *is*, both fulfilling the meaning of the sacraments of the old dispensation now past, and disclosing to us in full the meaning of the sacraments of the new dispensation. On this day, therefore, Christ is not removed from us – we are now to know Christ by other means, means which extend the *one* eternal liturgy, the liturgy of the end-time, into all times and places henceforth, *and* reveal the full meaning of what went before (the sacraments of the old dispensation) *and even* the 'sacraments' (significations) of (to borrow St Augustine's phrase) the *ecclesia paganorum* or church ('assembly') of the pagans.

In the *Processional* of the Dominican rite, the procession for this day proscribes that, before the office of Terce, the cross having been carried out in procession and returned to the Church, the Prior opens the prayer above not as a separate rite, but as itself *part* of the rite of the procession (and so without the usual salutation 'Dominus vobiscum'). The collect is addressed to the Father, and begins by noting, in a form entirely characteristic of the Roman rite, that his Son, who is on this day to the depths of the heavens 'powerfully ascending', has by this power (i.e. by his sacrifice) 'taken captive our captivity' (so ending with his sacrifice our captivity to sin). This later phrase is again taken from Psalm 67, a phrase paraphrased and amplified with its specific meaning for the new covenant by St Paul in his letter to the Ephesians.[15] St Paul explicitly comments on the Psalm to indicate that *in* Christ's ascending, grace is communicated through the structure of the Church until the coming of the end-times. St Paul names the whole structure and character of the Church in this context.[16] The liturgy for the day therefore makes an explicit and pronounced reference to the significance of the feast for the establishment and sacred activity of the Church before the chanting of the Gospel, emphasizing the significance of the symbolic exchange that will take place immediately after it in the extinguishing of the Paschal light.

This phrase, 'has led captivity captive', together with the one already indicated, is repeated in the alleluia chant for the Mass for this day in the Dominican rite, and in the Roman rite itself. Other forms of the Roman rite betray a different preoccupation: the alleluia chant, for instance, in the Carmelite rite is quite different, reflecting the more Gallican origins of its Gradual.

---

15 Psalm 67.18–19; Ephesians 4.7–8.

16 Cf. Ephesians 4.7–13. 'Unto to every one of us is given grace, according to the measure of the giving of Christ. Wherefore he saith: Ascending on high, he led captivity captive: he gave gifts to men. Now that he ascended, what is it, but because he also descended first into the lower parts of the earth? He that descended is the same also that ascended above all the heavens: that he might fill all things. And he gave some apostles, and some prophets, and other some evangelists, and other some pastors and doctors: For the perfecting of the saints, for the word of the ministry, for the edifying of the body of Christ: Until we all meet into the unity of faith and of the knowledge of the Son of God, unto a perfect man, unto the measure of the age of the fullness of Christ.'

Whereas in the Roman Gradual the alleluia chant ends 'captivam duxit captivitatem', the Dominican Gradual adds from Psalm 67 and St Paul's quotation of it 'he gives the gift to men':[17] also a clear reference to the collect of the processional, but extending its meaning and commenting on it. In the collect, the gifts refers not simply to those which Christ gives in leading captivity captive and rising up, but that the gifts are the multiplied effects of the *single* gift which Jesus Christ himself is. The collect emphasizes this by not ending with the usual '*per* Jesum Christum Filium tuum', but by connecting the clause that begins *ut dona* directly with an immediate transition to the divine name: *Jesus Christus Filius tuus*, and so by implication, 'by means of this gift Jesus Christ'. The central formula of the prayer suggests that by *these* gifts, which by his rising were bestowed on those present with him, may *this* gift (Jesus Christ), 'largiatur et nobis', be also extended to us. At the same time, inasmuch as those present to Christ's having been taken up are the inception of the Church (as Apostles) so may we also be included in the assembly, as ones also to whom the gifts (grace) are to be extended *now*.

A further oddity is the omission in the concluding formula of this prayer of any reference to the Spirit. However, we should understand that this also is not accidental, because of the ancient connection between the Ascension and the feast of Pentecost. All forms of the Roman rite frequently employ a device, textually and rubrically, whereby the very things to which our attention is to be drawn are hidden or omitted from the place we would usually expect to find them, so that by removing them from their habitual place they have to be seen in a different way, a way oriented toward disclosing the character of this or that specific liturgical action, event, or day.[18] This

---

17 'Dedit dona hominibus.' In fact the continuation of the chant is implied in the *Graduale Romanum*, which as so often in naming only the first verse of the psalm to be sung nevertheless would once have presupposed that the psalm could, and would, have been continued. It is entirely possible that the Dominican Gradual includes the additional text so that it is not left out, after it became the custom to truncate the chant only to the first verse named.

18 The whole Office and Mass for the Dead can only be explained in this way, as it is crowded with omissions and substitutions which, taken together, explicate the entire theology of praying for the dead.

practice of displacement is manifested here: the gifts given are given *through* the Spirit. The removal of the physical body is so that the Spirit of God, the Spirit of Christ, is made manifest through the future means by which the gift that Christ is, in the manner of its being given. The *dona*, or gifts, refer to what the Spirit will now confer.

The full liturgical meaning of the Ascension of the Lord is entirely disclosed in this collect. Christ is the gift of the Father to mankind and to the world, a gift which becomes visible in his sacrifice, and whose full energy and power takes captive our captivity to sin (thus freeing us) and leads us as ones freed up to the heavens. His powerful ascending, however, has power not because it is withdrawn to the outermost heavens, but because it is *extended from beyond, across the whole of the heavens and from the end of time.* It is precisely not taken away; it is *now* to be manifest everywhere, at all times and places. This is why it is *potens*, powerful. As powerful it rises up fully, *oriens in alta.* Christ is the gift, as *all* signs of Christ now bestow the gift that He is (through the Spirit): inasmuch as Christ as a gift is divine, so the gifts now given are, by virtue of their relation to the Spirit, also divine, and also indicate, and make us present to, the end-time.

The Ascension is not simply about a physical disappearance, but about the capacity to signify as such. Signification is the gift in and of itself: the signification in question is the liturgical causality – the signs are what they signify. The Ascension inaugurates the possibility of *Christian* liturgy, whilst authenticating and authorizing the liturgy of Israel and all true worship of God (the Church of Israel, the 'church' or assemblies of the pagans). What was given then, may it now also be extended over us – 'largiatur et nobis'.

If the liturgy for Ascension draws attention to the exchange in the way grace is to be received, and also indicates the essential connection of grace with the end-times, it does this again through the collect for the day in the Mass and the Office. The collect says:

| Concede, quæsumus, omnipotens Deus ut qui hodierna die Uinigenitum tuum Redemptorem nostrum ad cælos ascendisse credimus; ipsi quoque mente in cælestibus habitemus. | Grant, we beseech you, almighty God, that we who believe your only-begotten [Son] our redeemer this day to have ascended to the heavens, may also ourselves by means of the mind dwell among the things of heaven. |

The collect confirms that faith (in the redemptive power of the Only-begotten) leads us to dwell among the things of heaven (and so relates to the appearing of the angels with whom, and as whom, we will now dwell). The things of heaven are at the same time the things granted from heaven, the things given that heaven may be understood *mente*, by means of the intellect. Yet more, through the Ascension, what we would otherwise have known in direct contact through the senses we now are to know through the mind – i.e. that it is through the perfection of the mind that the 'things of heaven' are both obtained and understood, and are the very transporting of us *to* the end-time.

If, as I am clearly implying, the Ascension discloses that the liturgy is the basis of that possibility of signification and so transformation, then the liturgy ties together the truth of all things in Christ, and the truth of all things in themselves. We would have to be schooled in the sacred liturgy to understand things as God understands them.

From the Ascension itself the liturgy moves toward the giving of the Spirit as the means by which all of this is accomplished. The liturgy for the Sunday of the octave of the Ascension stresses in the Epistle and in the Benedictus antiphon: 'Then will come the Paraclete, whom I send to you, the Spirit of truth who proceeds from the Father',[19] pointing us toward Pentecost itself. It is, however, the octave day of Ascension where Matins completes the liturgical connections

---

19 *Breviarium Romanum* (1623), Lauds for Sunday of the Octave of the Ascension. 'Cum venerit Paraclitus, quem ego mittam vobis Spiritum veritatis, qui a Patre procedit.'

between Psalm 67 and the ecclesial meaning of the Ascension of the Lord itself – the reading in the first nocturn of Matins is Ephesians 4, which therefore discloses *at the end of the octave* the whole meaning of the entire cycle of the mystery in question.[20] The meaning of the Mass texts is therefore given as the celebration of the Ascension closes, indicating and performing the very perfection *mente*, by means of the mind, that the collect of the feast day names, repeated in each day of the octave.

This is recapitulated at Matins of Pentecost itself, and for the whole following octave: the central psalm of Matins on each of the days of Pentecost is Psalm 67.[21] By now, however, the giving of the Spirit, and the pedagogy of the liturgical texts and liturgical arrangement of the scriptural texts, enables us to see what is prophesied in the psalm. The real connection between the feasts is indicated in *reverse*, when we have been made ready by the grace given in the liturgical signs to understand the full meaning of what we have, in any case, already been given. This is how deification is effected. What we have already received *mente*, by means of the intellect, we will fully understand, *mente*, with the intellect as the intellect itself is perfected *by the very things received*. Nevertheless, what is received comes from the end-time, the time *from which* the Spirit is sent. It is for this reason that the liturgy of Pentecost draws attention to one word from the Epistle for the Sunday of Pentecost in the Chapter at Lauds and Vespers for the entire octave: 'et factus est *repente* de cœlo sonus'. This is usually translated as 'and suddenly there came a sound from heaven'. The word *repente*, however, indicates the direction – the word means something both 'unexpected' and completely new. It is sudden only in a dependent sense, in that it is a startling and unforeseen revelation. This is what 'has been done' (*factus est*). What is made present (*operatus*) is both unforeseen (it is nothing man can

---

20 This reading, with its critical importance for the ecclesiological meaning of the feast, was entirely removed from the cursus of Matins in the 1961 reform of the Breviary.

21 Recalling that because there is only one nocturn of what is nevertheless a festal office, the central psalm is not one of *twelve*, as in the ferial office (prior to 1911), but only *three* – thus there is even greater emphasis on this psalm.

have predicted) and is renew*ing* (it is the work that renews the eternal covenant). The Spirit, from the end-time, has been sent, and so that which is sent from the end-times has been made manifest, that we to whom it is manifest may by that means be transported in faith and in limited understanding by the 'things of heaven' (sacramental instrumentality and signification to understand *now* incompletely what we will *actually* in the end-time understand in full).

The entire dogmatic reflection discussed in the last chapter is therefore present here, *in every aspect* in the texts and their inter-twinement, in the sacred liturgy for the period of the Ascension to the octave day of Pentecost (which is itself the feast of the Divine Trinity and *outside* the Easter season). Pentecost is one of the octaves which is *de facto* and for important liturgical reasons actually less than eight days. Moreover, this understanding of the meaning is *already present*, in advance of the dogmatic reflection. Anyone schooled in these texts would have had the pedagogy required to make the transition that St Thomas himself had to make, from an understanding of causality which is essentially philo-sophical in its limitations, to a causality informed by grace and by the theology of deification that Bernhard Blankenhorn shows is St Thomas' mature view. All of this takes place, however, in the redemptive life-world that is the practice and fulfilment of the sacred liturgy itself. The liturgy authenticates the dogmatic reflec-tion, and not the other way round (which is why dogmatic concerns can never be used as the justification for the alteration of liturgical texts).

A non-rationalistic understanding of the sacred liturgy begins with the understanding that God is only discoverable insofar as he himself reveals himself (God can be indicated by the exercise of thinking, but he cannot be encountered, nor can the possibility or meaning of his encounter be anticipated, in advance of any encounter he himself initiates). The question is: how (for Christians) does God reveal himself? Increasingly this question has been resolved in two ways: *first*, we say, God reveals himself 'in Christ' through sacred scripture, that is, in the words of the *Catechism of the Catholic Church*, 'to culminate in the person and mission of the incarnate

Word, Jesus Christ':[22] *second*, this is accomplished by grace. In fact, however, this begs much, for unwittingly it introduces a kind of a circularity. The historical meaning of scripture is only disclosed and fulfilled by Christ. It is, paradoxically, only because we know who Christ is that we can read scripture, as we have already seen. Second, what is grace? Too often grace is conceived of as a kind of light, an illumination which flows from God to the creature. This, however, is only a metaphor. The light in question is the light of understanding: understanding has a character, a manner, a 'how', and it has a situatedness, it occurs in such-and-such a place and at such-and-such a time, it always springs from out of the particular world we inhabit (we need a body to understand anything). What understanding understands is never freed from the particularities and *existentialia* – the worldedness – in which, and at which, it understands. Nor is there ever a pure 'thing-understood' from which every aspect of time, place and character has been stripped off.

What we 'see' in the light we take too easily for granted as a kind of self-evidence, something which, in its standing for itself, stands there also for us. In fact it is not that simple – *we* have to be shaped to receive what is illuminated. Grace is not automatic, nor is it simple rays: it is the continual and virtuous accommodation *to* what is to be known: God does not come as a simple, dazzling, flash or vision, but through our repeated habituation to the means by which he discloses himself: the liturgy. Any impairment of the liturgy, however much it does not invalidate the liturgy itself, impairs its capacity to communicate the understanding which is at the same time preparatory to and for our deification.

This accommodation of the soul to God is not initiated by us, but rather it comes to us *from* somewhere else: in fact alone from God. It is not a *pre*disposition, but an *acquisition*. It is accomplished over time. Liturgical time, and what is disclosed in the time the liturgy gives, and in the places in which the liturgy is given, and in the character of what is given, is the manner of its accomplishment. This is

---

22 *Catechism of the Catholic Church*, §53. 'In Persona et missione Verbi incarnati, Iesu Christi culmen attinget.'

why not only the texts of the sacred liturgy are of such importance, but also the manner of their being carried out (faithfulness to the rubrics) *and* the character of the place and setting of their enaction. The *Ecclesia operans* is neither of incidental importance, nor of merely accidental character, nor is it merely arbitrary in its form.

So how does God signify himself and by what means? In God's self-signification, it is Christ who speaks and makes manifest the meaning of all that he says and that speaks of him: sacred scripture is uttered *through* the mouth of Christ (when we speak the meaning of scripture, it is with a christly tongue that we speak, using breath given by the Spirit). *What* is uttered, in the *manner of its uttering* is grace: grace is no thing, but a time – it is the giving to us *now* of an understanding that we will have *in full* when we are deified (God willing that we should be). This is not 'mere epistemology', nor is it a heap of bits of knowledge, but is our being drawn into our future deification even now.

Chapter 9

Liturgy as Revelation

I indicated in the previous chapters that although St Thomas Aquinas appears to give a speculative, rationalistic, account of the essence of God, and particularly with respect to time, in fact, and critically, St Thomas' whole understanding is informed by an outlook defined by scripture, which explains that understanding to be *only* in virtue of Christ and the activity of the divine Spirit of God. The knowing of the truth of everything that is true is known ultimately and actually alone through Christ, and in the Spirit. This is entirely in conformity with St Thomas' grounding outlook, that philosophy is both consonant with divine revelation, and subordinate to what revelation reveals to be true. What philosophy knows, it only knows in virtue of the truth that God is, and that truth is disclosed and is dynamically active only in Christ. This understanding is entirely in conformity with the prayer of which I have given a brief exegesis in the last chapter – a prayer to be made on the feast of the Ascension. A prayer that indicates that Christ is the gift, and that *all* signs of Christ now bestow the gift that He is.

We can see that St Thomas has extended the effects of this prayer: all that is known in Christ extends to knowledge even of things not salvific for man. For St Thomas, even the truth of those things that are false and evil is disclosed *not* in fact by the mere exercise of reason, but in virtue of the triumph of Christ. As such, it is not disclosed calculatively and in general (to reason means to calculate), but concretely in the light of God's having spoken through the person and actions surrounding his Son. The liturgy reveals that the

Ascension is not simply about a physical disappearance, but about the capacity to signify. Signification is the gift in and of itself, and St Thomas extends the effects of this signification beyond the mere signification of redemption, even to signifying the meaning of evil (so that we can reject it). The Ascension inaugurates the possibility of Christian liturgy, and it inaugurates the fullness of the understanding of truth. What was given then, may it now also be extended over us – *largiatur et nobis* – with respect to all things. The whole of the cosmos – the depths and heights in question – becomes the setting for the giving of the gift, which transforms that cosmos in its meaning.

Although drawing attention to its importance, we did not examine in closer detail the statement of Martin Heidegger that God is only discoverable insofar as he himself reveals himself. The question is, how, for Christians, does God reveal himself? How indeed does God speak to us now and by what means? In God's speaking, it is Christ who speaks and makes manifest the meaning of all that he says and that speaks of him: sacred scripture is uttered *through* Christ. The *Catechism of the Catholic Church* speaks of the transmission of revelation by all the means possible before reaching the one which really matters: it talks of the apostolic tradition; preaching; succession; tradition; scripture; the Church; the Magisterium; dogma; faith; catechesis, before finally mentioning, in the broadest terms, and without any amplification, 'worship'.[1] However, the apostolic tradition, the foundation of the transmission of revelation, is itself only visible *through* the divine liturgy. The Apostles are only Apostles insofar as their being is made manifest by that which participates in the liturgy of the end-times.

This is why bishops must pontificate at their cathedral altars in order to be who they are. It is why the fact that the papal liturgy, in its specific ancient form, is currently largely in abeyance is a scandal. The papal liturgy was the type for every pontifical (and abbatial) form of the liturgy across the Roman rite: in turn the pontifical and

---

1 *Catechism of the Catholic Church*, §§74–95. See especially §78, where worship (*cultus*) is given as a means of transmission of tradition *after* doctrine and the life of the Church – as if her worship were not her very life.

abbatial liturgy was the type for every other solemn form (most frequently Mass with a single deacon and subdeacon, but many dioceses had forms where numbers of deacons and subdeacons assisted a single priest). Once again there is a gradation – corresponding to the interrelations of heaven itself – at work here. The modern papal Mass has, until the present Pontificate, taken a form barely different from the pontifical form in any diocese, reversing this order of influence and destroying the hierarchy of the Church as a hierarchy *rooted in the altar and what occurs around it*, and so understood to be rooted in the very body of Christ.[2]

In other words the whole meaning and character of divine revelation is only possible as *we* can receive it in virtue of the means of signification inaugurated *for us* by the resurrection of the Lord, extended over all things through his ascension, and completed *in us* at Pentecost and by our subsequent receipt of what Pentecost bestows – the Spirit of God. Christ, the gift that has been given, the gift of grace itself, is given through the means of signification that is to be extended across the whole of the cosmos.

At its very heart, this question about revelation can be traced back to what the young Joseph Ratzinger's *Habilitation* study on St Bonaventure revealed to him. Here the inner unity of the scriptures and the liturgy can be made manifest in their whole meaning – in Ratzinger's understanding of divine revelation, an understanding that was widely understood in medieval theology.

---

2 Nowhere is this hierarchical character better demonstrated than in the ritual connections indicated in the ordination rites. In what is commonly interpreted as a form of concelebration, newly ordained priests in the preconciliar rite of ordination kneel, fully vested (although with, at this stage, the chasuble still folded or rolled up at the back) and say the Canon or prayer of consecration audibly with the bishop. Each priest is accompanied by another priest wearing a chasuble over his choir-dress. This has nothing to do with concelebration – it is a formal demonstration of the way in which each priest's future recitation of the most sacred prayer of the Mass is intrinsically linked to, and in concert with, what the bishop himself does, as the one to whom he is hierarchically tied, and so this action is a formal demonstration of *how* the priest acquires, and exercises, his right to say this prayer and effect the miracle of transubstantiation.

The idea that God's revelation of himself to man through his Son in the power of his Spirit is synonymous with the mere words of Scripture is, for the present pope, both now and as a young scholar, totally insufficient. At the same time the idea that all that matters in the liturgy is that Christ becomes present in the Mass when the words of consecration are pronounced over bread and wine – and that all else is just beautiful ceremonies, added on to an objective event – is for him just as inadequate. The idea that the community can come together and express its common fellowship as an act of its own making, and can 'decide' what scripture says, or that Christ has been truly present among them, is equally false as a description of God's self-disclosure in our worship.

In his early study of St Bonaventure, Ratzinger had come to notice something about the medieval understanding of God which, one might say, has even yet properly to be recovered. It is the central issue on which the Second Vatican Council had tried to touch, and which, I might suggest, is yet fully to have its moment of understanding. What we call divine revelation is God's approach *toward* man. God's divine self-disclosure – his revealing of himself, his *disclosing* of himself so that he can be seen to be true – is *God's*, not *our*, initiative: again, it is given in and through grace. This is in conformity with the remarks of Martin Heidegger. We do not work out in advance – i.e. by rational or philosophical means – *how* or *what* God's approach to us is or can take place, nor can we define in advance its limits or its content. Nor does such an initiative lie around undiscovered for when we can be still enough to notice it: it is always *for*, and so *given to* some*one*. It springs forth addressed *to* you and me in our *particularity*. This is why liturgy has to be prayed. Attending *to*, hearing, and praying, turn out to be much the same thing. The words and gestures employed make the attending *to*, the hearing, possible. We do not speak in praying, we learn to hear.

In commentating much later on in his life on his *Habilitation* thesis, Ratzinger notes that 'in Bonaventure (as well as in the theologians of the thirteenth century) there was nothing corresponding to our conception of "revelation", by which we are normally in the habit of referring to all the revealed contents of the faith'.[3] Too often revelation has been taken as simply the same thing as scripture, or as 'contained' in tradition, as if it were immediately obvious what that means. Revelation is an act – an act of God's self-communication to man. Above all, however, the believer is part of the body of Christ. The real subject of revelation is the Church herself, in the person of her faithful, each of whom is through the liturgy and its sacraments to be made a member of the body of Christ. The Church *lives* in the conversation between God the Father and the Son.

Coupled with this idea is that revelation is not what scripture is, but what scripture *contains*. Ratzinger says if Bonaventure is correct, 'then revelation precedes scripture and becomes deposited in scripture but is not simply identical with it. This in turn means that revelation is always something greater than what is merely written down ... because an essential element of scripture is the Church as understanding subject, and with this the fundamental sense of tradition already given.'[4]

It is clearly the work of the sacred liturgy in which God reveals himself in the person of his Son through his Spirit to the believer who anticipates God's self-disclosure in faith and hope. The liturgy is so suffused with scripture that in many ways the liturgy *is* the interpretation of scripture belonging to the Church. Here is a further reason why liturgy can never be 'made' – it is part of what is 'given' by God. Here is why the present pope has devoted so much energy to discussion and concern with the sacred liturgy, and why he has emphasized repeatedly the continuity between the liturgy as it was before the Second Vatican Council and the Liturgy after 1970. As

---

3 Ratzinger, Cardinal J., *Aus meinem Leben: Erinnerungen*, Munich, Deutsche Verlags-Anstalt, 1998 (1997), pp. 83f. 'Daß es bei Bonaventura (und wohl bei den Theologen des 13. Jahrhunderts überhaupt) keine Entsprechung zu unserem Begriff "Offenbarung" gebe, mit dem wir üblicherweise das Ganze der offenbarten Inhalte zu bezeichnen pflegen.'

4 Ratzinger, Cardinal J., *Aus meinem Leben: Erinnerungen*, p. 84. 'Dann liegt Offenbarung der Schrift voraus und schlägt sich in ihr nieder, ist aber nicht einfach mit ihr identisch. Daß aber heißt dann, daß Offenbarung immer größer ist, as das bloß Geschriebene ... daß zur Schrift das verstehende Subjekt Kirche gehört, womit auch schon der wesentliche Sinn von Überlieferung gegeben ist.'

Prefect of the Congregation for the Doctrine of the Faith the then Joseph Cardinal Ratzinger said only shortly before his election that it seems to him indispensable to continue to offer the opportunity to continue to celebrate according to the old Missal of before the Council: what was fundamental before 1969 remains fundamental afterwards, the liturgy is the same. It is this view which led to the relaxation of the restrictions on the use of the preconciliar rites in the motu proprio *Summorum Pontificum*.[5]

Does this understanding of revelation entail that God does not make himself known beyond or outside the Church? We have already seen how St Thomas extends the activity of the Spirit beyond the Church. It is not that God *could* not speak outside the Church, but rather that the Church is the recognized and guaranteed place wherein God always and continually makes himself present and discloses himself. By Church here is meant *not* primarily the Magisterium, but the liturgy. The liturgy is what the Church knows, in the objective and subjective sense. If this ordinary and continual revealing of his truth were not happening, God's self-disclosure beyond the Church could not even be recognized for what it is – even when the Spirit blows beyond the bounds of the Church, that breath returns to the Church herself. The Church is the proper place of God's self-revelation to man, it is its *home*, and its completion.

5 Benedict XVI, motu proprio *Summorum Pontificum* of 7 July 2007, Vatican, Libreria Editrice Vaticana.

Chapter 10

Liturgy as Communion

If we understand the liturgy as the place of God's self-disclosure to man, we can see that the Church is only an institution in a dependent sense – its institutional work is to safeguard and preserve God's continuing self-revelation: that is, the liturgy itself. Here is why the liturgy is of paramount importance as the means of divine self-disclosure.

The case this book makes out is that the liturgy is the founding possibility for God's gift of faith – a foundation that cannot be displaced, either by the supposed claims of the priority of scripture, or the claims of reason. An adequate understanding of this foundational character has been lost or relegated almost entirely to the background, and really for quite some time, so that – to give one example – many theologians have found it quite respectable to argue that liturgy has to be 'rational' (i.e. founded in reason), rather than arguing that the liturgy is what opens up the intellect to the activity – the self-disclosure – of God in his divine Son.

Perhaps the most crucial alterations to the liturgy were not the ones that began in 1964, in the wake of the Second Vatican Council, but much earlier, in fact beginning with the pontificate of St Pius X in 1903. We have already looked at the question of 'active participation', and suggested quite a different meaning for that phrase than the one which has come to predominate since the words first appeared in the Italian and Latin documents. Pius X's reforms to the practice of the communion of the faithful are now too-little understood, but they have also had a dramatic effect on lay and clerical perceptions of the liturgy. They were published in the decree *Sacra Tridentina Synodus*: 'Decree on the necessary dispositions for frequent and daily reception of holy communion'.[1]

The practices of attending Holy Mass and receiving communion have sometimes coincided, but *more* often as not, they have *not* been identical since the earliest times in the Church, until now. Even if communion followed immediately after Mass (as it frequently did) this is not the same as communion and attendance at Mass being identical. Now it is only the sick who experience communion outside of Mass. Until 1905 rarely would the faithful have made their communion within Mass, at least since the ninth century, if not long before: even when some did, most did not, except at Easter. Attendance at Holy Mass, and fulfilling one's obligation *to* the Mass, is not identical with the obligation to make one's communion. We know from remarks and complaints made in the fourth century by St John Chrysostom that the faithful had already long separated attendance at Mass with making their communion. The faithful took very seriously from the beginning St Paul's admonition 'for he that eateth and drinketh unworthily eateth and drinketh judgment to himself, not discerning the body of the Lord'.[2] In fact even when the practice among Christians appears to have been frequent communion (at least for the most pious), the normal place of communion seems to have been as often the home as the altar rail: the faithful took the Blessed Sacrament home with them in muslin bags. The significance of this for the sacred liturgy has almost never been discussed – the loss of the astonishing significance of the liturgy of the presanctified on Good Friday, when only the celebrating bishop or priest received communion from a host consecrated on Maundy Thursday morning, partially intincted in an *un*consecrated mixed chalice of wine and water, far from being a late medieval corruption (as is reported with wearying frequency by those modern liturgists who all

---

1 Pius X, *Sacra Tridentina Synodus*, in *Acta Sanctæ Sedis*, of 20 December 1905, vol. 38 (1906), Vatican, pp. 400–6. 'De dispositionibus requisitis ad frequentem et quotidianam Communionem eucharisticam sumendam.'
2 1 Corinthians 11.29.

too frequently make up reasons for what they do not fully understand) is actually much more likely to be a replication at the altar of the practice in ordinary Christian homes during the week, when the faithful took the sacrament home with them in the form of the precious body, and daily intincted the sacred species – in a gold mixed chalice of unconsecrated wine and water.[3] The abrogation of this ritual in 1955 represents the formal and final breach with one of the most ancient practices of communion *of the faithful* in the Church, as well as destroying an important theological point – that on Good Friday what *one* does has salvific effect for *many*, and that the proper place for the faithful on Good Friday is the place occupied by Mary the Mother of God and John, the beloved disciple – at the foot of the cross – unable to *do* anything at all while the most central saving act for mankind is completed in all its horror and splendour before our very eyes.

Equally, the practice of the *missa sicca* or 'dry mass' (known, in a slightly different form, as the *officium* by the Carthusians), of great institutional significance especially in pre-conciliar Præmonstratension practice but not restricted to the Norbertines, emphasizes the separation of Mass and communion even for the celebrant. The *missa sicca* was the practice of saying the entire rite except those prayers specifically pertaining to the consecration (because the priest had already offered mass at another time of the day). The first part of the pre-1955 liturgy of Palm Sunday, with the procession and blessing of palms, is effectively a *missa sicca*, for which the vetsments were red, becoming purple for the Mass itself (now the two rites are conflated into one, all in red vestments). Until 1905, various forms of the Roman rite – especially its papal and pontifical forms – specified who *must* receive communion in addition to the priest (in many diocesan rites the solemn form of the Mass specified that the deacon, and in some cases the subdeacon as well,

3 See Dix, G., *The Mass of the Presanctified*, London, Church Literature Association, pp. 18–25.

receive the sacrament, sometimes also in both kinds) – which indicates that ordinarily no one else did.

Barely anyone could now explain with proper justice the significance of the decision that followed the Fourth Lateran Council that the obligation to be present at the sacrifice is fulfilled once the priest has made his communion, and so be able to explain the critical fulfilment of intention indicated by that requirement. Yet not to understand the meaning of this injunction leads directly to the objectification of divine presence in the sacred species that Henri Cardinal de Lubac so assailed in his work *Corpus Mysticum*. The damage done to the Church's worship has been immense – it has even had the effect of objectifying the rite of Mass over against the offices, the celebration of which (especially for the faithful) in parish and even cathedral life has fallen into desuetude except as personal devotion in the private recitation of the Breviary. With this, the intimate inter-relationship of the texts of the offices with those of the Mass has all but disappeared from popular understanding. At the same time, many are receiving Holy Communion without having taken the due care and without the fearful reverence that would have characterized earlier ages: perhaps the words of St Paul in this century are left all too easily unheeded.

In common with several medieval writers, St Thomas Aquinas distinguished between two modes of receiving Communion. Full reception of the sacrament, say the medieval authors, is 'spiritual' reception, by which means we are joined to the body of Christ. This mode of eating is salvific for us: through it we receive the full benefits of our reception of the Eucharist. The second mode is 'sacramental' eating, which means that the sacrament imparts no spiritual benefit to the recipient – this is 'imperfect' eating. Then for Aquinas there is accidental eating – which means not even sacramentally. This is not a third means, strictly speaking, because, Aquinas says 'should even an unbeliever consume the sacramental species, he would receive the body of Christ under the sacrament: hence he would eat Christ sacramentally, if the word 'sacramentally' qualify the word on the part of the thing eaten. But if it qualify the word on the part of the one eating, then, properly speaking, he does not eat sacramentally, because he uses what he takes, not as a sacrament, but as simple food'.[4]

It is here that the medieval schools debated a question by means of a figure who could not even believe, let alone be an unbeliever. What, they asked, happened theologically speaking if a mouse managed to obtain some of the sacred species of the blessed sacrament? What would the mouse eat?[5] The mouse and the unbeliever strictly speaking do not eat even imperfectly, but only as if they were eating bread. This distinction (which is, we should note, not a real distinction), means that the sacred species remains in itself what it truly is, and at the same time withholds what it is in itself from both the unbeliever, and the mouse (and incidentally, from a believer who eats a host not knowing that it has been consecrated). The withholding has nothing to do with the miraculous, but is rather the dependence for a knowing based on faith on the prior possibility of what it is to know anything at all.

We *know* what the sacred species is, but this does not mean that the order of knowing is disturbed in the range of what is possible to be known by the unbeliever. Aquinas is adamant, and very careful to say, that in the transubstantiated species in every respect 'the accidents remain according to the being which they had before'.[6] 'Accidents' means here no more than outward appearances. The whole sentence means (and Aquinas goes into great detail about this) that the transubstantiated species will continue to behave in every respect like bread and wine, even though they are no longer these things: the appearance of bread will nourish (warm) if eaten, the

---

4 Aquinas, *Summa Theologiæ*, IIIa, Question 80, article 3, corpus ad 2. 'Etiam si infidelis sumat species sacramentales, corpus christi sub sacramento sumit. unde manducat christum sacramentaliter, i ly sacramentaliter determinat verbum ex parte manducati. si autem ex parte manducantis, tunc, proprie loquendo, non manducat sacramentaliter, quia non utitur eo quod accipit ut sacramento, sed ut simplici cibo.'

5 Quid sumit mus? The question was first raised by Guitmund of Aversa around 1073–7, when he asks in a treatise *On the Body and Blood of Christ Truly in the Sacrament* what would happen if beasts were to eat the sacred species. The question takes on the better-known formulation in relation to mice with Adam of Lille around 1190.

6 Aquinas, *Summa Theologiæ*, IIIa, Question 77, article 2, corpus. 'Remanent accidentia secundum esse quod prius habebant.'

appearance of wine has the actual power to make drunk, they will both also decompose over time. The unbeliever and the mouse also know what these things are for what it is possible for them to know without faith. A mouse that nibbles the sacred species will get fat on it: he will not thereby go to heaven. The point is that what we know in faith continues to be based on the normal, everyday appearances of bread and wine.

We, however, who know what these things are *in faith* are called to eat the sacrament spiritually. In contradistinction to corporeal eating, 'spiritual food changes a man into what it is itself',[7] and so by this means one who eats the body and blood of the Lord spiritually is thereby converted into the body of Christ. St Thomas is not alone in insisting that the sacrament may be 'eaten' spiritually by mental desire and so not always through physical eating.[8] He is clear about the conditions under which sacramental eating takes place: freedom from mortal sin; a desire to eat spiritually (in the sense described above); sufficient fervour and devotion. Although Aquinas does not develop the point at length, he also makes clear that sacramental eating of the sacred species can in no way guarantee or command spiritual eating.[9] There are two things given by spiritual eating of the sacrament: one is Christ himself, the other is incorporation into the mystical body of Christ which is the fellowship of the saints.[10]

To summarize: first, the sacramental conversion of bread and wine into the body and blood of Christ takes place through the infinite power of God; second, this conversion is known only through faith; third, what faith knows remains based on the persistent appearances of bread and wine; fourth, there are two ways of receiving Holy

---

7 Cf. Aquinas, *Summa Theologiæ*, IIIa, Question 73, article 3, corpus. ad 2. 'sed alimentum spiritualem convertit hominem in seipsum.'

8 Cf. Aquinas, *Summa Theologiæ*, IIIa: Question 73, article 3, corpus ad 2; Question 79 article 2, corpus ad 1; Question 80, article1, corpus ad 3.

9 Cf. Aquinas, *Summa Theologiæ*, IIIa: Question 80, article 1.

10 Aquinas, *Summa Theologiæ*, IIIa: Q. 80, art. 4, resp. 'Duplex autem est res huius sacramenti . . . : una quidem quæ est significata et contenta, scilicet ipse Christus; alia autem est significata et non contenta, scilicet corpus Christi mysticum, quod est societas sanctorum.'

Communion – spiritually, which means perfectly, and sacramentally, which means imperfectly. The other way of receiving the sacrament, 'accidentally', means that although the sacrament remains what it is in reality, to the one receiving only accidentally, this reality is withheld; fifth, not everyone who eats the sacrament will receive it perfectly; sixth, there are some who receive the sacrament spiritually – that is perfectly – who do not have physically to eat it to do so. Every one of these considerations is held to this day by the Catholic Church.

The dogmatic consequences of this can hardly be underestimated. At its most immediate, the body of Christ is not, and cannot be, simply coextensive with those who gather at Mass, since not all will receive perfectly. At the same time, it is not coextensive only with a smaller, privileged, group who gather for Mass, since there will be some who (not present in the gathering) in various ways desire to eat the species sacramentally but cannot, and whose very desire thereby conjoins them to Christ. This group, I would argue could be interpreted very broadly indeed, as at least implying all who, could they but hear it, would joyfully hear the Good News, and who long to know who God is. Whoever God *chooses* to be so, is conjoined to the body of Christ, but in a way only partially known to us *now* (although all will be revealed at the end of time). Of course, the one who makes the appropriate efforts to present themselves at the altar-rail with the proper dispositions may properly and entirely trust that they have fulfilled what is laid down – God is *not* arbitrary in his promises. This is a point entirely implicit in the documents of the Second Vatican Council, but to which insufficient attention has been paid, because to a very great extent we now construe the rite of the Mass as an action of a gathered assembly with a fixed beginning and a fixed end.

Of course the opportunity for, and injunction toward, more frequent communion in 1905 had a pastoral impulse whose significance seems obvious to us now, but in fact is not. St Pius X saw the immense care ordinary Catholics took in preparing themselves for their infrequent communion. Fasting, sacramental confession, prayer, diligence in remaining free from even venial sin, would have characterized the humble disposition of any Catholic who came to make his communion. This diligence represented a good practical and pastoral induction into what it meant to offer one's own flesh to be conjoined spiritually and sacramentally to the body of Christ. The practical, instinctive, disposition is toward the deification of the soul implicit in the event. How many modern Catholics could explain this now – even in what they do, if not in what they say? The question does not imply a judgement (this sinner in no position to judge). My point is this: even at the devotional level, frequent communion without the accompanying catechesis which explains it has robbed the Church of an essentially pastoral intuition – that salvation is not immediate, is difficult, has certain existential requirements, but is still *available*. How well is this understood today? How many Catholics regard attendance at Mass as giving them the *right* to communion, when in objective terms (and I make no judgement here, I simply cite the discipline of centuries) their ancestors would have trembled to go up, kneel, and present their tongues to the priest?

Moreover, attendance at the principal or Conventual Mass, which means the attendance at Mass as the central act of worship of a community, convent, house (even if one had said or heard Mass privately), was in former times clearly understood as a pious act, even an obligation in religious communities and Chapters, and as something to be given to God, irrespective of whether the one attending made his communion. Even the average Catholic before 1905 would have instinctively understood the decree that followed the Fourth Lateran Council – that the sacrifice was completed *by virtue of the priest's communion*, and the completion of the sacrifice had consequences for the one attending who did not make his communion, as well as for the world *and not just as an individual act for the priest.*

Chapter 11

Temporal Liturgy

The passage of time is the means by which the liturgy of the heavenly Jerusalem unfolds into human life. The liturgy itself, especially the part of it contained in the Missal and the Breviary, is primarily concerned with how the time is modulated and varies to indicate *across* time the whole mystery of our salvation. Taken as a whole – the texts of the liturgy, the rubrics (the manner and means of the way the work is to be done) and the calendar all work together to make each specific liturgical *action* part of a much greater, more complex fabric. Inasmuch as the liturgy is itself the means of the sanctification of time, the passing of time (by which here is meant the movement of the heavens) is the availability, and opening, of time itself to be sanctified. Time, as the rising and passing of the sun, the phases of the moon and the rising and falling of the seasons, 'lets unfold' the time of the *opus Dei*, the work of sanctification. The fabric, constantly woven together by the intertwinement of the sacred liturgy with the passage of cosmic time, is a fabric of meaning, a fabric that explains the being of the cosmos as God's letting of man into God's own self-understanding. As we ourselves are lifted up in the very weaving of this fabric, we share in the divine life and we are redeemed.

The changes in the liturgy that began during the pontificate of St Pius X and that have been most dramatic in their effects have been those to the calendar. The calendar was reformed in 1911, then multiple small changes were made throughout the pre-war period, with more major structural changes in 1955 and 1961, culminating with the complete reform of the calendar in 1969. Until 1970 these changes were often made without noticeably altering the texts of the Missal and Breviary – indeed, the changes of 1955 were specifically designed not to necessitate change in the actual texts. Taken together with the other changes St Pius X initiated, and the reform of the Breviary,[1] it is the changes to the calendar that unleashed a revolution of unparalleled transformation on the practice of the sacred liturgy and its capacity to signify the mystery of the divine life. And yet, superficially, these changes were often the least visible. Alcuin Reid, in his study of liturgical reform up to the Second Vatican Council, says of the 1911 changes (quite incorrectly, but I can see why he said it) 'the effect on the Missal was minor'.[2] The effect on the actual printed *book* may have been minor, but what the faithful experienced week by week, what they heard, and what was actually prayed and when, was quite dramatic. What is said and sung in the temple of the Lord is what really matters. The texts, and the books in which they are arranged, are there to facilitate what is to be *done* and so actually *affects* and *effects* our understanding.

The motu proprio of 1911, *Divino afflatu*,[3] which authorized the changes to the Breviary and the calendar, made only oblique mention of the calendar reform, but gave as its reason for the reform as a whole that the burden of the liturgy 'be not any heavier for the clergy'.[4]

In the reform of the calendar, a significant principle was established for liturgical reform, one that has become more pressing with each reform undertaken. The performance of the liturgy has ever-

---

1 This book will not discuss in detail the textual reforms to the Breviary (as opposed to the calendar reforms which affected both Breviary and Missal), which also began in 1911. To understand these, and their effects, see László Dobszay's 'The Bugnini-Liturgy and the Reform of the Reform', pp. 45–84. Dobszay concentrates on the reform of the psalter, which did indeed have dramatic effects on the texts and on its historicality. There were a multitude of more subtle changes, however, which gives the 1911 Breviary a less modulated, more penitential structure where the (more penitentially oriented) litanies occurred more frequently (until their virtual suppression in 1955) and there was less transition between the festal and the penitential aspects of liturgical prayer.

2 Reid, A., *The Organic Development of the Liturgy*, p. 75, note 8.

3 St Pius X, motu proprio of 1 November 1911, *Divino afflatu*, in Acta Apostolicæ Sedis, Vatican, vol. 3, pp. 633–7. See also *Rubricæ in recitation divini officii et in Missarum celebratione*, in Acta Apostolicæ Sedis, Vatican, vol. 3, pp. 639ff.

4 St Pius X, *Divino afflatu*, p. 636. 'Ut clero . . . non maius imponeretur onus.'

increasingly been subordinated to the stated requirement to address pastoral needs, and so increasingly the liturgy has to be tailored to the exigencies of daily life.[5] In no different spirit did *Sacrosanctum Concilium* extend this yet more widely to the Church as a whole, as we have seen, speaking in its very opening paragraph of the need to reform the liturgy to accommodate it to the 'requirements of the age'. In reality, changes done in the name of pastoral requirements have failed to understand the essential differentiatedness of Christian life (that different people have different vocations across the body of Christ), and have tried to make available the whole mystery of salvation to the *single* Cartesian subject rather than have it be a work of the whole faithful.

Two ideas here get conflated into one. On the one hand there is the minimal work of the liturgy to make available to a single man or woman the possibility of his and her salvation. In this respect, Baptism, regularity at the other sacraments, the minimum requirements of a Christian life (sacramental confession, catechesis, some understanding of the need for repentance, penance, fasting and so forth) are the minimal demands that make a Christian soul fit to stand in the Temple and be one of those who receives the approaching Bridegroom. The Liturgical Movement merely reflected the concerns of earlier movements in church life that had the desire to make the sacred liturgy more available to the faithful. For just one example, the baroque reform of church architecture from the sixteenth century onwards sought to make the performance of the liturgy more 'visible' to the faithful by removing every obstacle between the pew and the altar.

While this instinct is an entirely laudable one, it had consequences which have often been ignored. The sacred character of the way in which the laying out of a physical church as an analogue of the Temple and the whole cosmic order has been lost in the production of what are essentially liturgical 'theatre-houses' since the sixteenth century. The attempt to recover more ancient practices of church-building in the neo-Gothic architecture of the nineteenth century

---

5 Cf. Reid, A., *The Organic Development of the Liturgy*, p. 75; see esp. note 9.

(especially in Britain) had to struggle not only against a prevailing trend, but also against what had been lost and forgotten as the sacred *principles* of church construction. These principles are not worked out by the human mind and so in any way rational, although they are augmented by human experience. The churches dedicated to God are exactly *not* amphitheatres for the pagan (pre-Christian) Dionysian mysteries (which later became the dramatic performances), whose structure and arrangement is according to *logos*, to the *word* that is given to man. On the contrary, they are divinely revealed – this is the meaning of the scriptural passages which specify the lengths and quantities of the construction of the Temple.[6]

It is the 'hand of the Lord' (which means the Word of the Lord, Christ, the *Second* Person of the Divine Trinity), which commanded Solomon and Ezekiel to lay out the measures, spans and quantities both of the city of Jerusalem and the Temple. For the correct ordering of the Temple makes possible the presence of the Majesty of God with his people, so that he (as Bridegroom and High Priest) can dwell with them. This is not a metaphor: the building wherein God discloses himself also functions like a text: it discloses itself intelligently to the mind. The mind 'reads' the very structure of the building. The conversion of the liturgical place into a kind of theatre actually *eliminates* the building's textuality between the pew (or narthex – in older times there were no pews in the lay spaces of churches) and the altar. What this meant in the baroque period is that in directing more attention on to the altar, the rest fell into the background, and so fell out of focus. One might almost say that it is unsurprising that the celebration of Mass came so to predominate over the offices of the Choir (the offices contained in the Breviary) over the same period.[7] If the baroque manipulated the textual character of church architecture for certain effects, contemporary church architecture has (with some exceptions) simply become the architecture of the amphi-

---

6 Cf. Ezekiel 40.1–43.4.

7 Kevin Seasolz traces the development of baroque church architecture to the rise of the Jesuit Order, who were not bound to recite the offices of the Church in Choir, but only privately. Seasolz, K. R., *A Sense of the Sacred: Theological Foundations of Christian Architecture and Art*, New York, Continuum, 2005, p. 172.

theatre with even less reference to the ancient symbolic plan of what is divinely ordained.[8]

The minimal requirements of the liturgy for predisposing the Christian soul for salvation, however, are not to be conflated with the work that is to be undertaken for the sake of the sheer worship and love of God. The second idea that has been conflated into 'pastoral requirements' is that first in the order of the meaning of the liturgy is the return to God of the worship and love for the love once offered us on the cross. The Christian soul moves between these two require-ments – the minimal requirement of what is at the least necessary, and the maximal requirement to give glory to God. Where this understanding leads will preoccupy us as we proceed.

A recurring issue in matters of liturgical reform – from before Trent – is the question of the interrelationship of the temporal and the sanc-toral cycles. The temporal cycle is that which governs the Christian year, beginning in Advent, then Christmas and Epiphanytide (with Christmas ending on the fortieth day of the feast of the Nativity, with the feast of the Purification of the Virgin Mary in the Temple), Septuagesimatide, Lent, and Eastertide. I would like to reserve the question of 'green' or 'ordinary' time as a specific season, as I hope shortly to explain. The sanctoral cycle is of course the calendar of the saints, martyrs and prophets, which has inevitably grown and expanded over the centuries (although, and this is a point too rarely made in liturgical study, it has also been collapsed: the local celebra-tions of saints has in many dioceses dwindled to almost nothing: as many saints' days as have been made in recent centuries have been forgotten in those same years). *Divino afflatu* explicitly mentions the need to alter the sanctoral cycle and its effect on liturgical celebration because 'the offices of the saints have gradually been developed to

---

8 Much canon law still regulates the construction of church building and furnishing, although this has changed substantially between the 1917 Code of Canon Law and the 1983 Code of Canon Law. For a full liturgical commentary on the 1917 code see O'Connell, J. B., *Church Building and Furnishing: The Church's Way – A Study in Litur-gical Law*, Notre Dame, University of Notre Dame Press, 1955. See also Schulte, A. J. and O'Connell, J. B. (revised), *Consecranda: The Performance of the Rite of Consecration of the Roman Pontifical*, New York, Benziger Brothers, 1956 (1907).

such an extent that now the Sunday and ferial offices are hardly ever heard, with the effect that not a few of the psalms have been neglected'.[9]

There was a debate of this kind during the Tridentine reform of the liturgy. The calendar of 1568, published after the Council of Trent with the new edition of the Roman Breviary, and which inaugurated for the first time a genuinely universal calendar, was substantially pared back in the number of the obligatory celebrations. Only later, in 1623, did Pope Clement VIII return a substantial number of feasts to the Roman 'universal' calendar, which had the effect of universal-izing many holy days previously largely reserved to the Roman or Italian dioceses. In fact the intention of the 1568 calendar had been to make room for local, that is largely diocesan, feasts to be added to the calendar of Pius V, a facility which remains to this day. Signifi-cantly, however, no changes of the kind that followed from 1911 onwards were made – the essential, ancient, integrity of the inter-relationship between the temporal and sanctoral cycles was pre-served. An idea arose, really with the rationalism of the baroque period, and fuelled by the Jansenism that manifested itself in litur-gical matters in the rogue Council of Pistoia,[10] that the temporal and sanctoral cycles are at odds with one another. Some of the discus-sions around Trent attempted to support this view, but it is not really accurate, and these views did not prevail. Guéranger had defended the integral character of the two cycles vigorously, and as we shall see, there really need be no conflict between them. The idea grew up – it was a formal condition of Pistoia – that there could only be one liturgical celebration of one character at one altar (Pistoia also argued that each physical church should have only one altar).

---

9 Pius X, *Divino afflatu*, p. 635. 'In ipsorum vero honorem Officia de Sanctis sensim propagari coeperunt, unde fere factum est, ut de Dominicis diebus deque Feriis Officia silerent, ideoque non pauci negligerentur psalmi.'

10 Council of Pistoia, Scipio de' Ricci, 18–28 September 1868. A commission appointed by Pope Pius VI of four bishops and theologians examined the documents of the Council or Synod, and a congregation of cardinals and bishops subsequently pronounced on them, condemning the synod as a whole and anathematizing 85 of its propositions. In August 1794 Pius VI revoked the enactments of the Council and condemned it in the Bull *Auctorem Fidei*.

The reform of the sanctoral cycle of the calendar was specifically conducted to force it to conform to rationalistic principles. In the first place, saints were excised from the calendar who, it is thought, did not exist, or were unlikely to have done so. Secondly, aspects of saints' lives that were uncomfortable to modern ears, or whose legends were crowded with the miraculous, were edited with the clear understanding that what was retained in the liturgy had to be acceptable to contemporary tastes for what is credible. The revisers of the Missal raised as a matter of policy in editing the Missal of 1970 whether 'there are some orations which have lost their historical significance or are no longer in conformity with the norms of Christian life today' and proceeded on that basis.[11] For just one example, the antiphons and responsories at Lauds and Vespers referring to St Laurence as a Levite were excised, removing from the liturgy (as in other places) the ancient references to the connection between the present diaconate and the Levitical priesthood (where the Church's priests are understood to be the inheritors of the Melchisedech priesthood), and so suppressing the way in which the characters of ordination relate to the former dispensation, and to the Temple. These changes alone impair the way contemporary Catholics can understand their own relation to the one and eternal covenant with God, now made manifest in Christ, as the *same* covenant in both old and new dispensations.

The results, especially in the editing of the prayers, have often been themselves ahistorical even in the 'historical critical' sense. Certainly the policies employed in reforming the calendar have overemphasized the necessity for literary and 'factual' proof *over* the oral and legendary tradition. Of course, if it is possible to prove from specific records that some event did not happen, or did not happen in the way reported, and the specific records can be corroborated as accurate from other sources, then the independent written record must be respected. But if the record does not speak either way, then there is no reason to alter the calendar, or excise things from it, *for mere lack*

---

11 Placide Bruylants to the seventh General Meeting of the *Consilium* (October 1966), quoted by Pristas, L., 'The Orations of the Vatican II Missal: Policies for Revision' p. 641.

of evidence, or because of modern sensibilities concerning the character of the miraculous, or even the metaphorical. In fact oral traditions often preserve with great faithfulness understandings of events from the past, and should not be distrusted simply because they are, or were for a long time, unwritten.

Some alterations to the sanctoral cycle have lost or suppressed important aspects of the connection of the saints to the resurrected life of Christ. The feast of St Agnes has two dates in the old calendar, eight days apart, on the 21st and 28th of January. St Agnes was one of the most important female martyrs of the early Church, and is one of the women saints commemorated in the Canon of the Mass. Martyred in her thirteenth year in 304, she had at the age of ten consecrated herself to Christ. Her martyrdom occurred because the Prefect of Rome asked for her hand in marriage, which she refused. Surviving an attempted rape she was beheaded, and so strong was her espousal to Christ that her legend reports her as saying to the executioner 'strike without fear, for the bride does her spouse an injury if she makes him wait'. The antiphon at first Vespers reinforces this, quoting her addressing Christ: 'behold I hurry toward you, whom I have loved, whom I have sought, whom always I have held in the highest'.[12]

Her feast is repeated a week later, commemorating her (risen) appearance to her parents who had come to pray at her tomb. She appears surrounded by a choir of virgins (angels), and bathed in glorious light, saying 'I live with him in heaven whom with my whole spirit I loved on earth'.[13] The Magnificat antiphon at Vespers makes clear the significance both of the vision and the feast, when it says 'standing at her right [is] a lamb whiter than snow, Christ, consecrating her union with him and her martyrdom'.[14] The vision

---

12 *Breviarium Romanum* (1623), Feast of St Agnes 21st January, Magnificat antiphon at first Vespers. 'Et ecce venio ad te, quem amavi, quem quæsivi, quem semper optavi.'

13 *Breviarium Romanum* (1623), Feast of St Agnes 28th January, third reading in the (otherwise ferial) nocturn.

14 *Breviarium Romanum* (1623), Feast of St Agnes 28th January, Magnificat antiphon for the commemoration at Vespers. 'Stans a dextris eius agnus nive candidior, Christus sibi sponsam et martyrem consecravit.'

presents a clear parallel with the appearance of the risen Christ to Thomas and the others of the Twelve, on the eighth day. She (as with all Christians) who unites herself to Christ and who is faithful to the loss of her own life will be united to him as Bridegroom, as sacrificial lamb, and as High Priest. Her appearance on the eighth day of her death recapitualtes Christ's own identification of his body with the Temple, in his own reappearance on the eighth (rededicatory) day, so that the union of her soul with his can be seen on earth, and liturgically, to be complete and directly mirroring Christ's own resurrected appearences.

To illustrate how the calendar up until the 1911 reform integrated the temporal and sanctoral cycles it might be opportune to consider what would have happened under its terms on the Sunday after Christmas on the 31 December 2006. The octave day (1 January) is at the same time the feast of the Circumcision. On this day simultaneously would have been kept the octave commemorations of each of the major feast days after Christmas – St Stephen, St John, the Holy Innocents – in some places (especially in certain dioceses or churches with that dedication) St Thomas of Canterbury also had an octave commemoration, and the Sunday of the Nativity also had its own office, which, anything to the contrary notwithstanding, would have been the office for that day before Vespers. Vespers for that day would have been first Vespers of the Circumcision: at Vespers there would have been added a commemoration of St Silvester. Vespers is perhaps best illustrative of the complexity here: the psalms and antiphons, and the reading, hymn, responsory, Magnificat antiphon and first collect would have been of the Circumcision, but the commemorations would have been successively Christmas, St Stephen, St John, the Holy Innocents, and St Thomas (in some places), and St Silvester. The commemoration consists not just of a collect, but is preceded also by the Magnificat antiphon and then a responsory (reversing the usual order). The doxology of the collect would have been added to the first collect, and then not repeated again until the last, the collect of St Silvester. In all seven liturgical celebrations would have been recollected at Vespers, six at Lauds and six in the Mass. In the Mass the relevant sequences of commemorations would have taken place at the collect, the secret prayer (or prayer over the gifts), and the post-communion prayer.

This is (perhaps dizzyingly) complex, but it is possible to see here that the temporal cycle (Christmas and the Circumcision) is harmonized with the sanctoral, despite the fact that there is a crowd of feasts and octaves to commemorate. They do not displace one another, they overlap. Very often they overlap specifically in the readings, where (especially at Matins) although the office is of a festal structure (three nocturns instead of one), the readings and responsories at the first nocturn are those of the ferial office (or temporal cycle), not the festal office (or sanctoral cycle). This overlapping is, however, in itself not nearly as simple as it looks. If we return to Vespers, what we should note is that each of the commemorations in fact represents a reference to a complete celebration of the office, and implies with it the whole wider office including that of the Mass. The antiphons to the Benedictus and Magnificat canticles are invariably taken from the Gospel at Mass for that feast: they represent yet another of the interconnections between the office and the Mass at this point. What is commemorated therefore is a Vespers 'in miniature' for each of the overlapping liturgical obligations. But Vespers in miniature *here* will be Vespers in *full* anywhere where the dedication of the actual church or diocese is for that saint: in that place the saint in question takes precedence. The commemoration is not only a way of handling a relation to *time*, but also to *place*. The sanctoral cycle is not grounded, historically, in an abstract recollection of a saint or saints, or holy events. It is founded at the ground where the bones of that saint are kept, or some *place* and so location with a reference to the saint, event, or matter in question.

Vespers 'in miniature' presupposes Vespers in full in some other *place* sanctified above all by the saint or event in question. That place is brought *here* in every commemoration of the saint or event. This issue becomes clearer if we consider the question of what the liturgical calendar now calls 'ordinary time'. Until 1911 Sundays were of relatively low rank in the calendar – they could easily be displaced as the prime liturgical day by a feast of higher rank. Indeed, in many parts of Europe the Sundays most likely to be 'green' were already earmarked: in October for feasts of Our Lady – the Rosary was universal on the first Sunday of that month, but in France and other places could be added the Maternity of Our Lady (second Sunday of October) and Purity of Our Lady (third). Again in every Sunday where the ordinary Sunday office and Mass is displaced, a commemoration is nevertheless made of the Sunday in question. The Epistle and Gospel proper to the Sunday would in any case be said on the ferial days of that week.

The idea of 'green' or 'ordinary' time as a specific season is relatively late, perhaps in truth as late as in the minds of the liturgists of the twentieth century – something that is worthy of more scholarly consideration. The reform of 1911 substantially altered various other ways in which the calendar worked, which I will simply mention as adjunct to the complexity I have noted. To take a few examples: on each of the Sundays of Advent (and also in Lent) Vespers of the Sunday was to be followed immediately by Vespers of the dead. Advent is a season with a very strong connection with the theology of death – not least in the collects and the tradition of the connection of the Sundays of Advent with the preaching of the last things, but also because Advent above all is the most eschatological of the seasons, the season that ties together the appearing of the Christ both before (historically), already (in the life of the Church), and yet to come (at the end of time): Advent points to the overcoming of death for the ordinary faithful in fulfilling all the hopes of the various comings of Christ. These liturgical connections were suppressed in the 1911 reform. This commemoration of the dead is further fulfilled by a rubric requiring that on the first unimpeded day of January (i.e. the first non-festal day) the whole office for the dead is to be recited after the ferial (ordinary) office: the promises of Advent are fulfilled in the truth of the Incarnation, and this has a direct effect on the souls of the faithful departed.

Lent also is filled with these references to the dead. If sung, the office for Ash Wednesday begins, not with Matins, but before that with the recitation of the Gradual Psalms, together with their accompanying litanies and collects and on every following Wednesday until Holy Week. The first four of these psalms are sung as in the office for the dead, ending, not with the doxology, but with 'rest eternal grant to them O Lord, and let light perpetual shine upon them'. The lenten fast begins with a commemoration of the dead, and continues in the same vein: as well as reciting Vespers for the dead after Vespers of each Sunday, the whole office for the dead is recited on each Monday until Holy Week. This eschatological aspect of the Lenten office was suppressed in the 1911 reform.

The reform of the calendar in 1911 made other alterations to the cycle of prayer for the dead. What we now call All Souls day is in fact one of the octave days of All Saints, again making the eschatological connection between the attainment of sanctity and the hope of redemption for all the faithful departed much more visible. The office for the dead is to be *added* to the office for the octave, and throughout November the office and the Mass could be repeated on unimpeded days *ad libitum* for the sake of the dead. To reduce this to one day is to suppress and truncate the interrelation of the various feasts and aspects of the temporal cycle with its eschatological consequences in the hope of resurrection.

The loss of all the octaves and vigils except Christmas and Easter, successively at various points in the twentieth century up until the reform that concluded with the publication of the 1970 Missal, represents a further erosion of the complexity of the calendar. If we return to the Sunday of Christmas octave discussed earlier, it is worth mentioning that (depending on the community or diocese) significant discretion is available to celebrate votive masses of any of the *particular* days simultaneously commemorated: the conventual or principal mass of a church, or chapter, or monastic house, however, is of the principal day. The *missa sicca* was another way in which the multiplicity of liturgical celebrations on these days could be celebrated publicly. The same pertained in Lent and Advent, and in some cases in Eastertide – in the conventual mass of churches with chapters, the Mass was almost invariably strictly of the season, while other masses could be of saints or other commemorations depending on specific considerations.

In the liturgy as it has been reformed, all of this complexity has been truncated, for essentially rationalistic reasons. There are only a handful of days when commemorations are made in the post-1970 liturgy – the privileged days of Advent, and the minor feast days (or obligatory memorials) of Lent. There are only two octaves left. The current debate in England and Wales over the suppression of the holy days of obligation need not have arisen if the octaves and vigil days had been preserved – it seems to me entirely right that one can fulfil one's obligation, let us say, to the feast of Corpus Christi by attending the Mass of the Sunday of the octave, whilst preserving the ancient connection of that feast with a Thursday, the Thursday implied as the day of inauguration of the Holy Eucharist. The very reason for the suppression of the octaves – to allow the Sundays to take precedence – has itself been surpassed by the supposedly pastoral need of not forcing the laity to attend days of obligation in the week – and so feasts like the Ascension are transferred to the Sunday, destroying the symbolism that is in many cases (scripturally) intrinsic to their meaning, in the Ascension's case of being the fortieth day of Easter.

One of the reasons for all this simplification of the liturgy has been the supposed requirements of 'active participation', and the intelligibility of the sacred liturgy, which I have already discussed. What was at issue in the injunctions of Pistoia, that reappeared in the Liturgical Movement as it became more doctrinaire and rationalistic, and that took hold especially in the course of the most recent liturgical reforms, was the idea that a liturgical event should have only *one* character. I have already suggested that this destroys the inherent sense that the divine is a participation, and that divinization is participatory.

The idea that a single self can consummate in itself the entire meaning of every particular liturgical act as it is enacted – this is the real meaning toward which every definition of *actuosa participatio* has been driven by so much contemporary liturgical discussion – is foreign and indeed corrosive to the interior character of a complex and centuries-long symbolic language which uses the *differentiated-ness* of place, of time, and of the different vocations and stations of all of humanity, to mediate the full range of the drama of our salvation.

Too little has been understood of the way in which subjective intentionality has regulated and framed liturgical practice and understanding. The idea – well known in the East – that the entire liturgy must be fulfilled, but that it is impossible for any one person to fulfil it alone – was superseded in the West by the idea that every priest must complete the office and Mass daily and in full, which after Vatican II was extended, at least as a hoped-for possibility, to the laity as well. An attitude that developed as early as the appearance and growth of the mendicant orders, liturgy has increasingly come to be understood as something that I can (and therefore must, if I am to have subjective 'access' to the divine presence) 'do for myself' rather than something which the whole local church – monastic house, convent, diocese, and so forth – has to distribute across its membership and life for the sake of the *distributed* body of Christ as it manifests itself in particular places.

Here we see the conflation of the two ideas mentioned earlier at its clearest. On the *one* hand are those things required as a minimum for an individual to fulfil his obligations to the Church. On the other hand the *whole liturgy* is a work given by the Church to God, love returned for love once offered. It does not have to be intelligible in its essence all at once, and from out of the work as it is offered – it need only in the first instance be understood as what God has ordained should be returned to him, as that making fit of Jerusalem for the sake of the advent of the Bridegroom. Those who grow in sanctity, through the sanctifying effects of the grace communicated *through* the liturgy itself, will come to understand more deeply as they grow (over years) what God has provided. For some of us, the full meaning of what we offer liturgically *now* will become clear only *at the end of time*, when all is revealed.

Chapter 12

In Time for Liturgy

Far better than truncating rites to fit in with the demands of every-day life is the understanding implicit in more ancient practice that if I am dispensed from, or fail in, any part or office of the Church's sacred worship, then I owe a debt to God and to the Church which is nevertheless repaid through the work of others. Immediately in this understanding *I* as the worshipping person am taken out of the stranglehold where the subject of liturgy becomes liturgy *for* the (Cartesian) subject.

The loss of the sense of intertwinement of the sanctoral and temporal cycles is, theologically construed, the loss of an understanding of how the saints participate in the deity of Christ, and, in their sanctity, make it present. The astonishing aspect of the possibility of signification inaugurated by the event of the Ascension of the Lord is not that it becomes *possible* for earthly things – sacramental signs – to be significatory of Christ, but that *this is the way Christ is signified until the end of time*. Not only things – by which we include prayers, gestures, rituals and so forth – but *persons* signify Christ. Every religious order instinctively knows and explicitly teaches it. It is for this reason that the names of founders were introduced into the formulae of the *Confiteor* (I confess . . .) at Prime, Mass and Compline in almost all orders. The Order lives in a form of Christ communicated through and by the founder, and the Order is the extension and continuation across time and place of that form. A benedictine monk, for instance, lives in and through St Benedict's life in Christ.

The type of this communication is Mary the Mother of God. She communicates divine grace in the most direct, concrete way possible. She embodies it, and it is ushered forth through her flesh. Not wrong, despite all the exegesis to the contrary, is St Jerome's translation of the substantive participle *kecharitomene* ('one having been favoured') in St Luke's Gospel as 'gratia plena', 'full of grace'. She is full of grace because she already contains the fulness of grace, and she *is* the communication of that grace. St Jerome was perhaps not the first to translate in this way: the translation seizes the *essential* (by which we mean salvific, anagogical) meaning of the participle, in every sense. By long tradition, the Mother of God is said to have conceived her divine Son through her ear. Too often this idea is dismissed as a kind of metaphorical romanticism. It is exactly correct: the ear, even more than the eye, is the organ which attends to the Word, and which attends to what I have been calling signification all the way through. *Logos*, divine or otherwise, is its more proper name. This Greek *logos* is almost impossible to translate, meaning variously speech, speaking, language, signification, what Jacques Lacan has called the 'symbolic order'. We come close to understanding what it means when we hear at the deepest level the Greek understanding of man himself, man who is the *zoon logon echon*, the being that is held in and has the word. Living in the word – and here I do not yet mean the Word of God – is intrinsic to man's being – it *is* the being that he is.

The Word – the Word of God, who is from the beginning,[1] confirms the word in which man dwells. The opening words of St John's Gospel are normally translated as 'in the beginning was the word', but do not really say this at all. The Greek says *ēn arche*: from out of what originates – from out of the origins of time. The origins of time, however, lie not behind us, but ahead of us: they are what we are striving towards. The 'from out of' is the unfolding of time itself, not just the passing of the seasons and the unfolding of morning, noon and night, but their unfolding from out of where they are destined *to*. *Ēn arche*: the *ēn* here is the imperfect form of the verb 'to be' in the third person. We translate this into English as 'was'. In Greek, however, it means was-and-still-is: 'having been and yet is (and even

---

1 Cf. John 1.1.

yet will be)'. We would say: presences, not as formal pre*sence*, but presen*cing* as ongoing unfolding. The ecstatic Word which is poured out from the end of time, was and yet is, and will so be. It is *this* word which is *pros ton Theon*: God and *toward* God, directing us *into* God. The words of St John's Gospel speak of what the liturgy of the Ascension speaks of: the way in which *now* in the light of the Incarnation and its meaning-having-been-disclosed, *now* the Word given as this one, the Christ, transforms and unfolds all other words.

This Word is *eschatological*, it is fulfilled in what it promises (and this is the peculiar energy of every word that is true): it communicates and dispenses what it signifies. At its most basic level, the liturgy is the *logos*, the Word of God. We conclude, therefore, that in *this* word, *kai Theos ēn ho logos*, divine and God was and ever-is this word.

Mary, the Mother of God, by tradition conceives Jesus by receiving the Spirit in the words of the archangel through the ear. She who conceives through the ear attends to God and in so attending, is filled with divinity and ushers it forth into the world. She who conceives through the ear conceives what we must conceive: we also are to conceive through the ear – she physically, we sacramentally. The two orders are not different, but in the in-between time in which we *now* live are one and the same, as the feast of the Ascension attests.

This intertwinement that characterizes the sacred liturgy, however, is, in its full complexity, the making available through the passage of time the activity of divine *logos*, divine speaking. We attend to it, so that it speaks to us. Here is the most dramatically strange character of the sacred liturgy itself. How is a language learned? It is learned through repetition, through appropriating and making one's own the forms which language already inhabits. Here language is to be understood not just as the mere grammar and syntax, the vocabulary, but the whole *manner* of speaking, the character of the way in which what is said *is* said. Gesture, expression, citation, repetition – these also are the parts of speech. Not least of these is silence: what is not said in what is said; what remains to be said; what is yet to be said; what cannot be said; what in its being said is spoken as veiled. Who, during the silence in church of the recitation of the Canon (or prayer of consecration) of the Mass, said by the priest in a mere whisper – who does not yet know and instinctively understand what is being said? I hardly ever hear these words out loud, and yet I know each one intimately, and it speaks to me every time it is prayed. It does not have to be said out loud in order to be understood.

An essential aspect of the liturgy, especially true in the Roman rite, is that liturgy works through *hiding*. The silent recitation of the Canon is just one example, of which there are many. The sacred vessels, by always being veiled and hidden from visibility *except* when they contain the things to be consecrated (the *oblata*), or the sacred species once they have been consecrated, speak about what they are through this veiling. There are multiple uses of veiling and hiding in the language, the rubrics, the very use of the *fabric* of the sacred vestments in the liturgy, all of which make manifest not the visible presence of God, but that God the Father is the very Hidden One, the one revealed *as one hidden* in the Spirit, by the Incarnate Word.

The liturgy works by our inserting of ourselves into the words that are already given for us to speak. Above all, this is carried out through singing. Singing, not as performance, but as chorus, strophe and antistrophe, and song, entrains us to a kind of *return*, which, in our absorbing it, our making of it our own, and returning it as having been sung, schools us and lets us into participation in the conversation that the liturgy *is*. This is why the sung forms of the liturgy are more basic, more ancient, and prior to the said forms. It is also why the communal activity of the liturgy is always prior to any private form. Private recitation of the office is a dependent form of public celebration. I would go so far as to say that private recitation of liturgical texts has brought with it dangers for understanding what prayer is at all. The conversation which the liturgy is, is not less or other than the conversation between the Father and the Son, enacted throughout the cosmos – which is why it cannot be done as something in the heart, it *requires* the gift of the Temple, a physical building *adequate to the task*, 'adorned as a bride for her husband'. In liturgical prayer we are inserted into that conversation. If we make it our own, at the same time we are *constituted* by it: it makes of us what we are.

We are therefore required to ask, what is the effect of the transformations worked on the sacred liturgy by the process of liturgical reform that began with the turn of the twentieth century? In each of the processes of change that were initiated – frequent communion, the alterations to the structure of the Breviary (above all the arrangement of the psalter), and the transformations of the calendar, a kind of objectification occurred, entirely unforeseen by those commanding or executing the reform. I stress that these were beginnings – the processes of change continued right up until the publication of the postconciliar rites beginning with the first parts of the Pontifical from 1968 onwards. It could quite properly be argued that these changes were only possible because the direction in which they were driven had, in a sense, as changes already occurred in the minds of the experts and theologians who recommended them. The objectification of the sacred species of the Eucharist has been traced, with degrees of success, by Henri Cardinal de Lubac in his fundamental work *Corpus Mysticum*; the alterations to the Breviary exhibited, as László Dobszay and others have argued, an objectification of the liturgy as a whole – as something subject to papal fiat. Joseph Cardinal Ratzinger had said that 'after the Second Vatican Council, the impression arose that the pope could really do anything in liturgical matters, especially if he were acting on the mandate of an ecumenical council'.[2] Eamon Duffy has noted the paradox of the present Pontificate – that the one senior churchman and theologian who has understood the huge damage to the liturgy through exercise of that arrogation of papal power has paradoxically become pope – Benedict XVI, and it is for this reason that he has not unleashed on the Church another round of liturgical change.[3]

Benedict XVI himself has made the same point, when, in taking possession of the Lateran Basilica shortly after his election, he said, 'the pope is not an absolute monarch whose thoughts and desires are

---

2 Ratzinger, Cardinal J., *Der Geist der Liturgie: Eine Einführung*, pp. 142f. 'Nach dem II. Vaticanum entstand der Eindruck, der Papst könne eigentlich alles in Sachen Liturgie, vor allem wenn er im Auftrag eines ökumenischen Konzils handle.'

3 Cf. Duffy, E., 'The New Pope and the Liturgy', in Lang U. M. (ed.), *Ever Directed to the Lord: The Love of God in the Liturgy of the Eucharist, Past Present and Hoped For*, London, T&T Clark, 2007, pp. 6–9.

law. On the contrary: the pope's ministry is a guarantee of obedience to Christ and to his Word. He must not proclaim his own ideas, but rather constantly bind himself and the Church to obedience to God's Word, in the face of every attempt to adapt it or water it down, and every form of opportunism.'[4]

There is a fundamental connection in the liturgy between time and place. The reasons for this are very complex, and would require a much lengthier, more complex study to illustrate than I can undertake here. What has obtruded into the instinctive liturgical understanding of time is a rational concept of time: the same with place. The fact that in the liturgy and in liturgical action places can be indicated *here* by virtue of what happens *there* (the point of my concern with the multiplicity of commemorations in the last chapter) has been overlooked by liturgical theologians. The formal indication of place that, for instance, underlies the papal stational masses at Rome is another case in point. The Holy Father has himself understood the significance of the loss of the stational masses – both in his restoration of some of his attendances at the stational altars in Rome, and in the fact that he has commissioned a study, suitable for lay pilgrims, of the stational map of the diocese of Rome. The stational masses – briefly put – are the papal paralleling of our Lord's own pilgrim journeys around Jerusalem and the surrounding land: they reproduce in Rome the priestly significance of Christ's own movements in the Holy Land during his earthly life. They indicate the physical sanctification of the land, and by implication the whole of Christendom and the entirety of the world. This is why it matters that the papal liturgy takes place in Rome, and not in some other, arbitrarily chosen, city (and why, therefore, the pope has had to return to Rome either from Avignon or from exile at various times in history).

---

4 Benedict XVI, Homily at the Mass of Possession of the Chair of the Bishop of Rome, 7th May 2005, in *Acta Apostolicæ Sedis*, vol. 97, p. 751. 'Il Papa non è un sovrano assoluto, il cui pensare e volere sono legge. Al contrario: il ministero del Papa è garanzia dell'obedienza verso Cristo e verso la Sua Parola. Egli non deve proclamare le proprie idée, bensì vincolare constantemente se stesso e la chiesa all'obedienza verso la Parola di Dio, di fronte a tutti I tentative di adattamento e di annacquamento, come di fronte ad ogni opportunismo.'

A further example – the theology of blessings. Nowadays blessings are just so many happy words to be pronounced at various points, normally but no longer exclusively by the ordained, in 'pastoral' situations. I have never seen any serious theological treatment of the meaning of blessings, perhaps because none is possible. Until the 1983 code of canon law, many blessings required faculties, which were granted exclusively by bishops through their chanceries: the ability to give a blessing presumed a (faculty) of permission from the local Ordinary. The historic attack on this practice was, of course, justified on the grounds that many blessings came at a price, especially in the Middle Ages. In theological terms, that is neither here nor there. Blessings are facultative to bishops and abbots because they relate to *places*, and bishops and abbots have jurisdiction over place. That is what oversight – *episcope* – means. The sanctification authorized by a bishop relates that place to Christ, exactly through the character of sacramental activity I have tried, at least in outline, to describe.

The rationalism that was, among other places, indicated in Pistoia and which has dominated subsequent liturgical theology, especially since the war, has reproduced each liturgical act as a rational object – a quantifiable event, whose intricate connections with the other parts of the liturgy have been gradually and through successive reform loosened and even undone. This objectification means the laity in general have almost no appreciation of the importance or meaning of the intertwinement of the offices with the rites and texts of the Mass, and the clergy regard the Breviary as so much (and bluntly, there isn't much now) stuff to wade through, unwitting of the way in which the interconnectedness of the more ancient forms of the liturgy forms a commentary, and at the same time a pedagogy, of interconnection which unfolds not specific events but the whole web of time itself.

Since Aristotle, time has been counted as the successive passing of objective 'nows'. In this, time and place are detached from one another. But if you turn to Homer, to the Greek Lyric Poets, and to the most ancient conceptions of time in the West, you will find no such rational accounting for time. What you will find is something much more akin to the unreformed liturgical sense of time. Time is not something to be encountered, but something through which we are passed in successive, and contrasting, moods and determinations. We are 'timely': it is in this way the liturgy unfolds time *with respect to place. The liturgy is the sanctification of the time-places* that the world *is*.

Preachers can sometimes be heard to complain that they do not know what they will preach about at Holy Mass in the forthcoming Sunday. If they attended to the liturgy in its full historical richness, their problem would not be one of what to say, but how much they would need to leave out. The job of the preacher is not genius – which means he is not to come up with some personal message of breathtaking, unforgettable, rhetorical force – but to lay out for the faithful the full complexity of the liturgy *as it leads each one who prays it through itself to Christ, commenting on this journey as it proceeds.* This leading through and commenting on is at the same time the growth in understanding. Understanding of what? The understanding of the self-disclosure of himself that God ordains the sacred liturgy to be – to grow in understanding of what God already knows, to be inserted in a limited, creaturely way into the cosmic transparency to himself that God *is*. To grow in understanding of God's own self-understanding is nothing short of what it is to be sanctified, and so redeemed.

Chapter 13

The Subject of the Liturgy

It should be clear from what I have said so far that the actual possibility of liturgy speaking to us at all is because of a possibility inherent in language as such. Language has the power to move us – or to move things to and from us – both temporally and spatially. Liturgy – not just the liturgical texts, but the whole being of liturgy, gesture, rhythm, music, repetition, recapitulation, is nothing other than *logos*, than speaking-signifying as such. Liturgical language is as complicated a language as any other. There are some things which are phenomenologically basic to every language, and there are some which are specific to a particular language as such. What is specific to the language that the sacred liturgy is, is that it is the language of our salvation. In learning this language, in being appropriated to this language, we are at the same time to be saved. The liturgy is the language of salvation – it is how salvation speaks to, and in, us. In addressing the situation of the liturgy, those of a conservative bent have emphasized the need for what they have termed 'transcendence'. We must (and even Joseph Cardinal Ratzinger has said this) recover a 'sense of the transcendent'. We say this as if we knew what this meant, as if it were a kind of self-evidence. The central word here is *ekstasis* – it is part of the being of man to be with respect to what is already stood-out before him: world, as such. The world unfolds for man as already stood out for him.

What St Thomas understood as the inherent intelligibility of the world – that the world is inherently knowable for us – is a kind of gift. We need to go further even than this. As a gift, it is a gift to which

we are *bound*. We cannot be freed from existence. *Ex-istere*, ex-stare, is
the Latin form Greek *ek-stasis*. Since Descartes the world has become
for man specifically a mere field of objects: it has lost its inner unity.
This is because Descartes' whole philosophical *method* is world-
denying, such that having emptied the world for the sake of establishing the self, this pre-established self only then re-enters it. The world
becomes mere objects, essentially present 'for me'. Descartes says: 'The
seeker after truth must, once in the course of his life, doubt everything,
as far as is possible.'[1] This fundamental orientation to the world
transforms the world in a way at one and the same time so dramatic
and profound that it is barely visible. The entire ancient orientation in
being is reversed – this is the very 'subjectivism' that Casel named
earlier.[2] From now on, and increasingly so over the centuries, human
beings have seen the world not as something they are already *in*, but
something they essentially 'enter' and 'retreat from' from a kind of
outside.

This astonishing transition alters, not only our orientation to place,
to world, but also to time. Now we 'live' in a time-place 'outside' the
world: as a consequence, from now on we can enter 'multiple' worlds
('time travel' only becomes possible with this kind of understanding,
and also the 'private worlds' of the internet and so forth). What is most
significant about *ekstasis* is not that man is in his being, stood-out for
world and in world, but that in every being-stood-out, you and I are
always given to be in the *same* world. The struggle against relativism (a
struggle Benedict XVI has named repeatedly as a pitfall for modern
man) is the struggle to recover and show the binding character of this
same, necessary, *one* world in which we live.

In much of my other published work I have attempted to show
how, from the outset, what transcendence actually names, as it
becomes entangled with divinity, is derived out of an essentially
Neoplatonic reading of Aristotle's understanding of what he calls

---

1 Descartes, R., *Principiorum Philosophiæ*, in Adam, C. and Tannery P., *Œvres de
  Descartes*, Paris, Vrin, 1996 (1965:1641), vol. 8, p. 5. 'Veritatem inquirenti, semel in vitâ
  de omnibus, quantum fieri potest, esse dubitandum.'
2 See p. 58 above.

theorein, contemplation.[3] Transcending is the basic orientation of man. At the same time, as the phenomenological tradition (Husserl, Heidegger) has attempted to demonstrate, transcending *is* the experience of time. This experience is not something I go out and 'get', but is the way in which time already unfolds for me and ahead of me. All time flows from the future – even when I am asked to remember something, the memory comes from ahead – it does not stay present alongside me.

With these remarks in mind it becomes possible to see that speaking of 'a sense of the transcendent', or even 'the transcendent' as such raises certain difficulties. When we speak of 'the transcendent' we name something that we already appear to be held out towards. Since the medieval period we have wanted to say that this 'being-held-out-towards' is a kind of predisposition for, and toward, God. Many contemporary and twentieth-century theologians have wanted to say the same. Man is inherently disposed towards the being of God. But what the word *ekstasis* (in the Greek sense) named by indicating the character of human transcend*ing* is not (the Christian) God, but rather (in the pagan sense) the divine singularity of the world. This singularity, this unity and simplicity of the world was then *resolved* as at the same time the single, unitary, simplicity of God in the medieval synthesis because God was at once the prior cause of the being of all things, and, as highest being in Himself, the end to which they all tend.

Why does this matter? Because once again in the word 'transcendence' we have an *essentially* rational name for God, at a time when the rational access to God has been thrown into doubt by the death of God, by the current subjectival situation with regard to being. Modern Cartesian subjectivity teaches us that everyone is implicitly the same: anyone may implicitly perform any task in the social, political, religious, or moral sphere (irrespective of age, gender, disposition, or preparedness) but ancient philosophy never taught this, and the sacred liturgy could for centuries take for granted an

---

3 See especially Hemming, L. P., *Postmodernity's Transcending: Devaluing God*, esp. pp. 215–36.

understanding of the human person far richer and deeper than that which we are now accustomed to take for granted as true. With that understanding's long collapse, the liturgy must unfold in one of two ways – it must either continue to assert this richer understanding in the face of contemporary incomprehension, or it must be altered and modified to reflect the modern requirement.

This bifurcation or split is manifest in what Benedict XVI has called the 'hermeneutic of continuity'. In a speech to the whole Roman curia in December 2005 the pope suggested that the division in the Church is not between liberal and conservative, left and right, but between those who interpreted the Second Vatican Council within a 'hermeneutic of rupture', by which he meant that they interpret Vatican II as having made a conscious break with the whole past tradition of the Church, and those who seek a 'hermeneutic of continuity', whereby Vatican II can only be understood and implemented in continuity with the whole of the Church's past history and tradition. On this occasion he spoke of how for those who stressed the 'spirit of the Council', 'a vast margin was left open for the question on how this spirit should subsequently be defined, and room was consequently made for every whim'.[4] The motu proprio *Summorum Pontficum* corrects that 'misunderstanding'. At its heart is the claim in the supporting letter to the motu proprio that 'there is no contradiction between the two editions of the Roman Missal' – meaning that the 'law of prayer' as the 'law of belief' (*lex orandi, lex credendi*) contained in the Missal of 1962 is identical with that of the Missal of 1970.

In truth this is only partially the case. Lauren Pristas has illustrated with forensic precision examples of where the language of the preconciliar rites – and in reality much of the language of the prayers and rubrics date back to the very origins of the written texts of the Church, often to the fourth or fifth centuries – was edited for the 1970 Missal in such a way that it *could be* interpreted ambiguously.

---

4 Benedict XVI, Allocution to the Curia of 22 December 2005, in *Acta Apostolicæ Sedis*, Vatican, vol. 98 (2006), pp. 44–5.

One small example – the collect for the feast of St Albert the Great (November 15th) in the 1962 Missal says 'O God, who made blessed Albert, bishop and doctor, great in a human wisdom made subject to divine faith'. The 1970 Missal edited this to read 'O God, who made the bishop, blessed Albert, great in human wisdom combined with divine faith'.[5] The 1970 text is *susceptible* of an orthodox interpretation, but contains an ambiguity – it fails to clarify what the relation between divine faith and human wisdom is: the older text *requires* the orthodox understanding that human wisdom is subordinate to, and so is completed and fulfilled by, divinely granted faith.

The translation from the 1970 Missal is Pristas's own – the translation currently in official use says 'you endowed St Albert with the talent of combining human wisdom with divine faith',[6] rendering the divine gift to the saint like a kind of knack or aptitude. If, as Pristas has shown, there are (to say the very least) serious questions about the theological decisions that were made in editing and altering the ancient texts of the liturgy even in the revisions in the Latin language in the postconciliar reform, Catholics have been hugely disserved by the translations made into local vernaculars, and not only in English. The English re-translation of the 2002 edition of the 1970 Missal currently in an advanced state of preparation looks likely to remedy that and have a substantial impact on Anglophone Catholic worship, with (at least in the drafts that have become public so far) its far more sympathetic respect for the rhythm and nuance of the new Latin texts, having drawn on long traditions (predating even the

---

5 *Missale Romanum* (1962), collect for St Albert the Great: 'Deus qui beatum Albertum Pontificum tuum atque Doctorem in humana sapientia divinae fidei subiicienda magnum effecisti'; *Missale Romanum* (1970): 'Deus qui beatum Albertum episcopum in humana sapientia cum divina fide componenda magnum effecisti'. The collect is a late composition, as St Albert was only canonized in 1931, but it demonstrates the regulative way in which even late compositions invariably retained the theological force of earlier ones, right into the twentieth century. Cf. Pristas, L., 'The Pre- and Post-Vatican II Collects of the Dominican Doctors of the Church', in *New Blackfriars*, November 2005. For a full list of Lauren Pristas's articles on the collects of the Roman Missals of 1962 and 1970 see the Bibliography.

6 *Roman Missal* (English Edition), 1973, Proper of Saints, November 15th, Washington, ICEL (International Commission for English in the Liturgy).

Reformation) of rendering sacred texts into English – traditions on which even Cranmer drew in rendering the Sarum rite into protestant form in the Books of Common Prayer of the sixteenth century.[7]

A whole one or two generations of Catholics are now largely unfamiliar with worshipping in the Latin language (a language which, in my own pastoral experience, has provided little obstacle to anyone who does, irrespective of educational or social background). The earliest and early Christians in the city of Rome spoke Greek, not Latin, and it should be remembered that the shift of the language of the liturgy from the (vernacular!) Greek tongue of the Roman empire (where 'koine' or 'common' Greek was the dialect familiar across much of the world of late antiquity, until the fall of Rome) was to a *high* literary Latin. This shift took place in the fourth century under the pontificate of Damasus I, and did not represent a translation into the speech of the street from a language of the literate *but in fact the very reverse*, so that a sacral, formal tongue was developed and preserved for Christian worship that was quite separate from everyday life.[8] The prayers we make are addressed *to* God: the language must be accommodated to the divine hearing, not merely the ease of our own ears.

One of the purposes of this book has been to examine the dangers inherent in altering and 'modernizing' the liturgy. The entirely well-intentioned postconciliar reform of the liturgy in its desire to relate the sacred liturgy to the 'requirements of the age' failed to see the what would happen when the 'requirements of the age' were simply interpreted through the underlying conception of the human person, the Cartesian subject, that was taken for granted by contemporary thought. This 'taking for granted' affects all of us – whether we are inside the Church or without, unless we are able to exhibit the very 'taking for granted' in itself. That is the reason why this book has made continual philosophical detours – to try to indicate the presence and influence of the Cartesian subject in our midst.

---

7 The Books of Common Prayer of 1549 and 1552, which latter text became the basis for the Book of Common Prayer of 1662.

8 See, for a full discussion of the development of Church Latin in the liturgy and catechesis of the Church Fathers, Mohrmann, C., *Études sur le latin des chrétiens* (4 vols), Rome, Edizioni di storia e letteratura, 1958–77.

Every suggestion that the liturgy be 'inculturated' confronts the
awkwardness that the more the liturgy is accommodated to our own
familiar lifeworld, its power to make visible the New Jerusalem is
lessened. Jesus is difficult to see as the Messiah in the everyday byway:
the Bridegroom does not enter the high street but comes into his own
in the Temple, itself the most sacred precinct of the holy city,
Jerusalem, renewed, on high and in Sinaï. The sacred species are not
transubstantiated *next* to the bread and drink of our common tables,
but in distance, on the altar (not touched by common hand), at the
sacred table of the Lord.

The texts, rubrics, calendar and structure of the sacred liturgy
contain centuries of carefully sedimented openness to God's self-
disclosure in the coming of his Son as Bridegroom and High Priest
into the Temple decked out and fit to meet him. It is impossible now
to argue that the reforms that took place after the Second Vatican
Council, in fact the reforms since 1911, were not at times over-hasty,
driven by often rationalistic concerns. When the pope speaks of there
being 'no rupture' between the two forms of the Roman rite (the pre-
1970, and that of the 1970 Missal and its accompanying reformed
books) he asserts a truth which the Church has yet to discover in its
fullness – that when the 1970 Missal and the other reformed rites are
understood in the context of the former rites (as their very memory),
then their orthodox interpretation is assured, and all ambiguity is
removed. What the motu proprio *Summorum Pontificum* of 2007
does is make possible in the ordinary life of the Church that the
'rupture' proposed by adherents of the 'spirit of the council' can only
be healed through the Church's sacred activity of prayer and admin-
istration of the sacraments. What Benedict announces as a 'fact' –
that there is no rupture between the two forms of the rite will then
become an actual truth, one which will have effects in every aspect of
the Church's life. What he proposes is that the *living* presence of the
ancient rites – as themselves active vehicles of the Holy Spirit and of
divine grace – will ensure the freedom and health of the future
Church. If the liturgy is to have a future, it will be in rediscovering the
riches and wealth of its past. This past is not best enshrined in the
rites of 1962 – the ones specifically authorized by the *motu proprio* of

2007, but in the unreformed rites, prior to 1911, and in gaining a richer and wider understanding of the whole of the Roman rite(s), in detailed and careful exegesis of their texts and rubrics, their whole long history and their development.

How do we overcome the influence of the philosophy of subjectivity in the life of the Church's liturgy? Even much of the critique of the contemporary philosophy of subjectivity takes place from within the philosophy of subjectivity itself. Even in much contemporary theological discourse, Descartes' *cogito* and its effects are accorded higher status than the authorization which is God's self-disclosure of himself to men and women to whom he imparts the gift of faith.

But if philosophy is not to provide the authorization of Christian worship, from whence will authority derive? Surely, this authorization is given to us through divine revelation itself. Only from beyond and ahead of ourselves, from entirely without, can we be freed from what we would otherwise simply become. Only God dwells in this beyond, and yet only God is close enough to us, as one who became one with us in our humanity, to offer to and for us what else we could become. The sacred liturgy has traditionally implicitly taught that who each of us is can be understood not through a self-declaration, a mental act presupposed in every other mental act (the meaning of *cogito, ergo sum*), but *with respect to the altar*. It is the symbolic body of Christ, the divine Christ in his embodied full humanity, who reveals to us who we are and at the same time constitutes us in relation to His Father *through* the divinity which is *manifested by his body*, above all through the meaning that is disclosed by what happens to that body *in* and *after* its crucifixion. Symbolically the body of Christ is manifested in the structure of a church building, and in the liturgy through the altar itself, through the crucifix upon it, and of course through the presence in the tabernacle.

It is for this reason that traditionally the Mass and the other sacred actions of the liturgy are filled with actions which *defer to the altar*, and defer to its crucifix. In the preconciliar rites, when the sacred ministers and those in choir bow to each other in rank of precedence, they do so only with respect to their deference to the crucifix, and the altar. In other words, even when we acknowledge the differences between us – say between bishop, priest, deacon, etc., we do so only with respect to, and so in a way derived from, the sacred body of Christ, which demonstrates that who we are – who each of us is – is constituted only sacramentally and mysteriously through the relational character of Baptism, which gives us a right to consider ourselves in some sense identical and belonging to Christ.[9] At certain central moments in the traditional rites a bishop, when he vests to administer a sacrament (this is particularly evident in the sacrament of Confirmation), is vested *from* the altar. He does not take off what he comes to the altar with – his cassock and white rochet, but the amice, stole, cope and mitre are taken from the altar and placed over what he already wears, indicating in as clear a ritual way as possible that his whole identity *as bishop* is derived from the altar.[10]

This is the most radical challenge to our self-constitution in its description in the Cartesian *cogito*. There is no prior 'self' which is *then* redeemed (as one who cannot other than, as thinking, exist, and then discover its need to be redeemed). Rather my entire identity is received *from* and *with respect to* Christ, symbolically manifest in sacrament and altar, and in whose risen being I am then related to the Father. The identity I receive from Christ is not absolute, but *precisely relative*, 'with respect to some (other) thing', in the manner of that respectivity: with respect to what redeemed me – namely the sacrifice of the cross (which is at the same time the sacrifice of the altar). The theological point is this: that the meaning of the body of Christ, disclosed through the actions of the liturgy, succeeds and completes any understanding arrived at by philosophy, and *not* the other way round.

---

9 The theology here is directly from St Paul's letter to the Romans, 6.4–5. 'For we are buried together with him by baptism into death: that, as Christ is risen from the dead by the glory of the Father, so we also may walk in newness of life. For if we have been planted together in the likeness of his death, we shall be also in the likeness of his resurrection.'

10 In fact when a bishop is ritually present before an altar where the Blessed Sacrament is usually reserved, the sacrament is to be removed from the altar to another place, to intensify the understanding that the bishop, pontificating at an altar, represents Christ for the ritual work that is to be done – that it is really Christ who does the work.

With this understanding we return to the necessity that the liturgy is not underpinned by the Cartesian subject, nor even the humanity of the Son. Rather, the divinity of the Son and the hiddenness of the Father underpin the liturgy and make it true, in an underpinning which the Son's humanity makes manifest and is able, by no automatic or straightforward means, to exhibit. Above all this hiddenness is a gift of the Spirit, who constitutes us from out of the very future to which we are called. As we grow in perfection, and in understanding (through grace and the activity of the Spirit), we will *come* to understand what God already *knows to be true*. There is nothing wrong with experiencing God as hidden and mysterious *through* the opacity and difficulty of the rites, their *in*comprehensibility as well as their comprehensibility, that (we are confident, in faith) will make him manifest, because it is *we* who are to be made present to God, not *God* to us.

In the sacred liturgy *I* am recalled to the steps of Calvary, to the sacrifice and the sacred banquet which atones for my sins and the sins of the entire world, and which unites me to the whole Church both extant and gone before me in death, and those yet to come, through the sacrifice of Christ which ends my enmity with God. In that sense am I *em*bodied truly, in the body of Christ. I am included in the liturgical action by its very familiarity to me, to the central act of my redemption in its ritual form. I am assembled by the priest as one who is through Baptism (and my thereby having been sealed with the Spirit), through catechesis, through prayer, and through penance, and thereby am (made – by the Spirit) worthy to be present (and through the merits of Christ alone) to take my part in participating in, and sharing in, the offering of the divine sacrifice of the Son to the Father, *through which* I share in the eternal conversation between the Father and the Son in the Spirit. Only *now* might I yet become the subject and site of divine revelation. Subject means here, not the philosophical subject, the *cogito* in any of its forms, but a *ground* wherein the divine, salvific, Trinitarian, action is made manifest.

Chapter 14

Worship as a Revelation

This book seeks to explore the essentially revelatory character of the sacred liturgy. I have not sought to address the questions of the historical development of the liturgy because it is in becoming preoccupied with historical developments that the significance and meaning of the sacred liturgy has been obscured – the dangers of archaeologism are always to be avoided. Archaeologism was a term coined by Pius XII in his encyclical letter *Mediator Dei*, meaning falsely consecrating rites of the past, especially of what was supposed to have occurred in the early Church, in discerning liturgical questions.[1] At the same time I have wanted to avoid proposing 'solutions' to the liturgical question: to advocate a 'reform of the reform' is to presuppose that one fully understands what it is we are reforming, or reforming all over again.

If this book makes any contribution at all to current debates, it should by now be clear that we understand the historical and theological roots of the liturgy all too little. There has been too much reform – now is not the time for even more. Nor should we fear liturgical diversity – the whole history of the Church is a history of diversity in liturgical practice. The year 1970 was the only time in the whole history of the Western Christendom when there was an attempt to impose a *single* set of rites for use throughout the Western Church. The problem with attempting to 'assess' liturgical reform, and to decide what is and isn't 'organic' reform and so forth is that we

---

1 Pius XII, Encyclical Letter *Mediator Dei*, p. 546.

are forced constantly to become ones who judge what in fact is not ours to measure. Every standard of judgement becomes a measure set up from outside the liturgy – be it history, reason, or whatever, there is no adequate standard.

The liturgy, as I have attempted to show, *measures us*, it is the divine means by which we are gathered into God. Even the attempt to separate out what is divinely instituted from what is instituted 'merely' by the Church (historically speaking), as I hope I have indicated, is doomed to fail. The only measure the Church ever employed prior to 1911 was antiquity of continuity of use. Not just antiquity – which is the very archaeologism I mentioned earlier. Nor mere use, since there is a certain kind of liturgist who will beg, borrow and steal uses from anywhere to spice up a liturgical event, whether those uses belong in their new home or not. Above all, not novelty. One cannot fail to admire the breathtaking scale of work that was undertaken, principally between 1964 and 1970, in the course of the reform of the Roman Breviary and Missal. However, a reform of such short order could not be other than a product of its age. Nevertheless it is a source of grace and consolation for by far the greater portion of Catholics, and it will be with us for a good time yet, albeit, we can hope, in rather better, more faithful, and more enriching translations than we have had hitherto. Others are writing, and will write, on the specific theological problems raised by that reform – that is not my intention. If we must return to anything, it should be to a respect for antiquity of use, and to a more gentle kind of liturgical exegesis and theology that emphasizes the anagogical and soteriological, rather than the pastoral, aspects of liturgy.

The liturgy is a living thing, which developed not over years or even decades, but centuries. Its roots are manifold, but above all they are in the religion of Israel and in the Temple. However, and this is a point that has been made repeatedly by those who have discussed the postconciliar reform, the central texts – the Canon, the collects of the principal days of the temporal cycle, an overwhelming portion of the most important parts of the Breviary and the Missal, were all substantially in place, together with much of the most significant rubrics and ceremonial that provided their context and meaning, by the fifth and sixth Christian centuries at the latest. It is this pre-eminent edifice on which the medieval Church made its own constructions, in developments that were in extraordinary harmony with what went before. From then on the structure and character of the liturgy remained essentially the same. The reforms of the Tridentine era were minor, and even more so were subsequent changes to the Roman rite up until 1911.[2]

The divinely revealed character of the sacred liturgy is not easy to explain or account for. It is susceptible of few apodictic 'principles' or rules, and yet its very sanctity and delicacy demands caution and the utmost care. The successive reforms of the Breviary from 1911 to 1970 have left us with a liturgy of the hours that is barely recognizable when compared to the breviaries of 1568 and 1623 (and even that of 1568 had been simplified and truncated by Paul IV, both as pope and as Cardinal Carafa) and St Pius V. What has been of greatest importance is the disturbance and loss of the order of recitation of the psalmody in the Breviary, an order which in at least some of the offices appears to have been taken over from the Jerusalem Temple and predates Christianity itself. In its essentials the psalter contained in the Breviary of 1568 is identical to what preceded it, and is the same in its essentials as that laid down by St Benedict in establishing his *Rule*, and this was not an innovation. St Benedict was drawing on an established practice for the recitation of the psalms.[3] The argument used for these reforms of the psalter – that the ferial office was only rarely properly said and so some psalms were left out – is nothing short of bizarre when compared with its effects: liturgically some psalms were always more prominent than others, and in the current arrangement of the Breviary of 1970 some psalms are said barely once a month (in sections so small and across so many days that their integrity *as a single text* simply disappears) and some

2 This does not mean that there was not considerable debate – witness the reforms to the Breviary proposed by Cardinal Quiñones in 1533 and 1536 (the so-called 'Holy Cross' or *Santa Croce* Breviary, after Quiñones' titular church in Rome) or the various neo-Gallican rites that arose in eighteenth-century France and finally died out under the gentle zeal of Guéranger.

3 *The Rule of St. Benedict*, Collegeville, The Liturgical Press, 1980, pp. 202–17.

psalms have been excised altogether as 'inappropriate' for prayer, despite having been used liturgically for not hundreds, but thousands of years.[4]

There is no particular virtue or theological meaning to be derived in the mere rote recitation of the cursus of the 150 psalms week in and out. Some psalms have always been of greater importance than others (as we have already seen). The psalter provides the underlying structure of the offices, but is not mechanistic (like the workings of a clock). It does not matter that some psalms are hardly ever said (and must matter even less now that some are not said at all). That there is an underlying unity to the offices (the recitation of all 150 psalms in the week), but this underlying unity is rarely accomplished and is difficult to achieve, does indicate an important theological insight. There *is* an implicit unity to the work that is done in the liturgy, but it requires much patience and careful reflection to understand it – this unity only rarely becomes entirely visible, and yet it is always there, always *implicit*. To force this visibility is actually to impair the very richness and complexity of how this unity is given. László Dobszay has said of the 1911 reform of the Breviary that 'the rearrangement of the order of psalmody basically destroyed the system of the Roman office and erased its most traditional elements from the experience of two or three generations of priests'.[5]

In the matter of the redaction of texts for use in the liturgy, Lauren Pristas encapsulates an outlook that should be basic to all care for the liturgy itself when she says:

> first, the relevance of a particular oration for the Church universal is not something that can always be judged by persons of any one time or place. The prudent course is to trust the wisdom of our liturgical tradition to beg for what we need even when we cannot comprehend or imagine it. If changed histori-

---

4 The so-called 'imprecatory' psalms: 68, 108 and some verses of others.
5 Dobszay, L., 'The Bugnini Liturgy and the Reform of the Reform', p. 152.

cal circumstances give fresh relevance to this oration, perhaps no generation should permit itself to reject as unsuitable a petition that has enjoyed long use.[6]

What Pristas announces as a hermeneutic of prudence should have been extended to the whole of the liturgy.

I have already remarked on Benedict XVI's characterization of the need for a 'hermeneutic of continuity' in interpreting the postconciliar period of the Church's life. He has extended this interpretative key to the liturgy itself, by saying that 'the changes which the Council called for need to be understood within the overall unity of the historical development of the rite itself, without the introduction of artificial discontinuities', adding in a note: 'I am referring here to the need for a hermeneutic of continuity also with regard to the correct interpretation of the liturgical development which followed the Second Vatican Council.'[7]

Klaus Gamber has at times spoken very harshly of the postconciliar liturgy, saying 'after the Council . . . in the place of Liturgy as the fruit of development came fabricated Liturgy. We abandoned the organic, living process of growth and development over centuries, and replaced it – as in a manufacturing process – with a fabrication, a banal on-the-spot product.'[8]

In 1996, Joseph Cardinal Ratzinger gave a protracted interview to the German journalist Peter Seewald about the state and present situation of the Church. He spoke once again of his disappointment with liturgical developments in the postconciliar period, speaking of

---

6 Pristas, L., 'Theological Principles that Guided the Redaction of the Roman Missal (1970)', in *The Thomist*, vol. 67, 2003, p. 165.

7 Benedict XVI, Post-Synodal Exhortation *Sacramentum Caritatis*, 22 February 2007, §3 and note 6. 'Agitur reapse de immutationibus percipiendis, quas intra unitatem voluit Concilium, quae historicum ipsius ritus progressum, absque inductis facticiis fractionibus, designat'; 'De necessitate loquimur cuiusdam explicationis continuationis, ratione quoque habita rectae lectionis liturgicae post Concilium Vaticanum II progressionis: cfr Benedictus XVI, Sermo ad Romanam Curiam (22 Decembris 2005)'.

8 Gamber, K., *La Réforme Liturgique en Question*, Le Barroux, Éditions Sainte-Madeleine, 1992, p. 8.

how the liturgy has been 'flattened' and evacuated of mystery. Seewald put the following question: 'wouldn't it be conceivable to reactivate the old rite in order to work against this levelling and demystification?' The future pope's response is a clear indication that there are no short-cuts, no easy solutions to the present situation with respect to the sacred liturgy. Ratzinger replied:

That alone would not be a solution. I am of the opinion, to be sure, that the old rite should be granted much more generously to all those who desire it. It is impossible to see what could be dangerous or unacceptable about that. A community is calling its very being into question when it suddenly declares that what until now was its holiest and highest possession is strictly forbidden and when it makes the longing for it seem downright indecent. Can it be trusted anymore about anything else? Won't it proscribe again tomorrow what it prescribes today? But a simple return to the old way would not, as I have said, be a solution. Our culture has changed so radically in the last thirty years that a liturgy celebrated exclusively in Latin would bring with it an experience of foreignness that many could not cope with. What we need is a new liturgical education, especially of priests. It must once again become clear that liturgical scholarship doesn't exist in order to produce constantly new models, though that may be all right for the car manufacturing industry. It exists in order to introduce us into feast and celebration, to make man capable of the mystery. Here we ought to learn not just from the Eastern Church but from all the religions of the world, which all know that liturgy is something other than the invention of texts and rites, that it lives precisely from what is beyond manipulation. Young people have a very strong sense of this. Centres in which the liturgy is celebrated reverently and nobly without nonsense attract, even if one doesn't understand every word. We need such centres to set an example. Unfortunately, in Germany tolerance for bizarre tinkering is almost unlimited, whereas tolerance for the old liturgy is practically nonexistent. We are surely on the wrong path in that regard.[9]

What is the right path for understanding the liturgy? The liturgy *performs* its meaning, which means: makes its meaning available such that it *is* what it signifies. The liturgy is not a sacrament as such, but it has the same underlying structure of intelligibility that the sacraments possess. The 'subject' of the liturgy is Christ, which means the liturgy both discloses who Christ is, and in this disclosing, inscribes those to whom the disclosure is made into the very being of the one disclosed. This unfolding disclosure does not happen all at once: precisely not. It happens cyclically, through constant repetition, both within the day, and daily, and in its annual repetition, across a lifetime of faithful engagement and prayer. In the liturgy the ones participating are made present to Christ, as ones whom he receives as Bridegroom and High Priest in the Temple of the New Jerusalem.

---

9 Seewald, Peter, *Salz der Erde: Christentum und katholische Kirche im 21. Jahrhundert: Ein Gespräch mit Peter Seewald*, Munich, DVA Sachbuch, 1996, p. 188. 'Das würde allein keine Lösung sein. Ich bin zwar der Meinung, daß man viel großzügiger den alten Ritus all denen gewähren sollte, die das wünschen. Es ist überhaupt nicht einzusehen, was daran gefährlich oder unannehmbar sein sollte. Eine Gemeinschaft, die das, was ihr bisher das Heiligste und Höchste war, plötzlich als strikt verboten erklärt und das Verlangen danach geradezu als unanständig erscheinen läßt, stellt sich selbst in Frage. Denn was soll man ihr eigentlich noch glauben? Wird sie nicht morgen wieder verbieten, was sie heute vorschreibt? Aber eine einfache Rückkehr zum Alten wäre, wie gesagt, keine Lösung. Unsere Kultur hat sich in den letzten dreißig Jahren so radikal verändert, daß eine ausschließlich in Latein gefeierte Liturgie ein Fremdheitserlebnis mit sich brächte, das für viele unüberwindbar wäre. Was wir brauchen, ist eine neue liturgische Erziehung, besonders auch der Priester. Es muß wieder klar werden, daß Liturgiewissenschaft nicht dazu da ist, ständig neue Modelle hervorzubringen, wie es für die Autoindustrie passen mag. Sie ist dazu da, in das Fest und in die Feier einzuführen, den Menschen für das Mysterium fähig zu machen. Da sollte man nicht nur von der Ostkirche lernen, sondern von den Religionen in der Welt insgesamt, die alle wissen, daß Liturgie etwas anderes als das Erfinden von Texten und Riten ist, daß sie gerade vom Unmanipulierbaren lebt. Die Jugend spürt das sehr stark. Zentren, in denen die Liturgie ohne Mätzchen ehrfürchtig und groß gefeiert wird, ziehen an, auch wenn man nicht jedes Wort versteht. Solche maßstäblichen Zentren brauchen wir. Leider ist bei uns die Toleranz selbst für abenteuerliche Spielereien fast unbegrenzt, die Toleranz dagegen für die alte Liturgie praktisch inexistent. Damit ist man sicher auf dem falschen Weg.'

We make this assertion because this is what the liturgy itself tells us, in the very acts of making us manifest and like to Christ. The manifestation of the full meaning of Christ to the world is given in the Christmas cycle of the liturgy, beginning with the feast of the Nativity, the Incarnation itself. This feast was originally kept on January 6th, but probably following the arguments of Sextus Julius Africanus (supposedly relating the records of the Roman censuses to the birth of Christ), the actual birth of Christ was redated to December 25th. Guéranger reports that the Holy See 'obliged all Churches to keep the Nativity on this date [nevertheless] the Sixth of January was not robbed of its glory'.[10] So important was the date of the feast of the 6th January, however, that the established feast on that date remained, in both the East and the West.[11] We might say that the historical considerations were subordinated to their anagogical and theological significance, but this would not be quite correct, for the keeping of the Nativity as the actual birth of Christ was already subordinate to two other significations of the feast of the Epiphany – the baptism of Jesus and the commemoration of the wedding at Cana. The least of the significations of the feast (so much so, that it gets no mention in the liturgies of the East) is the appearance of the wise men or Magi from the East, the so-called 'three kings'.

The vigil of the Epiphany is not a penitential day (the vestments are white and there is no fasting), and it repeats in its essential elements the liturgy of the Nativity from the 25th December, recalling the ancient connection between the two feasts. The antiphons at Lauds of the vigil stress the significance of the Nativity and its

---

10 Guéranger OSB, P., *L'année liturgique*, vol. 3, p. 85. 'Les décrets du Saint-Siège obligèrent toutes les Églises à célébrer désormais, avec Rome, le mystère de la Nativité au 25 décembre, le 6 janvier ne fut pas entièrement déshérité de son antique gloire.'

11 It is often thought that the Eastern Churches keep the Nativity on the 6th of January, and only the Western (Roman) Church moved it to the 25th of December. In fact, if the Nativity is kept in January in the East it is kept on the 7th, according to the date of the Julian Calendar (so in fact on the Julian equivalent of the 25th December). The feast kept on the 6th in the West as the Epiphany is known in the East as the Theophany, and is the same feast, kept on the same day. The only ancient Churches that do not keep a separate feast of the Nativity from the Epiphany are the so-called 'Monophysite' Churches that did not subscribe to the Council of Nicea.

meaning with respect to the Christian faithful: 'O admirable exchange: the creator of the human race, assuming a living body, deigns to have been born of the Virgin, and comes forth as a man without human seed, his divinity has been extended to us.'[12] This divinity, *deitatem*, which is 'extended to us' (*largitus est*) is exactly that same gift that the liturgy of Ascension prays will be 'extended to us' (*largiatur et nobis*). The central importance of the feast of the Epiphany is that liturgically we are brought to see the connections between the Incarnation and the Resurrection. Not for nothing on this day in Rome and in many cathedral churches were the dates of Septuagesima, Ash Wednesday, Easter, the Ascension, Pentecost, Corpus Christi and the following First Sunday of Advent solemnly proclaimed in chant by the deacon after he had sung the Gospel for the day (in Rome many of these days still are proclaimed in this way). The Epiphany makes possible our sharing in the divinity which Christ extended to his own human body. The liturgy is the very making possible of this understanding. What is understood is at the same time what is effected: to understand is to be brought in to the divine *self*-understanding.

If the Vigil liturgy for the Epiphany reinforces the meaning of the Incarnation and its effect, the actual liturgy for the feast introduces a new and surprising note. The antiphons at Vespers, as well as mentioning the advent of the wise men, stress 'your light advances to you, Jerusalem, and the glory of the Lord has risen over you, and the peoples will walk in your light, alleluia.'[13] The chapter for Vespers and Lauds stresses this theme still more: 'Arise, light up, Jerusalem, for your light advances, and the glory of the Lord has risen over you.'[14]

It should not be missed that the Vigil liturgy reminds us of the creation of the world – the whole cosmic order – by the the one 'through

---

12 *Breviarium Romanum* (1623), first antiphon at Lauds for the Vigil of the Epiphany. 'O admirabile commercium: creator generis humani, animatum corpus sumens, de Virgine nasci dignatus est: et procedens homo sine semine, largitus est nobis suam Deitatem.'

13 *Breviarium Romanum* (1623), second antiphon at Lauds for the Epiphany. 'Venit lumen tuum, Jerusalem, et gloria Domini super te orta est: et ambulabunt gentes in lumine tuo, alleluia.'

14 Isaiah 60.1. 'Surge, illuminare, Jerusalem: quia venit lumen tuum, et gloria Domini super te orta est.'

whom all things were made' as that one who is born to the Virgin and is that one who alone has the power to extend his divinity to us, in the same way as he has assumed our humanity. The significance of the feast is Christ's taking possession of Jerusalem as his own, reinforcing the ancient Christian tradition that it is the *Second* Person of the Divine Trinity who created the world, and with whom Moses converses on Sinaï, and so it is the Second Person who is the presence in the Temple. The enthronement in question parallels that already discussed in relation to Psalm 67 at Ascension and during the octave of Pentecost ('the Lord is in Sinaï in holiness/the holy place').[15] The manifestation of who Jesus is – to the wise men and to all the Gentiles – is understood to be the very thing that is revealed through Jesus' Baptism. The Gospel of the Baptism is not read until the octave day of Epiphany, which closes the keeping of the major part of the Christmas cycle until the feast of the Purification of the Virgin. This latter feast takes place on the fortieth day after the Nativity, the ritual day for the sacrifices in the Temple in thanksgiving for a male first-born, and is celebrated on the 2nd of February.

The antiphon at the Benedictus on the feast of the Epiphany makes fully clear the entire significance of the feast: 'Today the divine spouse is joined to the Church, she whose sins Christ washed away in the Jordan: hurrying with gifts come wise men to the wedding feast, and wine is made from water to the joy of the wedding guests.'[16] The real significance for the feast of the Epiphany of the Baptism and the birth of Jesus as the divine Son is, as Margaret Barker has pointed out, that the Baptism represents the *heavenly* birth of Christ. It should be remembered that Origen had opposed the keeping of the feast of the Nativity of Jesus – 'of all the holy people in the scriptures, no one is recorded to have kept a feast or held a great banquet on his birthday. It is only sinners (like Pharaoh and Herod) who make great rejoicings over the day on which they were born into this world

---

15 See page 100 above.

16 *Breviarium Romanum* (1623), Benedictus antiphon at Lauds for the Epiphany. 'Hodie cœlesti Sponso iuncta est Ecclesia, quoniam in Jordane lavit Christus eius crimina: currunt cum muneribus Magi ad regales nuptiales, et ex aqua facto vino lætantur convivæ, alleluia.'

below.'[17] Origen, it would seem, opposed the keeping of the Nativity because it reversed the direction and order of the birth of Christ, from the eschatological order, the heavenly birth of the Saviour, to an emphasis on the temporal order, from the past. The Epiphany is greater in the order of feasts than the Nativity in what it reveals, because it retains the proper eschatological orientation – to the future, to the outpouring of the Spirit from the end-times – which is the proper orientation of all liturgical prayer.

It is for this reason that the liturgy really speaks of a double-birth of Christ in the Epiphany, and it speaks of the birth in far more eschatological terms, directly associating the birth with the meaning of Jerusalem and by implication Christ's identity with the Temple and his fulfilment of it in the new, heavenly, Jerusalem. Barker reminds us that the words recorded by St Luke as uttered by God, 'thou art my beloved Son: in thee I am well pleased',[18] are from Psalm 2 and Isaiah.[19] She shows that the psalm speaks of 'the birth of the divine Son who is set on Zion to rule the nations with a rod of iron. In Luke's original account of the Baptism, Jesus heard the words of this psalm: "You are my son. Today I have begotten you".'[20] Barker directly relates the events of the Baptism with vision in the book of the apocalypse, where the dragon waits to devour the child, 'but he is snatched up to heaven and enthroned, and then Michael and his angels defeat the dragon and drive him from heaven. This, briefly and enigmatically, describes the birth of the Son of God. There is no hint elsewhere in the New Testament that defeating the dragon was linked to the birth of the Son, but the consistent association of the dragon with Jesus' Baptism, and of his Baptism with his birth from above suggests that this was part of the original tradition.'[21]

The opening of the heavens to Jesus at his Baptism indicate his taking possession of the heavenly city, again recalling the text from

---

17 Origen, *In Levit.*, Homily 8, in Migne (ed.), *Patrologia Græca*, vol. 12, col. 495.

18 Luke 3.22.

19 Cf. Isaiah 41.1.

20 Barker, M., *Temple Themes in Christian Worship*, p. 110, quoting Luke 3.22 and Psalm 2.7.

21 Barker, M., *Temple Themes in Christian Worship*, p. 116.

the feast of the Dedication of a Church – 'I saw the holy city, the new Jerusalem, coming down out of heaven from God, prepared as a bride adorned for her husband.' In this case, however, the descent of the new Jerusalem is for the sake of the enthronement of Jesus, *for in his Baptism he takes possession of what is rightly his.* Barker explains carefully the parallelism of the opening of the heavens, the presence of the waters and the indication that Jesus had seen the cherubim throne of God as a parallel with the vision of Ezekiel in the Old Testament, a vision on which Origen had commented extensively.[22] She concludes: 'The open heavens, the water and the throne were elements in becoming a priest.'[23]

The significance of this is that in Jesus' Baptism he himself accomplishes his resurrection *and is aware of what he has accomplished.* This heavenly birthday reveals Christ to be the second Adam, fully human, and so reveals what it is that full humanity itself is, the full humanity to which we are destined. Adam was also anciently understood to be a priest.[24] What is disclosed is at the same time divinely authorized – this is the significance of God's own voice being heard and the Gospel account of the appearance of the Spirit over the person of Jesus. The actual resurrection will only make visible to all what has already here been accomplished. The readings in the first nocturn at Matins on the feast make this connection explicit, taken as they are from Isaiah. The responsory after the first reading at Matins says: 'Today in the Jordan the Lord is baptised: the heavens are opened, and the Spirit endures over him like a dove, and the voice of the Father is heard: "this is my beloved Son in whom I am well pleased".'[25] This responsory is said only on the actual feast and on the Sunday of the octave (the day when the Gospel of the Baptism is read): on the other days

---

22 Cf. Ezekiel 1. Barker notes that, coordinating the old temple calendar with the Roman calendar, the actual time in the year of Ezekiel's vision is coincident with the date of feast of the Epiphany.

23 Barker, M., *Temple Themes in Christian Worship*, p. 116.

24 A point discussed in detail by Margaret Barker in an unpublished paper, 'The Fragrant Tree'.

25 *Breviarium Romanum* (1623), first responsory at Matins for the Epiphany. 'Hodie in Jordano baptizato Domino, aperit sunt cœli, et sicut columba super eum Spiritus mansit, et vox Patris intonuit: hic est Filius meus dilectus in quo mihi bene complacui.'

of the octave a responsory commemorating the visit of the Magi is provided.

The Gospel on the feast day of the Epiphany is that of the adoration of the Magi, and at the point at which 'falling down they adored him'[26] is proclaimed priest, ministers and all present kneel. This gesture is, however, borrowed from the gesture at Matins on the same phrase. The feast of the Epiphany is unique in not beginning with the invitatory psalm, Psalm 94. This is because on this day the invitatory psalm is the seventh psalm in Matins, and it is recited at the third nocturn in the same way that on every other day of the year (except in the office of Tenebrae in the Triduum Sacrum) it is recited at the beginning of Matins, with the antiphon interspersed with the strophes of the psalm.

Psalm 94 is unique in the breviary as the only psalm taken over unaltered from the Old Roman psalter, and not from St Jerome's (later) Vulgate. The words 'Come, let us worship and fall down before him; and kneel before the Lord that made us' are expressly omitted from the Old Roman text, but are made present by the genuflection that is made at the point in the text where they would otherwise be found, a gesture which performs the text that has been omitted (they are restored in the 1970 Breviary, which suppresses the genuflection). Almost certainly the psalm was retained in its older translation because of the character of its liturgical use (could it even be that the adoration of the Magi became attached to this feast because of the parallelism of the words in this psalm and the Gospel?). The gesture which is indicated by these omitted words (so close to the words used in the Gospel – the verbs are identical) is 'borrowed' from Matins to be used in the Gospel. The point, however, is clear: the kneeling down and worshipping is because of what has been made manifest in the 'heavenly' birth of the Saviour. At the same time, the heavenly birth indicates the cessation of the very wrath of God named in the psalm, by which God proclaims: 'I swore in my wrath that they shall not enter into my rest.' Epiphany proclaims the renewal of the Covenant and the restoration of the priesthood in Jesus Christ as High Priest.

---

26 Matthew 2.11.

The importance of Psalm 94 as a psalm specifically connected with the event and meaning of the Epiphany, and specifically the Baptism of the Lord can be best understood through the problematic translation of its first verse. The first verse is often translated in one of two ways: *either* 'let us make temple-singing to the rock [of salvation]' or 'let us meet with the face/presence [of the Lord] with temple-singing'. The disputed word in the Hebrew poetry is *ṣur*, which can be translated as either 'rock' or 'face/presence'. The old Roman translation makes a decisive choice, with the Septuagint, for 'face/presence', saying 'iubilemus Deo . . . præoccupemus faciem eius': 'let us sing joyfully to the Lord . . . let us come before his face' (Jerome's translation, and the New Vulgate also reflect this translation). To go to the Temple is to be moved to where the face/presence of the Lord is to be found, but this is also the meaning of the injunction in Exodus, 'thrice a year shall all thy males appear before the Lord thy God'.[27] The injunction is a command to make pilgrimage to the Temple: 'to appear' is ambiguous. In the Septuagint the verb is passive, and means, as it could mean in Hebrew 'to be seen' i.e. to be seen and so met with by one whose presence is *already there*, waiting and present. To enter the Temple is to enter the Presence and to be met with by God. This is also the meaning of Psalm 79: 'let thy face shine that we may be restored'.

To enter the Temple (and make temple-singing) is to encounter the Lord (the Second Person of the Divine Trinity) as he really is, he who in his Baptism was confirmed (for himself) in seeing the face of the *First* Person of the Divine Trinity. This psalm is moved into the body of the Matins office because *this is its proper home*, of which the Invitatory is the recapitulation on every other day (excepting the three days of the Triduum). The Invitatory makes a daily connection between us and our coming into the sight of the Lord (Christ) as the one who is identical with, and makes manifest the meaning of, the Temple; he whose identity is made manifest by his own 'coming into the sight of' and meeting with the Presence of the Father.

---

27 Exodus 23.17.

The Gospel that is sung on the octave day of the Epiphany, however, is that of St John, not St Luke, although the elements are identical. St John records the Spirit hovering over and descending on Jesus. The other theme of the liturgy of Epiphany, the wedding at Cana, indicates formally two things. First, the very conversion of the water into wine reflects the 'admirable exchange' of the Vigil antiphon, but in reverse – just as the divine Christ becomes fully human, so now can *we* men and women of flesh and blood share the divine life and be deified. The offertory prayers at Mass reflect exactly this understanding when they speak of the mixing of water and wine in the chalice as the 'mystical union of this water and wine [by which] we may be made partakers of [Christ's] divinity, who vouchsafed to become partaker of our humanity'.[28] The second indication of the wedding at Cana, however, is the Eucharist itself, the very wedding banquet referred to in the antiphon at Lauds. It is this 'admirable exchange' which brings joy to those called to the feast. In the Gospel of St John the miracle at Cana follows immediately after the baptism of the Lord: the significance of this, however, is that the miracle at Cana confirms the identity of Christ as Melchisedech. Philo had noted that the significance of Abraham's encounter with Melchisedech was that Abraham had expected the hospitality of water from Melchisedech, and had in fact received the higher hospitality of wine. This parallelism between the water and its conversion into wine (to the astonishment of the wedding guests) confirms that this is the first manifestation of Jesus as the returned Melchisedech, the restored High Priest – only possible after Jesus' own self-understanding at his Baptism.

The liturgical and anagogical parallelism of the feast of the Epiphany is between the Baptism of the Lord – where the Lord is enthroned as High Priest and Bridegroom, marked by the appearance and indwelling of the Spirit, as one who then makes available

---

28 *Missale Romanum* (1884), prayer said after the blessing of the water at the offertory. 'Da nobis per huius aquæ et vini mysterium, eius divinitatis esse consortes, qui humanitatis nostræ fieri dignatus est particeps.' A version of this part of the prayer was retained in the same place (although there is no blessing) in the Missal of 1970.

and extends to all humanity the possibility of its very deification –
and the risen Lord's appearance to the disciples 'the doors having
been closed', above all a Eucharistic appearance, where at the same
time he says 'receive the Holy Spirit'. The liturgies of Epiphany and
Pentecost are mirror images of each other, and they at the same time
explain each other. For it is only in our own being baptized that we
are able to see Christ as he is, enthroned as High Priest and Bridegroom, entering a Jerusalem 'decked out and fit to meet him'.

The Christmas cycle ends with the feast of the Purification of the
Virgin Mary. The Virgin goes to the Temple to fulfil the requirement
of the law to make sacrifice in thanksgiving for the first-born who
opens the womb. The patristic commentators note that a mother is
required to be purified in the Temple on the fortieth day of the birth,
which is in fulfilment of the requirement that the sacrifice be made
(and her own purity restored) on the thirty-third day after the child's
circumcision (itself on the eighth day after the birth, counting inclusively). According to the law this was to have been a lamb or alterna-
tively two young pigeons or turtle-doves. The renaming of the feast
to the 'Presentation of the Lord' in the reform of the calendar in 1969
erases the significance of the event, and erases the way in which the
cosmic significance of Mary's identity is bound *ritually* and *textually*
to the identity of her divine son. The readings at Matins of the feast
specify that Mary makes the sacrifice out of obligation to the law.
However, the Virgin is not obliged to fulfil *this* law, as her mother-
hood is already beyond ordinary laws: she takes the child with her
(itself an extraordinary matter) as the physical proof of her exceptional status (there is no mention of Joseph in either the Gospel or
the liturgical texts, in contrast to the later visit to the Temple in Jesus'
infancy). The antiphons at first Vespers are the same as those at Lauds
on the Vigil of the Epiphany, again reiterating the 'wonderful
exchange' of the creator of the world becoming man, that divinity
might be extended to the whole race of men.

At the centre of the liturgy of the feast is the prophetic canticle of
Simeon, used every night in the non-Monastic office at Compline,
with its reference to Christ the light who enlightens all nations and is
the glory of God's people Israel. This is the light referred to in the

liturgy for the Epiphany, the light which will brighten Jerusalem, the light which will 'rise up' and illuminate the holy city. The other part of the liturgy of the Purification is the procession before the Mass for the day, from which the feast gets its other name, of Candlemas. On this day the candles for use during the whole year in the church are blessed. There are in total six collects of blessing, but it is the fourth collect which both explains the ritual meaning of the use of candles, and the way in which Simeon prophetically understands the coming of Christ into the Temple.

The fourth collect speaks of the necessity of keeping lamps burning permanently 'before your face', according to law.[29] The Latin is 'conspectum' which means variously sight, face, presence. The light which Simeon recognizes in the infant in the Virgin's arms is the light of the Presence, the light to be kept permanently burning in the Temple. The light is the light of the menorah, the lampstand which stands in the place of the Presence in the Temple, the ritual symbol of the tree of life (the tree which Eve and Adam shunned, choosing to eat of the tree of knowledge of good and evil). Simeon recognizes the connection between the light and the tree, which is why he prophecies the piercing of Mary's heart. The light of the Presence represents the presence of the Lord, but *as* the presence in the world (the Second Person of the Divine Trinity).

Mary, however, is that one who also symbolizes the lampstand itself, for she is the one who, in reversal of the choice of Eve, chooses fruit from the tree of life. Mary is the one who bears fruit from the tree of life, the tree which Eve was ordered to eat but did not. Mary is not purified, she *is* the possibility of the purification of Israel, she is that one who gives flesh to the Christ and so enables the 'marvellous exchange' to come about. She is the lamp-bearer to Christ, the light of the presence. The place of the menorah in the Temple (and its possible different placing in the first and second Temples) is a problem repeatedly alluded to in Margaret Barker's work. In the book of Revelation the symbolic place of the menorah has moved, from the south

---

29 *Missale Romanum* (1884), fourth collect of blessing of candles on the feast of the Purification of the Virgin Mary. 'Ante conspectum tuum.'

side of the Temple to the Holy of Holies itself. Is Simeon's prophecy also, therefore, part of the prophecy of the restoration of the five missing ornaments of the Temple (the fire, the ark, the menorah, the Spirit and the cherubim)?[30] That the presence of the Lord in the world has been taken *into* the Holy of Holies would confirm the ritual meaning of the liturgy of the Ascension, and the interlocking of the liturgies of the Ascension and the Epiphany. A further ritual connection with the feast of the Ascension should not be overlooked. Every light to be burnt in the churches in the coming liturgical year is blessed on this day except *one* – that which is blessed on Easter Day, the Easter candle. This one light – the Easter light, symbolizing the light of understanding that comes to men from the resurrection (which reveals to men what is already known to God) – is extinguished on the day of the Ascension, restoring the ritual eminence of the other lights, which now burn with a renewed brightness, in consequence of the enlightenment given through what the resurrection reveals – a revelation given to men on Easter Day, but to Christ on the Epiphany, of Jesus' identity as High Priest and Bridegroom. The liturgical interlocking of the Christmas and Easter cycles is further disclosed even in the Church's ritual articulation of the meaning of its lights.

The liturgy is none other than the means by which, and the manner in which, Christ the High Priest and Bridegroom enters the new Jerusalem where he can be found, the light to enlighten the nations, and the glory of Thy people Israel. He enters by means of the cross, which is why on Palm Sunday, at the Procession, readmittance to the church is gained only after the Subdeacon has struck the (closed) church door with the foot of the processional cross.[31]

---

30 Cf. Barker, M., *Temple Themes in Christian Worship*, p. 57, citing *Numbers Rabbah*, XV, 10.

31 This ritual gesture was suppressed in the reforms of the Holy Week ceremonial in 1955.

Glossary of Principal Figures

St Thomas Aquinas OP (c.1225–74)
Canonized on 18 July, 1323. Italian theologian in the scholastic tradition. His principal works are the *Summa Theologiae* and the *Summa Contra Gentiles*.

Pope Benedict XVI, Joseph Ratzinger (1927–)
Elected pope on 19 April 2005. Formerly Prefect of the Congregation for the Doctrine of the Faith (1981–2005), Archbishop of Munich and Freising (1977–81) and professor of theology at Regensburg and Tübingen. Author of numerous theological works, among which are *God of Jesus Christ* (1978); *Feast of Faith: Approaches to a Theology of the Liturgy* (1986); *The Spirit of the Liturgy* (2000).

Lambert Beauduin OSB (1873–1960)
Belgian monk who founded Chevetogne Abbey, previously a monk of the Benedictine abbey of Mont Cesar (Leuven) and a leading figure in the Liturgical Movement in Belgium.

Annibale Bugnini CM (1912–82)
Named archbishop in 1972, he oversaw the reform of the Catholic liturgy that followed the Second Vatican Council of 1962–65. Secretary to the Commission for Liturgical Reform (1948) which was responsible for the reform of the rites for the Easter Vigil (1951) and then for the whole of Holy Week (1955) and the Code of Rubrics (1960). Secretary of the Pontifical Preparatory Commission on the Liturgy (1960), the body which drafted *Sacrosanctum Concilium*, the Second Vatican Council's Constitution on the Sacred Liturgy.

Odo Casel OSB (1886–1948)
Benedictine monk of Maria Laach in Germany, Editor of the prestigious liturgical journal *Jahrbuch fur Liturgiewissenschaft* (Yearbook for Liturgical Science) until 1941. One of the most influential writers in the field of liturgical theology in the first half of the last century.

Pope Clement VIII (1536–1605)
Elected pope 30 January 1592. Instituted the Forty Hours' Devotion and issued revised editions of the Vulgate (1598), the Breviary, the Missal, also the *Cæremoniale* and the *Pontifical*.

Louis-Marie Chauvet (1942–)
Professor in Sacramentology at the Institut Catholique, Paris.

René Descartes (1596–1650)
French philosopher, mathematician, scientist and writer. A highly original philosopher, who established the idea that truth in philosophy can attain to certainty through the pursuit of method.

Gregory Dix (1901–52)
Monk of the Anglican Benedictine community at Nashdom Abbey, and liturgical scholar. Author of the highly influential *Shape of the Liturgy*.

László Dobszay (1935–)
Leading scholar in the Institute for Musicology in the Hungarian Academy of Sciences in Budapest and on the faculty of the Ferenc Liszt Academy in Budapest. A musicologist of international renown, he is founder of the Schola Hungarica. Expert on the Antiphonary of the Roman Rite.

Klaus Gamber (1919–89)
Head of the Liturgical Institute, Regensburg, his principal works include *Sacramentarium Gegorianum* (1966); *The Modern Rite* (2002); *The Reform of the Roman Liturgy* (2006).

Romano Guardini (1885–1968)
Catholic priest and academic, Guardini was a major influence on the liturgical reforms of the Second Vatican Council. Major works available in English include *The End of the Modern World* (1998); *The Art of Praying: The Principles and Methods of Christian Prayer* (1994); *The Lord* (1996); *Living the Drama of Faith* (1999).

Prosper Guéranger OSB (1805–75)
Benedictine monk. Guéranger sought to re-establish more filial relations between France and the See of Rome. He re-established the monastery of Solesmses, which in turn set a universal standard for the singing of plainchant. A prolific writer, he prepared a 15-volume commentary on the liturgy, *The Liturgical Year* and fought in France to have the Roman liturgy re-established in the dioceses that had abandoned it.

Martin Heidegger (1889–1976)
One of the most original and important philosophers of the twentieth century but also among the most controversial, his thinking has contributed to such diverse fields as phenomenology, existentialism, hermeneutics, political theory, psychology, theology and postmodernism. His main concern was ontology, or the study of being.

Ildefons Herewegen OSB (1876–1946)
Benedictine abbot of Maria Laach and sacramental theologian.

Pope Blessed John XXIII (1881–1963)
Beatified on 3 September 2000; elected pope 28 October 1958. John XXIII called the Second Vatican Council (1962–5) although he did not live to see it to completion.

Pope John Paul II (1920–2005)
Elected Pope 16 October 1978. Principal works include *Veritatis Splendor* (The Splendour of the Truth); *Fides et Ratio* (On the Relationship between Faith and Reason); *Evangelium Vitae* (The Gospel of Life) and *Orientale Lumen* (Light of the East).

Joseph Jungmann SJ (1889–1975)
Historian of the Roman rite and leading figure in the Liturgical Movement. Principal works include *The Mass of the Roman Rite* (1948) and *The Place of Christ in Liturgical Prayer* (1962).

Archdale Arthur King (1890–1972)
A renowned commentator on the liturgy, writing numerous descriptions of the various forms of the Roman rite as well as an introduction to Eastern Orthodox liturgies, *The Rites of Eastern Christendom*.

Henri Cardinal de Lubac SJ (1896–91)
French Jesuit priest, one of the most influential theologians of the twentieth century. His writings and doctrinal research played a key role in the shaping of the Second Vatican Council. His principal works are *Catholicisme: les aspects sociaux du dogme* (1938), translated as *Catholicism: Christ and the Common Destiny of Man* (1950); *Surnaturel* (1946); *Exégèse médiévale* (1959, 1961, 1964) and *Corpus Mysticum* (1941, 1949).

Friedrich Nietzsche (1844–1900)
German philologist and philosopher of extraordinary originality. He was made Professor of Classical Philology at the University of Basel at the age of 24 but resigned in 1879 because of ill health. His health progressively worsened until by 1889 he was mentally incapacitated and an invalid. His work, immensely controversial, discussed such ideas as the will to power and the eternal reccurence of the same.

Origen (c.185–c.254)
Early Christian theologian. Traditionally held to have been an Egyptian who revived the Catechetical School of Alexandria. His works and commentaries are extensive. In *Peri Archon (First Principles)*, he articulated an exposition of Christian doctrine in relation to Greek philosophy.

Walter F. von Otto (1874–1958)
German classicist, produced important work on the impact of Greek religion and mythology. Principal works include *Dionysus: Myth and Cult* (1933) and *Homeric Gods* (1954).

Pope Paul VI (1897–1978)
Elected pope 21 June 1963. The work of the Second Vatican Council was completed under his papacy. His principal encyclicals are *Sacerdotalis Caelibatus* and *Humanae Vitae* (1968).

Pope St Pius V (1504–72)
Canonized 24 May 1712, elected pope 7 January 1566. His principal work is *In Coena Domini* (1568). He was responsible for the editions of the Missal and Breviary that were issued after the reforms of the Council of Trent.

Pope St Pius X (1835–1914)
Canonized 29 May 1954, elected pope 4 August 1903. Pius X worked to increase devotion, particularly in the Liturgy of the Hours and the Holy Mass. In addition to restoring the Gregorian Chant to prominence, he

placed a renewed liturgical emphasis on the Eucharist. His principal works include *Catechismo della dottrina Cristiana, Pubblicato per Ordine del Sommo Pontifice San Pio X* (1908). He reformed the Breviary in 1911 and announced plans to reform the Missal that were never undertaken.

Pope Pius XII (1876–1958)

Elected pope 2 March 1939. Pius XII is one of only two popes to have invoked papal infallibility by issuing an apostolic constitution, *Munificentissimus Deus*, which defined *ex cathedra* the dogma of the Assumption of the Blessed Virgin Mary. He also promulgated 40 encyclicals and initiated the reform of the Missal from 1948 onwards.

Pope Leo XIII (1810–1903)

Elected pope 20 February 1878. Leo XIII's encyclical *Rerum Novarum* focused on the rights and duties of capital and labour. His 1893 encyclical *Providentissimus Deus* gave new encouragement to scriptural sudy while warning against rationalist interpretations which deny the divine inspiration of scripture. His 1879 encyclical *Aeterni Patris* restored the work of St Thomas Aquinas to prominence as a theological authority in the Catholic Church.

St Prosper of Aquitaine (c.390–c.455)

Disciple of St Augustine, in his *De vocatione omnium gentium* (The Call of all Nations), Prosper appears as the first of the medieval Augustinians. His principal works are *Epitoma chronicon* (covering the period 379–455) and *De gratia Dei et libero arbitrio* (432).

Edward Schillebeeckz OP (1914–)

First theologian to win the Erasmus Prize (1982). A major study on sacramental theology is still expected to appear but his principal work to date is *De sacramentele heilseconomie* (The redeeming economy of the sacraments).

Pope Urban VIII (1568–1644)

The last pope to expand the papal territory by force of arms. Urban VIII issued the Papal bull of canonization for Ignatius Loyola and Francis Xavier. He issued a new edition of the Breviary in 1623.

Cipriano Vagaggini OSB (1909–99)

Benedictine theologian and liturgist, his principal works include *Theological Dimensions of the Liturgy* (1958); *The Church and the Liturgy* (1965); and *The Canon of the Mass and Liturgical Reform* (1967).

Bibliography

Aquinas, St Thomas, *Quæstiones disputate de veritate*, Rome, Marietti, 1953 (2 vols). Translated by Robert W. Mulligan SJ as *Truth* (3 vols), Indianapolis, Hackett Publishing Company, 1994 (1954).

Aquinas, St Thomas, *Summa Theologiae* , Rome, Marietti, 1962. Translated by L. Shapcote OP as *Summa Theologiae*, Oxford, Blackfriars, 1924.

Aristotle, 'Posterior Analytics', in *Aristotle: Posterior Analytics: Topica*. Translated by Hugh Tredennick and E. S. Forster in *Loeb Classical Library*, Cambridge (Mass.), Harvard University Press, 1997 (1960).

Barker, Margaret, *Temple Themes in Christian Worship*, London, T&T Clark (Continuum), 2007.

Barker, Margaret, *The Great High Priest: The Temple Roots of Christian Liturgy*, London, T&T Clark (Continuum), 2003.

Benedict XVI, Allocution to the Curia of 22 December 2005, in *Acta Apostolicæ Sedis*, Vatican, vol. 98 (2006), pp. 44–5.

Benedict XVI (Joseph Cardinal Ratzinger), *Der Geist der Liturgie: eine Einführung*, Freiburg, Herder, 2000. Translated by John Saward as *The Spirit of the Liturgy*, San Francisco, Ignatius, 2000.

Benedict XVI (Joseph Cardinal Ratzinger), *Aus meinem Leben: Erinnerungen*, Munich, Deutsche Verlags-Anstalt, 1998 (1997). Translated by Erasmo Leiva-Merikakis as *Milestones: Memoirs 1927–1977*, San Francisco, Ignatius, 1998.

Benedict XVI (Joseph Cardinal Ratzinger), ed. Stephan Otto Horn and Vinzenz Pfnür, *Gott ist uns nah. Eucharistie: Mitte des Lebens*, Augsburg, Sankt Ulrich Verlag, 2001. Translated by Henry Taylor as *God is Near Us: The Eucharist, The Heart of Life*, San Francisco, Ignatius, 2003.

Benedict XVI, Homily at the Mass of Possession of the Chair of the Bishop of Rome, 7 May 2005, in *Acta Apostolicæ Sedis*.

Benedict XVI, Post-Synodal Exhortation *Sacramentum Caritatis*, 22 February 2007.

Benedict XVI, motu proprio *Summorum Pontificum* with accompanying explanatory letter to the bishops, 7 July 2007.

Benedict XVI (Joseph Cardinal Ratziner), *Salz der Erde: Christentum und katholische Kirche an der Jahrtausendwende*, Stuttgart, Deutsche Verlags-Anstalt, 1996. Translated by Adrian Walker as *Salt of the Earth: The Church at the End of the Millennium – An Interview with Peter Seewald*, San Francisco, Ignatius, 1997.

Benedict, St, *The Rule of St. Benedict*, Collegeville, The Liturgical Press, 1980.

Berger, David, *Thomas von Aquin und die Liturgie*, Cologne, Editiones Thomisticæ, 2000. Translated by Christopher Grosz as *Thomas Aquinas and the Liturgy*, Naples (Florida), Sapientia, 2004.

Blankenhorn OP, Bernhard, 'The Instrumental Causality of the Sacraments: Thomas Aquinas and Louis-Marie Chauvet', in *Nova et Vetera*, vol. 4 (2006), pp. 255–93.

Breviarium Romanum, 1568, 1623, 1914, 1961, Vatican.

Bugnini, Annibale, *La riforma liturgica (1948–1975)* (2nd edn), Rome, Edizioni Liturgiche, 1997 (1981). Translated by Matthew J. O'Connell as *The Reform of the Liturgy (1948–1975)*, Collegeville, The Liturgical Press, 1990.

Casel OSB, Odo, *Das christliche Kultmysterium*, Regensberg, 1959 (4th edn) (1948). Translated by Burkhard Neunheuser OSB and edited by I. T. Hale as *The Mystery of Christian Worship and Other Writings*, London, Darton, Longman and Todd, 1962.

Catechismus Catholicæ Ecclesiæ, Vatican, Libreria Editrice Vaticana, 1997. Typical edition of the *Catechism of the Catholic Church*, London, Geoffrey Chapman, 2000.

Cekada, Anthony, *The Problems With the Prayers of the Modern Mass*, Rockford, Tan Books, 1991.

Chauvet, Louis-Marie, *Symbole et sacrement: Une relecture sacramentelle de l'existence chrétienne*, Paris, Éditions du Cerf, 1987. Translated by Patrick Madigan SJ and Madeleine Beaumont as *Symbol and Sacrament: A Sacramental Reinterpretation of Christian Existence*, Collegeville, Pueblo (The Liturgical Press), 1995.

Corbon, Jean, *Liturgie de source*, Paris, Éditions du Cerf, 1980, p. 44. Translated as *The Wellspring of Worship* by M. J. O'Connell, San Francisco, Ignatius, 2005 (1988).

Descartes, René, *Meditationes de Prima Philosophia*, in Adam, C. and Tannery, P., *Œvres de Descartes*, Paris, Vrin, 1996 (1965:1641), vol. 7. Translated in a bilingual edition by George Heffernan as *Meditations on First Philosophy*, Notre Dame, Notre Dame University Press, 1990.

Descartes, René, *Principiorum Philosophiæ*, in Adam, C. and Tannery, P.,

Œvres de Descartes, Paris, Vrin, 1996 (1965:1641), vol. 8. Translated by John Cottingham, Robert Stoothoff and Dugald Murdoch in *The Philosophical Writings of Descartes* (3 vols), vol. 1, Cambridge, Cambridge University Press, 1985, pp. 177–291.

Dix, Gregory, *The Shape of the Liturgy*, London, T&T Clark, 2005 (1943, 1978).

Dix, Gregory, *The Mass of the Presanctified*, London, Church Literature Association, pp. 18–25.

Dobszay, László, 'The Bugnini-Liturgy and the Reform of the Reform', in *Musicæ Sacræ Meletemata*, vol. 5, Front Royal, 2003.

Duffy, Eamon, 'The New Pope and the Liturgy', in Lang, U. M. (ed.), *Ever Directed to the Lord: The Love of God in the Liturgy of the Eucharist, Past Present and Hoped For*, London, T&T Clark, 2007.

Fortescue, Adrian, *The Ceremonies of the Roman Rite Described*, London, Burns & Oates, 1918.

Gamber, Klaus, translated by Klaus D. Grimm, *The Reform of the Roman Liturgy: Its Problems and Background*, San Juan Capistrano, Una Voce Press, 1993.

Gamber, Klaus, *La Réforme Liturgique en Question*, Le Barroux, Éditions Sainte-Madeleine, 1992.

Guardini, Romano, *Vom Geist der Liturgie*, Freiburg, Herder-Bücherei, 1959 (1917). Translated by Joanne M. Pierce as *The Spirit of the Liturgy (Milestones in Catholic Theology)*, New York, Herder & Herder (Crossroad), 1998.

Guéranger OSB, Prosper, *L'année liturgique* (15 vols), Paris, Oudin, 1875 (1844–8). Translated by Laurence Shepherd OSB as *The Liturgical Year* (15 vols), Fitzwilliam, Loreto, 2000 (1867).

Harper, J., *The Forms and Orders of Western Liturgy from the Tenth to the Eighteenth Century: A Historical Introduction and Guide for Students and Musicians*, Oxford, Clarendon Press, 1991.

Heidegger, Martin, *Aufenthalte*, in *Zu Hölderlin – Griechenlandreisen*, in *Gesamtausgabe*, vol. 75, Frankfurt, Klostermann, 2000.

Heidegger, M., *Die Grundbegriffe der Metaphysik: Welt – Endlichkeit – Einsamkeit*, in *Gesamtausgabe*, vol. 29/30, Frankfurt, Klostermann, 1992 (1983). Translated by William McNeill and Nicholas Walker as *The Fundamental Concepts of Metaphysics – World, Finitude, Solitude*, Bloomington, Indiana University Press, 1995.

Heidegger, Martin, *Geschichte der Philosophie von Thomas von Aquin bis Kant*, in *Gesamtausgabe*, vol. 23, Frankfurt, Klostermann, 2006.

Heidegger, Martin, *Identität und Differenz*, in *Gesamtausgabe*, vol. 11, Frankfurt, Klostermann, 2006 [1957]. Original edition *Identität und Differenz*, Pfullingen, Neske, 1957, translated by Joan Stambaugh (ed.), as *Identity and Difference* in a bilingual edition, New York, Harper Torchbooks, 1969.

Heidegger, Martin, *Parmenides*, in *Gesamtausgabe*, vol. 54, Frankfurt, Klostermann, 1982. Translated by André Schuwer and Richard Rojcewicz as *Parmenides*, Bloomington, Indiana University Press, 1992.

Heidegger, Martin, *Sein und Zeit*, in *Gesamtausgabe*, vol. 2, Frankfurt, Klostermann, 1977 (1927). Translated by John Macquarrie and Edward Robinson as *Being and Time*, London, SCM Press, 1962, and by Joan Stambaugh under the same title, New York, SUNY, 1996.

Martin Heidegger, *Seminare*, in *Gesamtausgabe*, vol. 15, Frankfurt, Klostermann, 1986.

Hemming, Laurence Paul, 'The Experience of God: Aquinas on the Identity and Difference of Divine and Human Knowledge', in Laurence Paul Hemming and Lieven Boeve (eds), *Divinising Experience: Essays in the History of Religious Experience*, Leuven, Peeters, 2005.

Hemming, Laurence Paul, *Heidegger's Atheism: The Refusal of a Theological Voice*, Notre Dame, Notre Dame University Press, 2002.

Hemming, Laurence Paul, *Benedict XVI Fellow Worker for the Truth: An Introduction to his Life and Thought*, London, Continuum, 2005.

Hemming, Laurence Paul, *Postmodernity's Transcending: Devaluing God*, Notre Dame, Notre Dame University Press, 2005.

Hull, Geoffrey S., *The Banished Heart: Origins of Heteropraxis in the Catholic Church*, Sydney, Spes Nova League, 1995.

John Paul II, Apostolic Letter *Ordinatio Sacerdotalis*, Vatican, Libreria Editrice Vaticana, 1994.

Jungmann SJ, Joseph A., *Missarum Sollemnia: Eine genetische Erklärung der römischen Messe* (2 vols), Vienna, Herder, 5th rev. edn, 1962 (1952). Translated by F. A. Brunner CSSR as *The Mass of the Roman Rite: Its Origins and Development*, Blackrock, Four Courts Press, 1986 (1950).

Kant, Immanuel, *Opus Postumum* (Adickes, E. ed. and arr.), Berlin, Kantstudien Ergänzung, 1920.

King, Archdale A., *Concelebration in the Christian Church*, Oxford, Mowbray, 1966.

King, Archdale A., *Liturgies of the Past (Rite of Aquileia, Rite of Benevento, Gallican Rite, Celtic Rite, Rites of Mediaeval England, Rite of Nidaros – Trondheim)*, London, Longmans, Green & Co., 1959.

King, Archdale A., *Liturgies of the Primatial Sees. (The Rites of Lyons, Braga, Milan and Toledo)*, London, Longmans, Green & Co., 1957.

King, Archdale A., *Liturgies of the Religious Orders*, London, Longmans, Green & Co., 1955.

King, Archdale A., *The Rites of Eastern Christendom*, Rome, Catholic Book Agency, 1947.

Kocik, Thomas M., *The Reform of the Reform: A Liturgical Debate – Reform or Return*, San Francisco, Ignatius, 2003.

Koenker, E. B., *The Liturgical Renaissance in the Roman Catholic Church*, Chicago, Chicago University Press, 1954.

Lang, U. M., *Conversi ad Dominum: zu Geschichte und Theologie der christlichen Gebetsrichtung (Neue Kriterien)*, Einsiedeln, Johannes Verlag, 2003. Translated and augmented by the author as *Turning Towards the Lord*, San Francisco, Ignatius, 2004.

Leo XIII, Encyclical Letter *Æterni Patris* of 4 August 1879, in *Acta Sanctæ Sedis*, vol. XII, Rome, Propaganda Fide, 1879, pp. 95–115. Translated in J. J. Wynne SJ, *The Great Encyclicals of Pope Leo XIII: Translations from Approved Sources*, New York, Benziger, 1903.

Lubac, Henri Cardinal De, *Corpus Mysticum*, Paris, Aubier, 1948 (1944). Translated by Gemma Simmonds CJ, and Richard Price and edited by Laurence Paul Hemming and Susan Frank Parsons as *Corpus Mysticum: The Eucharist and the Church in the Middle Ages*, SCM Press and Notre Dame University Press, London and Notre Dame, 2006.

McDade SJ, John, 'Jesus: Son and Priestly Companion of God's Throne', unpublished paper.

Macy, Gary, *The Theologies of the Eucharist in the Early Scholastic Period*, Oxford, Clarendon Press, 1984.

Macy, Gary, *Treasures from the Storeroom: Mediæval Religion and the Eucharist*, Collegeville, Pueblo (The Liturgical Press), 1999.

Martimort, A. G., with others, *The Church at Prayer* (4 vols), London, Geoffrey Chapman, 1988.

Missale Romanum 1884, 1962, 1970, 2002, Vatican.

Missale S. Ordinis Prædicatorum, Rome, Santa Sabina, 1933.

Mohrmann, C., *Études sur le latin des chrétiens* (4 vols), Rome, Edizioni di storia e letteratura, 1958–77.

Mosebach, Martin, *Häresie der Formlosigkeit: Die Römische Liturgie und ihr Fiend*, Munich, Karl Hanser Verlag, 2007 (2002). Translated by Graham Harrison as *The Heresy of Formlessness: The Roman Liturgy and its Enemy*, San Francisco, Ignatius, 2006.

Nichols OP, Aidan, *Looking at the Liturgy: A Critical View of its Contemporary Form*, San Francisco, Ignatius, 1996.

Nietzsche, Friedrich, *Der Wille zur Macht*, in Nietzsche, *Sämtliche Werke*, Stuttgart, Kröner, 1996 ([1901]1911, 1930). Translated by Walter Kaufmann and R. J. Hollingdale as *The Will to Power*, London, Weidenfeld & Nicolson, 1968 (1967).

Nietzsche, Friedrich, Colli, G. and Montinari, M. (eds), *Nachlaß 1887–1889*, in *Nietzsche*, vol. 12, Munich, de Gruyter, 1996 [1980].

O'Connell, J. B. (ed. and trans.), *Simplifying the Rubrics of the Roman Breviary and Missal: A Translation, with Commentary, of the Decree 'Cum Nostra'*, London, Burns & Oates, 1955.

O'Connell, J. B. (ed. and trans.), *Sacred Music and Liturgy: Instruction of the Sacred Congregation of Rites September 3rd 1958*, London, Burns & Oates, 1958.

O'Connell, J. B., *Church Building and Furnishing: The Church's Way – A Study in Liturgical Law*, Notre Dame, University of Notre Dame Press, 1955.

O'Connell, J. B. and Schulte, A. J., *Consecranda: The Performance of the Rite of Consecration of the Roman Pontifical*, New York, Benziger Brothers, 1956 (1907).

Origen, *In Levit.*, in Migne (ed.), *Patrologia Graeca*, vol. 12.

Paul VI, audience of 17 March 1965, in Osservatore Romano, 18 March 1965, p. 1. Translated in *Documents on the Liturgy, 1963–1979: Conciliar, Papal, and Curial Texts*, O'Brien, T. C. (ed. and trans.), Collegeville, ICEL, 1982.

Pérès, Marcel, *Chant Cistercien du XIIIe*, Paris, Fondation, 1992.

Pérès, Marcel and Huglo, Michel, *Aspects de la Musique Liturgique au Moyen Age*, Paris, Éditions Créaphis, 1991.

Pickstock, C., *After Writing*, Oxford, Blackwell, 1998.

Pius X, motu proprio of 1 November 1911, *Divino afflatu*, in *Acta Apostolicæ Sedis*, Vatican, vol. 3, pp. 633–7. See also *Rubricæ in recitatione divini officii et in Missarum celebratione*, in *Acta Apostolicæ Sedis*, Vatican, vol. 3, pp. 639ff.

Pius X, motu proprio of 22 November 1903, *Tra Le Sollecitudini*, in *Acta Sanctæ Sedis*, vol. 36, Vatican, 1904, pp. 329–39.

Pius X, *Sacra Tridentina Synodus*, in *Acta Sanctæ Sedis*, of 20 December 1905, vol. 38 (1906), Vatican, pp. 400–6.

Pius XII, Encyclical Letter *Mediator Dei*, November 1947, in *Acta Apostolicæ Sedis*, vol. 14, pp. 521–95.

Pristas, Lauren, 'The Pre- and Post-Vatican II Collects of the Dominican Doctors of the Church', in *New Blackfriars*, November 2005, pp. 604–21.

Pristas, Lauren, 'The Orations of the Vatican II Missal: Policies for Revision', in *Communio*, vol. 30 (Winter, 2003), pp. 621–53.

Pristas, Lauren, 'The Collects at Sunday Mass: An Examination of the Revisions of Vatican II', in *Nova et Vetera*, vol. 3 (Winter, 2005), pp. 5–38.

Pristas, Lauren, 'Theological Principles that Guided the Redaction of the Roman Missal (1970)', in *The Thomist*, vol. 67 (April, 2003), pp. 157–95.

Processionarium Iuxta Ritum S. Ordinis Prædicatorum, Rome, Santa Sabina, 1949.

Prosper of Aquitaine, *Capitula Cælestini*, in *Patrologia Latina*, vol. 51.

Ratzinger, Joseph Cardinal *see* Benedict XVI.

Reid, Alcuin, *The Organic Development of the Liturgy*, San Francisco, Ignatius 2005 (2004).

Righetti, Mario, *Storia Liturgica* (vols 1–4), Rome, Ancora, 1998 (1964).

Rituale Romanum, 1752, 1884.

Robinson *cong. orat.*, J., *The Mass and Modernity: Walking to Heaven Backward*, San Francisco, Ignatius, 2005.

Rubin, M., *Corpus Christi: The Eucharist in Late Medieval Culture*, Cambridge, Cambridge University Press, 1991.

Seasolz, Kevin R., *A Sense of the Sacred: Theological Foundations of Christian Architecture and Art*, New York, Continuum, 2005.

Seewald, Peter, see Benedict XVI, *Salz der Erde*.

Sokolowski, Robert, *Eucharistic Presence: A Study in the Theology of Disclosure*, Washington DC, Catholic University of America Press, 1994.

Tanner SJ, Norman (ed.), *Decrees of the Ecumenical Councils*, London, Sheed & Ward, 1990.

Taft SJ, Robert, *The Liturgy of the Hours in East and West: The Origins of the Divine Office and its Meaning for Today*, Collegeville, The Liturgical Press, 1986.

Vatican Council II, Dogmatic Constitution on the Sacred Liturgy *Sacrosanctum Concilium*, 1963.

Vagaggini OSB, Cipriano, *Il senso teologico della liturgia*, Rome, Edizione Paoline, 1965 (1957). Translated by Leonard J. Doyle and W. A. Jurgens, Collegeville, The Liturgical Press, 1976.

Vellian, Jacob (ed.), 'The Romanization Tendency', in *The Syrian Churches Series*, vol. 8, Kottayam, 1975.

Index

CPSIA information can be obtained
at www.ICGtesting.com
Printed in the USA
LVHW021935020620
657247LV00007B/755

9 780860 124603